FRONTIERS OF THE CHRISTIAN WORLD MISSION

FRONTIERS OF THE CHRISTIAN WORLD MISSION

SINCE 1938

Essays in honor of
Kenneth Scott Latourette

Edited by Wilber C. Harr

HARPER & BROTHERS PUBLISHERS
NEW YORK AND LONDON

FRONTIERS OF THE CHRISTIAN WORLD MISSION
Copyright © 1962 by Wilber C. Harr
Printed in the United States of America

FIRST EDITION
C-M

Library of Congress catalog card number: 62–7288

CONTENTS

v

INTRODUCTION

The National Association of Professors of Missions is a comparative newcomer in North American academic circles. Its fifth biennial meeting was held in June of 1960 at Union Theological Seminary, Richmond, Virginia.

The executive committee of the association set for itself a pleasant but almost impossible task. It should be added that the committee has had no regret that it planned on a large scale.

The decision was made to honor Dr. Kenneth Scott Latourette at this meeting. The general theme chosen for the biennial meeting was "The Christian Mission Since 1938." The committee held that the Tambaram Conference of the International Missionary Council was an important focal date (1938). The fact that Volume VII of Dr. Latourette's *The History of the Expansion of Christianity* carried a 1945 date made the general theme possible and also significant.

In subdividing the general theme it was felt that area studies were important but that they could not do full justice to the theme. The chapter titles thus show a variation between topical and area treatment.

At least three simple propositions entered into the planning of this material. First, many of us who teach in the area of the Christian world mission stand convinced that Kenneth Scott Latourette has done a remarkable work in making studies of missiology vital and respectable. Second, because of the great range and competence of his own study we believed it fitting that we attempt to honor him. In doing this we are aware of a number of things. On the one hand it was known that there might be no comparable competence to follow up his study which closed with the date 1945. We also knew that the entire field could not be covered in a conference lasting only three days. Consequently we made no attempt to survey the whole field in a comprehensive way. Let other writers bridge the great gaps which we have allowed to stand open. Certainly the gaps need to be filled in the days ahead. Lastly, it was believed that the last twenty-five years of mission of the Church of our living Lord had much to say to us. In that confidence it was felt that honor could be given to a great teacher and friend.

These essays were prepared for presentation in 1960. This fact in no way diminishes their relevancy to the present situation. Instead, the papers stand as an illustration of the dynamic times in which the Christian mission must find its way.

Dr. Latourette attended the Richmond meeting of the National Association of Professors of Missions. The warmth of his person and his wise counsel remain with all who attended as a splendid memory. The papers do not adequately express our appreciation, but any limitation here is only the limitation of our minds and not of the affection of our hearts.

WILBER C. HARR

FRONTIERS OF THE CHRISTIAN WORLD MISSION

CHAPTER I

The Protestant Enterprise in China, 1937-1949

M. SEARLE BATES
Union Theological Seminary
New York, New York

Foreword

The present essay seeks a provisional understanding of the confused and imperfectly documented period from the beginning of the Japanese War to the establishment of the (Communist) People's Republic of China. Its brevity requires severe selection, with consequent risks of misjudgment and misinterpretation.

Not one year of the thirteen years 1937–1949 passed free from major struggle in China. Invasion and occupation brought the long War of Resistance, 1937–1945. Muffled civil war then moved toward and into full conflict, with the control of China as its prize, before the Japanese forces were dismissed from the stage. Communist triumph was achieved in 1949, with completion and consolidation quick at hand.

Not one year from 1937 to 1949 saw all Chinese churches able to communicate with each other and with related mission agencies. The usual processes of reporting, study, and publication were fractured, cramped, or stopped. *The China Christian Year Book*, since 1912 a major channel of reporting and interpretation, appeared only in two double issues before it ceased in 1940. *The Chinese Recorder*, which from 1867 had maintained a great tradition, sank under repeated blows and disappeared with 1941. In the thirteen years there was no comprehensive survey and no form of national Christian conference. The last "normal" meeting of the National Christian Council (Eleventh Biennial) was held in May, 1937. The Twelfth

1

Biennial was possible only in December, 1946. It had an extraordinary if not an emergency character, as did that of 1948.

Although considerable stocks of piecemeal information exist, they are scattered, incomplete, and essentially unorganized. Many important papers, usually sent from the offices of the National Christian Council in Shanghai (1937–1941; 1945–1949) and in Chungking (1941–1945), were received—and, as a rule, were mimeographed for appropriate officers of mission agencies—by the Committee on East Asia of the Foreign Missions Conference of North America, New York, and by the counterpart body in London. Reports of the various denominational missionary organizations and of special bodies aiding educational, medical, and general relief services, plus many report letters by competent individuals, help to fill in the specifics. A number of books by missionaries and others, diverse in quality, sought to record and to interpret the scene, or portions of it, at particular moments and in contemporary perspective. The period deserves book-length treatment in the perspective of ten or a dozen years after its close.

1. *The National Scene. The Church in Society*

Despite pervasive poverty, heavy illiteracy, and disease largely unchecked, China in 1937 seemed to most of her people and to most Christian interests to be on a better course than at any time in modern history—with the one great cloud of Japanese expansion proceeding from Manchuria into North China and threatening yet more. Two decades of fragmentation, marked by continual civil wars, were rounding off in relative order, with faulty but substantial steps toward modernizing government, which was extending railroads and highways, improving the banks and currency, and enlarging education. The Communist threat seemed less dangerous since the government had at last eliminated it from the central geographical position in Kiangsi province, and since the joint understanding of 1936–1937 in the face of the advancing might of Japan. After bitter decades of old-style and new-style anti-Christian attitudes of the ruling groups, by no means departed, here was a government with several top-rank men professing Christianity and with many Christians and graduates of Christian schools among other grades of officials. Not a few Christians were alert to new possibilities of good citizenship, joining in national reconstruction at a time of critical opportunity when the well-being, perhaps the very existence, of China was at stake. The government, on its part, was seeking the co-operation of Christians in many service enterprises, such as public health, mass education, the New Life Movement, rural improvement.

Nevertheless, not all was easy. The government, like the Chinese people, still did not understand the nature of a church or provide for it a tolerable legal and public status. In 1936 one major church body did secure registration with the government, but only in a category of guilds, unions, student associations, and the like, where the church had to accept, in principle, guidance from the Kuomintang, political decision on any meeting out of routine, and the obligation to expel any member who "violates the law." In practice, these conditions were ignored both by officials and by church, but the problem of status remained awkward and was never satisfactorily solved. Various "organizing" political activities, especially among youth, plus wide extensions of military and police control of many phases of public and even of neighborhood life, disturbed churchmen. Dr. W. Y. Chen, Secretary of the National Christian Council, who in general approved and led Christian co-operation with constructive governmental programs, boldly declared, "A fascist movement seems to be under way in China."[1]

The full-scale Japanese invasion from July, 1937, with its vast brutalities and dislocations, followed by exploitation of the occupied areas and thousands of air raids upon the free areas, rallied all responsive elements to national resistance under General Chiang's leadership. The immense humanitarian services undertaken by the Christian organizations themselves, and their conspicuous or substantial roles in other social services, were rewarded by grateful appreciation which lessened old prejudices and fostered new understanding of Christian and missionary motives and character. A number of the messages delivered through radio and press by Chiang Kai-shek on Christian occasions such as Good Friday, Easter, and Christmas were lay sermons that emphasized the unconquerable faith and courage, the will to serve and to sacrifice, even through the Cross, which Jesus Christ set before men in living example. Nevertheless, Christian involvement in public service brought prob-

[1] Eleventh Biennial Meeting of the National Christian Council, Shanghai, May 5–10, 1935. Also quoted by *Chinese Recorder*, Vol. 68 (1937), p. 343.

lems of bureaucratic and even of quasi-totalitarian procedures, of close association with prominent persons who could be honored for Christian name and merit but also distrusted and hated for individual and social faults, some actual and some produced or multiplied by partisan slander. One could not serve largely in that mixture of good and evil and keep unspotted from the world. Moreover, the higher a man stood then in public or quasi-public services, the greater would be the peril for his life or his good name after the Communists took power.

When, in 1943, the United States and British governments renounced the treaty privileges of extraterritoriality and other extraordinary rights, missionaries strongly approved and the Chinese exulted. It was not expected that this change would have important practical results, since for some time Christian effort had not depended upon the treaties. But the anxiety over the legal position of the churches was enhanced, and the government did nothing substantial to improve that position. Meanwhile, the persistence of Western supporters of the Christian enterprise in China and of related wartime benevolence was severely tried by a fixed exchange rate amid rapidly advancing inflation. The Chinese government's financial plight was indeed desperate. But it was hard to maintain extraordinary giving when the Treasury, in effect, took a large part from each American dollar or pound sterling. (This hardship was at last overcome in 1944.) By 1945 the price level had gone upward of 1,000 times prewar, and emergency measures of many sorts barely kept alive people who depended on money incomes.

During the war period the Communists were desperately seeking medical and other supplies, besides useful personnel. They welcomed and flattered Christians, emphasizing similarity of aims and their own devotion to freedom. Nevertheless, the total experience of the Christian workers resident in Communist areas, and the limitless need of freer regions which possible reinforcements would have to cross before reaching the Communists, plus the deterrent influence of the National government, prevented any noticeable inward movement.

The Japanese reluctantly recognized foreign missionaries as persons with "rights" and influence in the occupied areas, and the churches as valid but dubious institutions. They forced most of the British missionaries out of North China in 1939 and interned or exchanged practically all missionaries (save Germans) after Pearl Harbor. Meanwhile they were attempting, with the help of Japanese pastors, to organize the Chinese churches in a manner to facilitate direction and control. This effort was drastically successful in Manchuria and formally so in North China. In each case, however, Chinese and Japanese Christian elements, in unexpected relationships, secured certain minimum benefits of protection and fellowship.

The close of the war eliminated the Japanese; saw the Communists expanded from their prewar 3,000,000 subjects to some 90,000,000 and set to advance their power yet further; and found the National government sadly unequal to its overwhelming tasks of recovery. To say nothing of the Japanese and puppet currencies, two successive national currencies disappeared in Gehenna, with portentous consequences psychological and political, as well as economic. As soon as the necessity of resistance against the Japanese was past, the Chiang regime was no longer supported or accepted as the symbol of national survival but was judged corrupt, incompetent, and unable to secure internal peace either by negotiation or by force. Only a fundamental change could make life tolerable. The great majority did not want the Communists to be the rigorous and exclusive agents of necessary change. But if the government would not or could not usher in a better day, as each month of 1947–1948 taught more and more people to feel, millions would gradually move from reluctance to acquiescence and even to hope in the one possibility of strong-willed peace with an empowered program *to do something* about the plight of the country. The great part of the Japanese and of the Communists in bringing about the catastrophic situation is not forgotten. But we are concerned with the situation in which most Christians had to live and work, and also with their response to it.

Christian leaders were grievously disappointed, indeed outraged, by the continued suffering of the people in privation and in warfare, after eight long years of the Japanese invasion. They could not influence the Communists. They did issue public statements of moral and humanitarian judgment and appeal.[2] Moreover, in something of the temper of Hebrew prophets, they spoke privately to high personages in Nanking, including Chiang himself, declaring the loss of

[2] As, for example, in the "Statement from the Council," Twelfth Biennial Meeting, December 3–11, 1946.

popular confidence in the government, "because of its corruption
and apparent lack of interest in the welfare of the people," and pre-
dicting that, unless more was done for the people's living and for
freedom, the government's war effort would fail, "with dire and
disastrous consequences . . . for generations to come."[3] They were
ready to join in a program of improvement, the best weapon against
Communism. Thenceforward they continued to suffer the displeas-
ure of Chiang and others because they would not endorse all-out
mobilization of human and material resources, as prominent Roman
Catholics had done. Meanwhile, the accumulating evidence of persecution and restriction of Christian effort in Communist areas was
somewhat blurred after 1947, even for the Catholics, by efforts of
the Communists to gain a name for moderation, and the consequent
hope of Christians that they might have more living room than they
had feared.

2. *The Churches and Missions. Size and Growth. Relations*

Quantity is not the first Christian concern. But it is one indicator
of the quality that cannot be measured; and it certainly is related,
though not simply, to vitality and growth. Were the churches seriously set back by the long period of war? Did they enter the Communist era in vigorous condition?

The 1936 figure for communicant members was 536,000. To this
could be added 31,000 for Manchuria and possibly 10 per cent not
reported, chiefly Chinese sects. (That would mean some 623,000.)
The reported baptized non-communicants were 82,000, to which
Manchuria would add 7,000. Leaving aside the complications, the
basic figure of 536,000 shows a doubling in the scant twenty years
from 1917, despite the civil wars and the Nationalist revolution, the
anti-Christian movement, and the Great Depression. The Church
was growing substantially, not spectacularly.

The postwar picture is difficult to draw. Before the losses and the
accessions for 1937–1945 had been counted, civil war and the Communist damage were extending rapidly and without possibility of

[3] National Christian Council, Stencil 62-3, Strictly Confidential, "Report on a
Visit to Nanking," July 11–12, 1947, with some eighteen persons representing
Protestant Christians.

measurement. But some significant data are available in the reports of the denominations for a *Directory of the Protestant Christian Movement* (1949 and 1950);[4] in the statistics of 777 local churches answering a questionnaire late in 1946; in the statistics of 44 church districts, comprising 2,031 local churches with 241,000 total membership, for the same season; and in some competent generalizations of other evidence. The 1950 *Directory* figures were for "Christians" including all baptized, and could be added to show a total of some 900,000, which some persons gleefully compared with the 536,000 of 1936, communicants only. But the later figures included Manchuria and Taiwan. Moreover, they also added 125,000 for the True Jesus Church, and 30,000 for the continuing Presbyterian Church (which did not enter the Church of Christ in China), both of them reports impossible to check but probably subject to discounts of 50 per cent or more. On the other hand, no statistics were reported for the China Inland Mission after the thirties (then 85,000 to 95,000), and so their old figure has to be repeated without change. For a number of the church bodies one fears that in the manifold disturbances of the period most additions to church rolls were gladly reported but subtractions were less dutifully made, and that some entire local churches were left for verification by Him who seeth the invisible.

An effort has been made to compare carefully the figures for 1950 with those for 1936, in the reports of each of the larger church bodies, with results only partly convincing. Tentatively, we put forward the following hypotheses: (1) The older and familiar bodies may have gained 20 per cent. (2) An important and disproportionate fraction of the total increase was among Chinese sects. On the other hand, realistic reports of losses in the war years and of the crushing of church life in Communist areas before 1950, plus evidence of weakness noted in 1946–1950, make us wonder anxiously whether new accessions all along could so generously have offset the losses. The 44 church districts reported late in 1946 covering some 30 per cent of all Protestant members showed a growth of 15 per cent over 1936. Some—not all—of the reports on rural churches, an important component in totals, were gloomy indeed. All in all, the

[4] National Christian Council, Shanghai, preliminary and revised editions, respectively.

net change in the period, including a postwar rally in many areas, but probably not allowing adequately for fresh losses, seems to show growth which was a true achievement in the persistently adverse circumstances. The rate of growth, however, was much less marked than the rate before 1937.

Taking 1937 as the base, 5,800 organized churches and 7,000 other places of regular worship were served by 14,500 Chinese evangelistic workers, of whom 2,135 were ordained. There were just above 6,000 missionaries, of whom 1,084 were ordained. Many of the missionaries were engaged in educational, medical, and other services, though they might also aid churches directly.

Among ecclesiastical bodies, the Church of Christ in China was the largest, comprising 123,000 communicants or some 23 per cent of the total. It was built up through successive unions of the churches developed by sixteen missions and churches of British, American, Canadian, New Zealand, Korean, and Chinese rootage. Presbyterian and Reformed stocks led the way, with contingents of Congregationalists both British and American in type; British Baptists; United Brethren; United Church of Canada, which included in China a Methodist component; and an association of independent Chinese Churches. This geographically extensive union was relatively loose, allowing great liberty to each constituent synod, which might maintain much of prior denominational tradition; but it was steadily gaining in spirit and in combined action. The related missions continued to assist the Church with some 1,150 missionaries and financial grants, especially on the institutional side. Missionaries as such had no constitutional authority but might be elected or appointed to various responsibilities just as were Chinese. About one-fifth of the delegates to the General Assembly in 1937 were missionaries.

Next in numbers were the churches related to the China Inland Mission and its affiliates, with 85,000 communicants and 1,350 missionaries. A definite theological outlook was firmly maintained, but no general church order was established. Local associations of churches were strongly influenced, however, if not actually controlled, by the pattern, instruction, and advice of missionaries, more or less grouped according to their denominational inheritance. Concentration upon evangelism alone had its advantages but was accompanied by serious weakness in the training of Chinese workers. At the end of 1936 there were, for 1,253 organized churches and double that number of outposts, only 61 ordained Chinese pastors and a total of paid Chinese workers in all grades only slightly above the number of missionaries. The Mission and its affiliates were well-organized powers, while there was no recognized church body of greater range than a district.

Other churches with more than 20,000 communicant members were those developed by the Methodist Episcopal Church, North; the Anglican fusion with Protestant Episcopal; the Lutheran Church of China, which combined eight bodies of Scandinavian, German, and American origin; the churches founded by the Southern Baptist Convention; and those of the Methodist Missionary Society of Great Britain. The evident process of union within a denominational family was carried forward in 1940 by the union of Methodist Episcopal Churches, North and South, and the Methodist Protestant Church, made possible by the union of those bodies in the United States; and, in the postwar years, by the accession of eight more bodies to the Lutheran Church of China, including two important German missions that contained Reformed elements.

All told, in 1937, 134 Protestant mission boards, societies, and specialized organizations were working in China. Twelve churches, or well-known families of churches—if the latter term has real meaning—covered all those with more than 5,000 members; and these held 86 per cent of all members and included 73 per cent of all missionaries. Consolidation proceeded far enough so that the nearly complete *Directory* of 1950 showed some 35 church bodies while the number of missions and assisting organizations remained at about 135. (These two figures cannot be put into direct ratio with each other, but each is fairly sound in its own category.) Further light on Protestant relationships appears through the National Christian Council, in which 16 churches (8 of them among the larger churches) of 306,000 communicants (61 per cent of all communicants) were members. The China Inland Mission churches, the Lutherans, the Southern Baptists, and the Seventh Day Adventists were not. Various procedures of *ad hoc* co-operation for relief and other "practical" purposes, especially in wartime, included these last and some other bodies, however. Important unions in educational, medical, and literary work carried their obvious merit but had a local or specific character, often without comprehensive significance for bodies that also had denominational enterprises in the same fields of work.

The intent and spirit of the missions co-operating with the National Christian Council and of a number of other missions were concisely stated thus by Dr. Earle Ballou, who was in a central position in 1935–1940:

> Christian work in China is no longer primarily the activity of a missionary body scattered widely over the country. It has not been for years. . . . Neither the missionary, nor the missionary society in the homeland, nor the mission station on the field, but the church is the vital and creative center of the Chinese Christian movement.[5]

Nevertheless, fact lagged behind the faith thus declared. The task and the need of the Church were so great, its personnel and resources so limited, that the participation of a considerable body of missionaries was a major part of its tradition, of its image before the public, of its motor and steering mechanism. The ratio of the missionary factor to the Chinese factor varied widely from body to body, even among those that held the same outlook as to the primacy of the Chinese Church. Some missionary groups appeared to others peculiarly self-deluded as to their humility. On the other hand, some Chinese seemed to ascribe to reprehensible mission dominance difficulties which were inherent in the Church or in the total Chinese situation.

The war experience and the deterioration in Chinese personnel and resources tended to enhance the importance of missionaries and of mission aid, though this trend was incommensurably offset by the decrease in the number of missionaries—catastrophic for 1941–1946 and again at the close of the period—and by other factors favoring Chinese responsibility, including the late effort to prepare the Christian enterprise for Communist rule.

In its desire to keep up with needs and changes in China, and to lead the tardy in North America, the China Committee of the Committee on East Asia (Foreign Missions Conference of North America) voted thus, late in 1944:

> That the China Committee recommends to the Boards that in cases where they have not already done so they transfer administrative re-

[5] *Dangerous Opportunity* (New York, Friendship Press, 1940), p. 25.

sponsibility for the work now under the control of the missions, including the direction of all missionaries, to the Chinese Church with which they are connected, or to administrative bodies representing it, and that, to avoid misunderstanding, the mission cease to function, other provision being made for matters affecting the personal living and finances of the missionary, such as salaries, children's allowances, housing, and health.

It is plain, first, that the China Committee saw need among some boards for such recommendation or prodding; and second, that it definitely favored for China having the church body absorb the missionaries, rather than a mission organization separate from the autonomous church but necessarily affecting the program of that church. In general, the further adjustments called for by the new situation of 1948–1950 were made in excellent spirit, with missionaries willing to serve as needed and desired by the Chinese church but resigning particular posts or withdrawing entirely when that seemed best for the church. In 1948 and 1949 there were a number of responsible statements by Chinese Christian leaders, appealing for missionary colleagues to stand by them in person during the transition to the new era; and appeals were made, even after the publication of the famous "Manifesto" of 1950, for the continuance of financial aid, at least for a time. In sum, relationships in the crisis years were in many bodies essentially good. The statements just mentioned throw a softening light upon the harsh repudiations of missionary imperialism which were to pour forth from 1950 onward.

3. *The Life and Work of the Church*

Brief treatment of the life and work of the Church from 1937 to 1950 must necessarily take for granted the usual and the local, selecting a few developments distinctive to that time and large in scale.

One extreme was found in the considerable numbers, more prominent in some bodies than in others, for whom verbalizing without much education or much action in a narrow but intense pattern of emotion and of moralism, and with an individualist emphasis, tended to ignore the *doing* of God's will; though they might learn in the *community* of love the possibilities of His Kingdom. The opposite extreme was seen in those for whom organized social service and devotion to public problems constituted the religion of Christ. Some churches served but little. Some schools and hospitals evidenced little of explicit evangelism.

But the commitment to evangelize was generally strong and in some quarters stifled the need for nurture. Ralph Felton, who studied rural churches in the Far East in 1936–1938, wrote that "The zeal for extending the Gospel among the Chinese Christians has certainly been as great as in any occidental country"; and again, "Evangelism is even today the greatest concern of the average pastor." On the whole, it was not too hard to gain hearers and marginal response. All analytic studies and reports indicate that the problems of follow-up, instruction, and serious enlistment in the life and work of the Church were more difficult than those of first contact.

Free-lance Chinese evangelists were becoming increasingly prominent. Their meetings were characterized collectively by highly dramatic preaching with emphasis on the Last Judgment and Second Coming and other phases of the hereafter; an ethic of prohibitions of specific sins of indulgence; simultaneous individual prayers spoken to be heard of men; simple choruses, often using Chinese tunes; confession of sins, sometimes to be publicly spoken, and some form of reconversion—both of these tending to draw Christians more than non-Christians, and to draw them away from previous church allegiance toward sectarian groups; biting attacks upon the historic or familiar churches and their leaders; a tendency to extreme separatism, even in the term used for God and the editions of the Scriptures used to maintain that term. As might be expected, the judgment of other Christian workers upon such "evangelism" included warm approval for reviving some dead Christians, anguish over dubious teachings, and hostility toward proselytizers and workers of division. The steadier programs of evangelism undertaken by local churches, by denominational organizations, and by the co-operative efforts in cities, often taking cues and materials from the National Christian Council, were directed rather more to non-Christians and comprised a larger element of teaching comprehensive Christian truth. There was, however, no hard line of separation between the two types mentioned.

The Chinese Home Missionary Society (nondenominational) and a number of denominational home mission efforts stimulated out-

The Protestant Enterprise in China, 1937–1949   13

reach into pioneer areas and frequently approached a foreign mission outlook in directing their work to non-Chinese tribespeople in the western provinces. They did not, for the most part, discover methods markedly different from those known to the missions from abroad; but they were a healthy stimulus and outlet for Chinese devotion.

The excellent union effort entitled *Hymns of Universal Praise* fortunately became available in 1936. Its superior selection and translation of standard hymns from the Church Universal, plus some seventy hymns and tunes, old and new, originating in China, in a few years earned sales of 300,000 copies, about one for every two communicant members in the country. The spiritual values in this instrument of common worship were so great as to inspire gratitude for its thorough establishment before 1950 and regret that its remarkable range of use could not include all the major bodies.

The years 1937–1950 saw the fruits of long preparatory work in personnel, experiment, study, and materials in religious education, chiefly under the auspices of the National Committee on Christian Religious Education (NCCRE), serving both the National Christian Council for general church purposes and the China Christian Educational Association for school uses. Its courses for children, for youth, for middle school students, for lay workers, and for rural folk arose out of the experience and devotion of trained persons at work among these groups. Moreover, the great advance in effort for the Christian home belongs in this same grouping, both by organizational relationships and by the methods followed. The *Handbook for Christian Homes Week* used by local workers sold 7,000 copies in the distraught year 1948. The *Guide Book for Christian Homes*, an item of over a hundred pages, required within a year (1948–1949) four printings in Shanghai totaling 50,000, and another in West China.

Responsible Chinese leaders and missionaries were deeply concerned over the ministry, which had grown well before 1937 but was falling far short, both in numbers and in training, of the needs of the expanding Church in a developing nation. Chinese traditions, the doctrine of self-support, the West's depression and China's devastating war, the attractive inducements of alternative forms of Christian or altruistic service—all worked against recruiting and persistence in the ministry. A very small and declining number of col-

lege graduates entered theological seminaries, as did a number, inadequate and declining, of senior middle school graduates. Much of
the local work was done by men and women, some of them both
devoted and intelligent, who had a junior middle school training or
less, followed by three years or less in a Bible school. This level was
much above that of the short institutes, which provided the distinctive training in the underdeveloped regions, often for candidates
coming from primary schools. The war period was very hard on the
training institutions and on recruiting. An earnest struggle was put
up, nevertheless, and real recovery was evident by 1948–1950, with
advances at some points. A number of the seminaries and training
institutions in 1937 (and, when they could, thereafter) were improving their training in religious education and for the rural ministry,
while developing also their refresher courses and short institutes for
pastors in service, more than usually important at the close of the
exhausting and limiting war.

Brief reference was made earlier to the emergency services of the
war period, as Christian responses to immense human need in the
national scene. Refugees totaling millions were, at one time or another, aided with shelter, food, medical service, necessities of travel,
and, when possible, protection against violence and abuse by Japanese soldiers. Relief services of longer range attempted to help some
most grievously in want, including at times personnel of schools and
hospitals. Child-feeding projects, necessarily selective, were important. Support for such relief work, beyond local contributions in
labor and in buildings, came largely from Christian sources in Britain
and North America. The National Christian Service Council for
Wounded Soldiers in Transit, the YMCA Emergency Service to
Soldiers, the New Life Movement Service Corps, the Chinese Industrial Cooperatives—these suggest a wide range of enterprises in which
Christians played important parts as organizers, workers, supporters,
along with other personnel and backing by public or general funds.
There is voluminous testimony not only to the quality of service
rendered but to the Christian example and witness in living service,
an identification with acute need throughout the long crisis. The
effort of missionaries to stay by and to serve in the darkest times
was rewarded by unprecedented acceptance as a part of Chinese
life, appreciated in various public tributes which are now important
for historical accounting to offset the condemnations of later years.

4. *Some Major Auxiliaries of the Church*

Christian activity in education was peculiarly important in China, where the teacher was held in honor and the priest in contempt. By 1937, Christian primary schools were less needful and less serviceable to the Church than formerly, but there were still 2,800 reported, with 175,000 pupils. Ninety per cent of the teachers were Christians. Most of these schools were conducted in close relation to local churches. The churches and missions operated 255 middle schools, with 53,000 students, two-thirds of them in the coastal provinces. By 1939 the war had closed 37 schools, though about 15 of them continued to provide informal classes, and had combined 37 others into 9, in a major trend away from the coast and the central cities, but a minor, contrary trend into the temporary safety of Shanghai and Hong Kong. Fewer schools soon reached the same total of students, with increases in the ratio of girls and in the schools receiving both girls and boys. The percentage of students who were Christian, who enrolled in classes in religion, who were baptized during a school year, gained noticeably. Japanese attacks upon the United States and Great Britain cut off missionaries and their funds from the occupied areas, which areas were gradually extended, and destroyed the security of Shanghai and Hong Kong. These changes closed many middle schools; but in 1943–1944, 117 were known to be operating in free territory, besides a few irregularly elsewhere. Half of the 117 were on their own sites. Concentration was heavy in Szechuan and in Fukien. This skeleton report barely suggests the immense hardship for all concerned, and the tremendous burden carried by devoted people, in which the missionary share had declined. Relief grants of various sorts were necessary in the general impoverization of students and the mounting inflation.

Postwar removals, reopenings, rehabilitation, all in the midst of inflation and other economic troubles, brought further emergencies met partly by the missions and partly by relief funds, with tuitions doing more for ordinary maintenance. By 1947, 226 schools were known to be open, with at least 15,000 more students than before the war, of whom 37 per cent were Christians or inquirers—a ratio below the wartime best but about the same as in the thirties. Over 3,000 baptisms in one year were reported, a top figure. Even in the

fateful year 1949 the experienced Lautenschlager spoke to 87,000
students in 120 schools, Christian and government, securing nearly
5,000 decisions for a Christian life. It was clear that the middle
schools were an important element of Christian service and influence. They were in serious financial and administrative trouble soon
after the Communists took over any area.

In 1937 one-seventh of the college and university students of
China were in the fourteen Christian institutions, several of which
had outstanding merit in medicine, the natural sciences, agriculture,
English language and literature, the juxtaposition of Western liberal
subjects with the Chinese, and select elements in Chinese cultural
interests. Still small by some standards, the enrollment of 6,400 students had doubled in ten years, one cause for the complaint that the
Christian factor and influence in the colleges were not growing proportionately. Better than a fifth of the staff were missionaries, especially prominent in the medical schools. In a pattern of rising budgets
and expanding programs, income from Chinese sources had risen to
36 per cent of receipts, up from 20 per cent in 1930 and 10 per cent
in 1925.

The displacements and special services of the wartime are well
known. Only one institution was able to continue on its own campus
throughout the war—and it was host to four refugee institutions;
some had to move more than once. A great many research and training projects and undertakings of social service were directed to
urgent needs of the immediate region, while often of wider value.
Nutrition, the improvement of Chinese educational and medical supplies, study of men and nature on the little-known western bor-
derland, all sorts of technical aid to struggling industries and to
Christian enterprises of rural church, literature, religious education,
were instances of characteristic service. The extraordinary financial
needs of the wartime and postwar periods were met in considerable
part by the Associated Boards (latterly the United Board) for Christian Colleges in China, New York, and co-operative aid from London. Kuomintang political controls and activity in the colleges were
troublesome all through the years we are considering, despite general
friendliness and a modicum of financial aid from the government.
Toward the end the Communist agitation was difficult. Nevertheless,
the Communist public power did not, generally speaking, crash
heavily into the colleges until after 1950, though early disturbance

by laborers, underlings, and malcontents was fostered, and the staff were closely watched for their seriousness in "reforming themselves" during a preliminary stage of indoctrination and adjustment.

Christian medical service was, in 1937, a vast enterprise, providing 240 or more hospitals, according to the definition, besides some 600 additional dispensaries, clinics, or health stations. These latter tended to dwindle as the burdens upon the hospitals exceeded their strength and the government began to emphasize extensive and preventive medicine rather than full hospital service. Only 600 missionary doctors and nurses were in service, but 530 Chinese doctors and 1,000 graduate and 4,000 student nurses composed the core staff. The usefulness of the hospitals and their personnel was tragically enhanced by the long, harsh war and the great list of civilian casualties plus the increased incidence of disease among the poorly nourished. The problems of supply and support mounted also and were met in some fashion only through special and general relief services. Moreover, the war struck directly at the very existence of hospitals, besides drawing continually upon their inadequate personnel. Using a count of 268 for the year 1936, by 1939 no less than 62 had been destroyed, forced to close, or significantly damaged or looted. Of 217 in service in 1940, 121 were in occupied territory, where most of them were soon to pass out of recognizable character, if not entirely out of existence; 42 were in what were then listed as "fighting areas," a number of them to be taken by fresh Japanese advances and all subject to damage and stoppage of supplies. Only 54 were in safely free areas, some of them under air raids. As of that time, in the entire country, over 60 per cent of all the hospitals and hospital beds open to civilians were Protestant Christian.

At the end of 1942, a survey on a different basis showed 127 Protestant hospitals operating free of the Japanese. Of the five medical schools, only West China's was functioning fully—it was, indeed, even strengthened. Fewer than 40 of the prewar 143 nursing schools, with under 1,400 students as against the former 3,800, were continuing. And this was not yet the nadir, as hospitals and staff continued to diminish. Fewer than 100 missionary doctors were in service in 1945–1946, and the need for trained Chinese was terrifying.

Rehabilitation was accomplished only with great and continuing aid from various international agencies, important support from the missions, and much hard work for an impecunious public. In December, 1946, 203 hospitals were open, the majority under Chinese doctors. By 1947 the hospital beds were up to 17,000—still far below the prewar 22,000. But new blows from the Communists came while precarious recovery was yet incomplete. In the summer of 1948, 172 hospitals were in service, mostly south of the Yellow River, and all five of the medical schools. When strong foreign aid was cut down or cut off, various supplies could not be replaced, political interference with staff and discipline developed, and measures adversely affecting the flimsy finances were enforced or threatened. Most of the hospitals were at the end of human endurance before the close of 1950, or by the time they were actually taken over by the Communist authorities.

The extensive circulation of the Bible in China is well known. In 1936, 76,000 complete Bibles, plus 87,000 Testaments and over 9,000,-000 portions (usually single Gospels), were extant—rather high figures for a church membership of some 600,000, incompletely literate and very poor. Despite the advantage of one central language, 28 tribal or special languages and versions were used. The program of Christian literature was poorly co-ordinated despite persistent and devoted efforts, which achieved some highly useful co-operation, subject to criticism from every quarter. Distribution was probably the weakest link in the chain of work. The 160 periodicals published, most of them highly local or sectarian, had an aggregate circulation of 300,000. The Seventh-Day Adventist *Signs of the Times* supplied 70,000, and the relatively new *Christian Farmer*, with a simple vocabulary, which was found to reach seven readers for each copy, 30,000. Wartime damage to the publication, transport, and distribution of the Scriptures and of Christian literature was beyond understanding. One can only be grateful for the devotion and sacrifice that made possible extraordinary effort and reduced results, the more to be prized because of the need and the desire for them. The quantitative and qualitative rally at the close of the war culminated in the emergency effort of 1948 and 1949 to push distribution and sales, while providing three years' supply of Scriptures in the depots of thirteen cities, extraordinary stocks of hymnals in nine centers, and unusual reprinting of selected books in Shanghai and West China.

The YMCA and YWCA loomed larger in China than in some countries because they appealed to students, to young people, and to educated urban groups for whom the Church had inadequate attraction. Also, they successfully made Chinese leadership and responsibility, with the development of Chinese personnel, their first and central principles of work. In many centers their secretaries were indispensable leaders of co-operative Christian endeavor. The war hit hard their student work and their strong programs in eastern cities but gave them extraordinary opportunities for service, valued the more in hard times. Both of them undertook some new work in western cities, besides emergency and relief services to refugees, to students, and to soldiers. The versatility and competence of their staffs were almost a liability, in the sense that voluntary and governmental service organizations pressed hard for such talent and character.

5. *Faith and Thought in the Chinese Church*

The relative weakness of the Chinese Christian movement in thought-out and formulated theology and in recognition of the place of the Church in Christian life and understanding is familiar. The radical dislocation, hardship, and emergency demands of the war period were not generally conducive to quiet, persistent thought; and the stimuli of publication and conference diminished, especially after 1941. On the other hand, many Chinese were experiencing and developing faith, in prayer and in service, through suffering and response to suffering, through fresh confrontation of evil and the issues set for faith by the flourishing of evil. The collapse of many of the ordinary supports of life left some spirits free to turn more earnestly to God, or impelled them so to turn. Despite the many aspects of exhaustion, those who by faith endured to the end of the eight years' international war—the mature among them previously prepared by civil war, revolution, and the anti-Christian agitation—were surely better equipped in spirit to enter the testings of 1948 to 1950 and beyond than were neophytes or men in other countries of calmer experience.

In brief compass, we had best attend to Dr. T. C. Chao, one of the most helpfully productive of Chinese Christian thinkers and writers, unique as any leader is unique, yet representative in the sense that he shared widely in the fellowship of the Church and stood for the actualities and potentialitis of those who worked near him as colleagues and followed him as teacher, pastor, author. The Japanese invasion and its portents as to the weakness of Chinese institutions, culture, and morals; faithful concern for the spiritual future of the Chinese people; the relative seclusion of "occupied" Peiping after 1937, combined with requests for his own contributions to the great ecumenical conferences of 1937 and 1938, brought Chao to a clarified and empowered understanding of the Church. This understanding was wholesomely reached and declared, both in direct theological grasp and in Christian comprehension of the function and place of the Church in society, and in relation to the nation's fate. His most careful and complete formulation was in the paper prepared for the International Missionary Conference at Madras (1938) entitled "The Future of the Church in Social and Economic Thought and Action," where he had in mind the concrete Chinese realities of desperate economic problems, the National government, the Japanese, and the Communists. "The up-to-date Chinese Christian," he declared, "is really at heart and in spirit a Confucianist under a different name; for the force of circumstance has turned Jesus into a Confucius. Those who follow him do so because of his character, not because of his religion." Then Chao turned to his positive message: "It is high time to build up the Church as such, a divine-human institution whose foundation is Jesus Christ, revelation of God, and the word Incarnate, whose function it is to transform men and women, through faith in Jesus as Savior, and through reconciliation to God in such a faith, and to be a power for utmost social regeneration. . . . For the Christian, the Church should be the *sine qua non*. It should be the mediator between two worlds, the world of eternal truths and the world of historic changes."

After considering directly the issues of economic systems, of democracy, of the family, Chao concluded: "The Church makes and must make its impact upon society in social and economic matters, as well as in other matters, through trained spiritual leadership of various grades and by spiritual means. So it is, that its distinctive contribution to the making of a nation is primarily in its becoming its full and developed self, embodying forth the love and power of God in dynamic and loving personalities."[6]

In carefully prepared papers of 1947 and thereabouts Chao set

[6] *China Papers for Madras, No. 3*, National Christian Council, 1938. Also complete in *Chinese Recorder*, Vol. 69 (1938), pp. 345–354, 437–447.

forth his critical appreciation of Chinese culture and his realization of its failure to meet the demands of the modern world; "But today Chinese life is shaken to its very foundations. Its philosophy, ethics, religion, art, language and everything else, are falling to pieces." Chinese thinkers lack the ability and the cultural base to conserve selectively the values worth continuing. "Christianity alone has the power, not only to redeem Chinese men and women as individuals, but to redeem their culture and fulfill their aspirations." Chao then stated the orthodox Christian creed as bringing to China the transcendental faith without which her own idealism had proved futile.[7]

In his study for the Whitby Conference of 1947 on "The Problem of Communication," entitled "The Articulate Word," he faced various aspects of the work of the Church in China. "Fears have been expressed in some quarters, that in Communist areas the preaching of the Gospel will not be permitted—as though preaching were the only means of 'communication.' No Communist regime, however rigid and fierce, can prevent the fellowship of love and the communication of the Word by contagious conversion. Doors in such areas, I believe, are not closed but left open, for the daring and spiritually adventurous to enter."[8]

Chao's moving essay "Christian Faith in China's Struggle" is a weighing of the weakness and strength of the Christian position, with despair seeming to prevail over confidence in the future of the Church. Exhaustion of the Church's servants and deficiencies in high leadership are evident. Some prominent Christians "represent only corruption, avarice, and shame," while others have absolutely no connection with the worship and service of the Church. "The most popular religious appeal in China today is contained in selfish teaching and selfish enthusiasm for salvation." Not a few young people, willing to lose themselves, "go over to the Communists. They see slight hope in the Church for salvation of their nation."

On the other side, Chao recounted the familiar contributions of Christianity to China, from the nineteenth century forward, including "parental tyranny" among the evils fought and conquered, "freedom, love, and equality" among the ideas spread, "the upbuilding of

[7] *International Review of Missions,* Vol. 35 (1947), pp. 482–489; also, with variations, in the Whitby report cited in footnote 8.

[8] C. W. Ranson (ed.), *Renewal and Advance,* a report from Whitby, pp. 124–133.

the small Christian home" among the achievements told. He distinctly says of Christianity, "It encouraged patriotism and gave many of its useful, active church members to the service of the nation." "Twenty years ago, the Christian Church in China was stigmatized as the forerunner of foreign imperialism, . . . as the dispenser of spiritual opium that incapacitated the people for services to their nation. . . . But now, all this is changed. Even Communists, who are generally and traditionally against Christianity, declare that religious freedom should be given. The general public has faith in the Church and in its auxiliary organizations." Chao maintained, secondly, that the Church stands for faith and moral life, which have disappeared or sunk low in China; thirdly, that "this faith is backed up by a definite philosophy of life, which China seeks blindly today," spiritual freedom and equality rooted in the love of Christ, a dynamic for true democracy; fourthly, that the Church has, although divided, real life and strength in each local group, which, joined with the great institutions and service agencies, is reconstructing the spiritual life of the people; fifthly, that there is a growing will to unite and strengthen the Church "to meet the unprecedented opportunities and dangers ahead of us"; finally, that, weak and weary though the Church in China is, "It can count on the support, spiritually, morally, and practically, of the worldwide Christian fellowship." Indeed, Chao affirmed, "No power can cut its spiritual connections with Christian forces throughout the earth."

But, after reflecting upon the contemporary scene and the helplessness of the Church within it, Chao concluded soberly: "If, speaking as one without faith, on account of its inability to meet practical issues in China's struggle for democracy and peace, the Church should weaken and dwindle to nothingness, what will be the cause? Will it not be the weakness of the Church itself, its clergy or its evangelism, the weakness of the heart of the Christian movement? It does not seem impossible for the Christian faith to be eliminated from China a third time!" But from this prospect Chao drew back: "Of course, this possibility is still quite distant. The Church is today a living factor in Chinese life. . . ."[9]

---

[9] The entire essay is found in the collaborative volume, *Christian Voices in China*, Chester S. Miao (ed.) (New York, Friendship Press, 1948), pp. 4–32.

CHAPTER II

The Christian Mission Since 1938:
In Southeast Asia

WINBURN T. THOMAS

Commission on Ecumenical Mission and
 Relations of the United Presbyterian
 Church in the U.S.A.

New York, New York

Bibliographic Introduction

My primary source of information concerning the Christian movement since 1938 has been personal experience. From the year 1933 to late 1940 I was a missionary in Japan. One summer was spent in China and Korea. From 1940 to 1942 I continued my research into the history of Asia at Yale University. In 1948 I returned to Asia and for the next ten years traveled constantly, from Japan to Pakistan. Seeking material for *The Christian Century* and the Ecumenical Press Service I inquired concerning the progress of the Church at each stop. Because of my background in Japan and China, and conscious of the extent to which each of these nations had been affected by the Japanese occupation, I sought answers to the questions which comprise the material in this paper. The first draft, therefore, was written without consulting any outside sources.

The best single record is the annual surveys found in the January numbers of the *International Review of Missions*. Occasional articles deal with the situation in particular countries. The book reviews indicate any important works in the field. These numbers were then consulted for the purpose of filling in details.

Few major works have been written in this twenty-two-year period by Christian workers in the area about the church situation.

The symposium edited by Bishop Raja Manikan, *The Church and the Asian Revolution,* is an exception. Dutch and German scholars have written several important studies in the Dutch and German languages, which on the whole are profounder than the works of American and British writers. When Dr. Latourette's present *magnum opus* is concluded we will have a definitive story of the churches for these years, but it will be some months before the last volume of his series is off the press.

The churchmen in Asia are not yet history conscious. They are too involved in the struggle to strengthen the life of the churches to record the process, or to ascertain what has already happened. This has been true even of Japan, China, and India, where the peoples are much more conscious of historical process than are those of Southeast Asia. The best work has been done concerning Indonesia, and most of it by Dutch, German, and Swiss missionaries and scholars. They have brought to their task a background in the "science of missions" obtained from their continental studies in theology, and also in Warnecke's Mission School in Germany. Some of the most helpful articles in the *International Review of Missions,* for instance, are translations from Dutch missionary magazines.

Two recent world events have stamped their imprint upon the whole Christian movement throughout Southeast Asia, namely, the Japanese occupation and the communization of the Chinese mainland. The Japanese occupation tactics varied from country to country, but in each instance the military regime cut off the churches from their sources of mission subsidy and curtailed Christian activities. The exclusion of Protestant missionaries from China by the Communists reminded the sending agencies for the second time within a decade of the necessity for the younger churches to be able to stand alone. These two experiences have accelerated the trend toward self-government and self-support. The churches of Asia in 1960 are much more self-sufficient and self-conscious as independent entities than they were in 1938.

During the postwar years, relations between most sending societies and church bodies were resumed, and in several of the lands new missions entered, some because they had been excluded from China, others because of enlarged horizons, still others because of the affluence of America made possible by the multiplication of sectarian missionary activities. The achievement of political independence and the holding of regional political meetings, such as the Bandung Conference of twenty-nine Asian and African peoples, strengthened the regional solidarity of Christian groups. Asian churches became conscious of their mutual missionary responsibilities, which led in several instances to their undertaking of foreign missions. The ecumenical experiences of Asian Christians led to a strengthening of national as well as of regional movements committed to unity and mission. In addition to the traditional evangelistic, educational, and medical approaches of missions, stimulus was given to literacy work, industrial evangelism, the expansion of literature programs, the utilization of audio-visual aids, and a new emphasis upon home and family life, all of which had been emphasized by the Madras assembly of the International Missionary Council in 1938.

The War

As the Japanese forces moved southward into Indo-China in 1940 and into the remainder of Southeast Asia after December, 1941, they reorganized the political, economic, and social life of each country. Save for Thailand, all the occupied lands were under alien rule. Thailand long had retained its technical sovereignty as a buffer between the three rival colonial powers, Great Britain, France, and the Netherlands. A direct consequence of the Japanese occupation was the emancipation of each of the subject lands, in some instances by fiat of the imperial power, in others as a consequence of war and revolution.

The Japanese varied their policy from land to land, depending upon the reaction of the peoples to their coming, and to a lesser degree upon the value to Japan's war machine of the raw products, and the attitudes of the military officers. In each instance a puppet government was organized, conforming to Japan's ideology of "Asia for the Asiatics." In some cases the slogan had little effect; in others the Japanese propaganda was accepted in the beginning, but as Japan displayed a colonial policy no less harsh than that of the displaced European powers, hostility developed, resulting in rebellions and guerrilla fighting. The Evangelical Church of Timor resisted the

Japanese army's efforts to utilize it as a propaganda instrument—
surprisingly, in view of the spiritual immaturity of this church body.[1]

When the Japanese occupied the areas, the Christian movement
suffered loss of property and personnel. The leadership of the
churches in Malaya devolved primarily upon the Chinese and Indians, though the Anglican Bishop and two chaplains were permitted
for one year to conduct their ministry. Missionaries in Thailand were
either interned at the University for Political and Moral Science,
Bangkok, or escaped overland through Burma to India. Some of the
missionaries in Indo-China were permitted to continue literary work
and Bible translation while interned in the hill station. The Annamese Bible Training School at Tourane and the Mission Press in
Hanoi continued to operate until 1945. The Burma Christian Council
was removed to India; Christian workers refugeeing in Jubbulpore
prepared literacy materials and planned their return strategy. Four
Thai and 100 Burmese Christians were executed for their refusal to
co-operate with Japan. National Christians kept the Burma Christian
schools in operation at peril of their lives. Thai churches were used
as military billets, so the congregations worshiped in private homes.

Christianity was identified as the religion of the Western powers.
Japan sought to play up Buddhism and Islam. A Conference of Mus-
lims was held at Singapore in 1943.

A district conference for Indo-China was held in Saigon in March,
1943, and a Christian youth conference at the same time. A skeleton
staff of missionaries continued to work until March, 1943, when they
were moved to Dalat. After August all were interned save a French
missionary couple.

The Japanese sought to exploit some Christian communities as reconciling elements in dealing with civilian populations. Assurances of
religious freedom were given, but in execution it served the Japanese
religious practices and aims.

The holding of conferences and assemblies was possible in some
places, not in others. The work of the General Assembly of the
Church of Christ in Thailand was carried on during the war by the
Executive Committee. In Malaya the Methodists held annual conferences until 1944. Conferences were held annually in Indo-China.

---

[1] G. C. Oosterhuizen, *Theological Discussions and Confessional Developments in the Churches of Asia and Africa* (Franeker, T. Wever, 1958, pp.
322), p. 184.

The Japanese military set up a special department as liaison between the army and the churches to implement the military decisions. In some instances, as in South Borneo, where the Protestant-military representative was a devoted pastor from Japan, every possible aid, including some financial subsidy, was given to the churches.

The Japanese catered to the dominant religion of the area, as an aspect of their self-determination policies. Thus Buddhism used its position in Thailand and Burma in anti-Christian activities, forcing some Christians to repudiate their faith. The Moderator of the Church of Christ in Thailand was among those who capitulated to the Buddhist demands of the wartime puppet government. Churches were closed on Timor, even though Protestantism was the dominant faith, for Moslem Java was the principal island in the pseudo-independent state of Indonesia. The Batak Church, isolated from Muslim influences, grew by 100,000 members during the occupation, but the growth was not an unmixed blessing. There was a relapse among many of the members to native Batak practices such as visiting and bathing in so-called "holy waterfalls."[2]

The dislocations incident to the war took pastors and members away from their churches and closed Christian schools; church hospitals were impressed into military use. The more than forty mission hospitals in Indonesia were taken over by the Japanese military and subsequently surrendered to the Indonesian government. Many of them have not yet been returned to the churches.

The churches suffered financially both because of termination of Western subsidies and because of the economic dislocations of being geared into the Japanese war economy. Some funds were made available through the Orphaned Missions fund raised by the International Missionary Council especially in aid of the German Rhenish Mission work in Sumatra. The issuance of occupation "Mickey Mouse" currency by the Japanese military, which became highly inflated, and the struggle for bare existence reduced the capacity of the churches for self-support, for which they had been ill prepared during the preceding missionary era.

Church properties were requisitioned for Japanese military purposes. They were not kept in repair, so that at the end of the war even those which had escaped battle fire and bombings were in bad condition. Since they served as military installations, they were the

[2] *Ibid.*, p. 188.

objects of Allied bombings in Timor and in Minahasa with the result that most of the large structures were completely destroyed. Refurbishing and rebuilding them was a heavy drain upon mission and church resources after the conclusion of hostilities.

One salutary consequence of the war was that New Zealand and Australian Christians became aware of their neighbor to the north, the Netherlands Indies—now Indonesia. Airmen shot down by Japanese and rescued by Indonesian Christians reported their experiences in their home churches. Several Protestant agencies in Australia and New Zealand are now working in Indonesia in co-operation with Indonesian church bodies, as an outcome of this war-born experience.

The Japanese-sponsored Federation of Evangelical Churches stood in direct line of development from the Evangelical Union in 1901, the National Christian Council organized in 1928, and the Philippine Federation of Evangelical Churches organized in 1937. Immediately upon the Japanese surrender, the prewar Federation was rejuvenated with committees on church union, Christian education, and youth work.

The Federation-sponsored Evangelical Church of the Philippines was promoted by two ministers, both of whom were tried by court-martial at the close of the war. One was convicted, the other freed by a 4–3 vote. The moral deterioration was marked by stealing, lying, and looting. Ellinwood Church in Manila was spared only because an elder stood guard during the hectic days after the city was recaptured by the Allied troops.

The end of the war found 80 per cent of all the church property destroyed. Congregations had fled the towns into the mountains. Pastors who had been killed had been replaced by laymen. Professor M. Gambon stated, "The major task of the Evangelical Church is to recapture that sweetness and fineness of character for which the Filipinos are noted." Methodist Bishop D. D. Alejandro pointed out in 1946 that while anti-Japanese feelings were natural, these primitive emotions were evoked by resentment and hatred and were marks of self-centeredness. The new world order required that the Filipinos remove the barriers which would be a bar to mutual understanding and a detriment to the national character. If the Philippines are to live up to their reputation as a Christian nation, he charged, "we must love our enemies."

When Hitler invaded Poland in 1939, German missionaries in

Sumatra were no longer able to communicate with their homeland or to receive funds. The Missionary Consulate in Batavia cabled the International Missionary Council for aid, and the Dutch allocated some of their limited funds to help. The orphaned missionaries continued until Germany invaded Holland in May, 1940, when the German missionaries were interned by the Dutch. Funds from the IMC helped continue the work of the HKBP (Batak church) until the Japanese occupation. With the end of the war, the men interned in India and their families in Sumatra were helped for the eighteen months before return to Europe was made possible. They finally reached Germany in July, 1947, almost two years after the ending of the war in Asia.[3]

The effects of the war were both horrible and helpful. Loss of life, leadership, buildings, the deterioration of morale and morals were commonplace. Balancing these evil effects certain values emerged:

1. Servicemen were befriended by the native Christians and in many instances led into full-time postwar Christian service. Australian airmen shot down over Timor returned after the war to find their benefactors, and the Methodist and Presbyterian churches of Australia established personnel relations with the Synod of Timor.

2. The fact that the churches were required to shoulder responsibilities during the war isolation demonstrated that churchmen of Southeast Asia can carry much of the work formerly performed by missionaries. Mission boards recognized that such aid as might be extended in the postwar years would need to be along lines worked out by the indigenous churches. At Whitby it was openly declared, "The church emerged strengthened by the experience of suffering." The church in Malaya deepened its spiritual roots and learned self-reliance. While Indonesian churches list a loss of 30 per cent of their leadership, the young wartime leaders emerged as the head of the postwar church.

3. The outstanding need of the younger churches is for manpower, which must be recruited and trained from within their own ranks.

Ten new churches were constructed in Annam during the war years, four of them during the last year of the fighting. The churches

[3] William Richie Hogg, *Ecumenical Foundations* (New York, Harper & Brothers, 1952), pp. 304–305.

in Cambodia and Battambang made progress in self-support. The church in Laos, less ready for emergencies than elsewhere in Indo-China, suffered greater losses.

Postwar Revolutions

The Japanese surrender was the prelude to a new kind of war rather than peace in many of the countries of Southeast Asia. Thanks to the first taste of independence, and to the influence of Communist and religious elements in the populations, civil war wrought more physical damage in all the lands, save Thailand, than the Japanese occupation or the Allied liberation. The nature of the prewar Western imperialism helped to determine post-1945 events.

Japanese military commanders turned over to Vietnamese nationalists military supplies, saying, "We have lost the war, but not you." Thus the Vietnamese rebuffed the French attempts to re-establish control over Indo-China. Moscow-trained Ho Chi-minh led the Vietnamese resistance, establishing a national state with Hanoi as its capital. Serious fighting in 1949 leveled much of the city. The inability of the French to subdue Ho's forces resulted in the partition of Indo-China into four separate states, with northern Viet-Nam under Communist control. Few of the Christians from this area fled to the south. Little is known officially concerning the status of the church in North Viet-Nam today. Long-time guerrilla war had taken its toll of village church installations. The nationalistic aspirations having been shared by Christians as well as non-Christians, many of them were arrested by the French forces.

The Hukbalahaps, who had fought the Japanese, offered opposition to the return of America to the Philippines. Stimulated by Communist elements, and exploiting the rural poverty and absentee landlordism, they harassed large areas of the countryside until Magsaysay, first as Defense Minister and subsequently as President, pacified them. During the time they terrorized the land the work of the churches was affected, and the farmers from central Luzon who were transmigrated to Mindanao included some Protestants. These were sufficiently numerous to be organized subsequently by the Methodist bishop into a dozen or more congregations. This action necessitated a rethinking of the comity agreement previously ob-

served by the churches comprising the Federation of Christian
Churches, since Mindanao traditionally had been a field of the Congregational mission, and the congregations were related to the United
Church of Christ in the Philippines. The Protestant Churches recognized the threat inherent in the Huk and Communist challenge and
began a systematic study of Communism. The Philippine congregations received considerable assistance from the mission boards and
churches in America in the reconstruction of their many churches
destroyed or damaged in the guerrilla fighting or the fighting and
bombings incident to the Allied liberation.

Malaya likewise experienced civil war after the Japanese surrender, which hampered reconstruction activities. The Communist-led
guerrillas, while numbering hardly more than 5,000, were so dedicated, and such skilled jungle fighters that they constituted a difficult
security problem for the armed forces for more than a decade after
1945. In order to isolate the guerrillas, the government constructed
"New Villages" as new homes for over 400,000 Chinese, in which
curfew was observed. These became the locus of intensive work by
Christian agencies, organized under the Malayan Christian Council.
Fighters willing to surrender were concentrated in rehabilitation
centers. After two years of satisfactory conduct, they were freed
to return to their families. Limited Christian work also was conducted among these men.

Thailand technically had been an ally of Japan, so that nation
suffered a minimum of destruction. The church properties were
scarcely damaged, but morale had deteriorated. The church suffered
some fragmentation, thanks to Carl McIntyre's influence, including
the withdrawal of one who had served as wartime moderator. He
continues to constitute a severe problem for organized Protestantism.
Evangelistic campaigns were conducted around the country which
led to a doubling of the church membership. The Theological Seminary was reopened, and efforts were made to train a ministry, which
had been sadly depleted. Permission to open a Christian University
was also sought, but without success. The Church raised funds for
the erection of a fine air-conditioned office building. Thus Thailand
emerged from the war with the least damage, and the church was
able to resume operations more readily there than in any other land
in Southeast Asia.

The chaos which characterized Burma at the time of the Japanese surrender was compounded by civil war. At one time the government itself considered the advisability of going underground, so many were the factions engaged in civil war. Most of these were left-wing groups which differed among themselves as to the correct formula for rebuilding the nation. The assassination of the national leaders in 1947 was a severe blow to reconstruction efforts. Travel inside the country was hazardous. Christians were under a cloud because one of the warring factions was the Karen group, 40 per cent of which tribe were members of the Protestant Church. The Karens demanded their separation from the predominantly Buddhist nation. In the end they were given a semi-autonomous status within the nation, and the fighting was brought to an end. U Nu, who became Premier in 1947, since then has been in and out. For almost two years the government was under the control of General Ne Win, though he was replaced by U Nu, following a general election early in 1960.

The country which has experienced the most protracted civil war is Indonesia. When the Japanese took over from the Dutch, they established an Indonesian state with Sukarno and Hatta at its head. On the eve of the Japanese surrender, Sukarno proclaimed the islands an independent republic. After the Dutch began to return, incidents led to fighting, United Nations intervention, and in 1949 the transfer of sovereignty. For a brief time order prevailed in most of the islands, but increasing tension between Djakarta and the provinces led first to the revolt of the Moluccas in 1950 and then to another civil war in Sumatra and the Celebes beginning in 1957. This was terminated by the surrender of the rebels late in 1961. An abortive Communist-led *coup d'état* also occupied the Republican forces for a time during the struggle for independence. While the churches suffered from the Japanese occupation and from the civil strife, they received little from the Western sending societies to aid in their reconstruction. As this is written, conditions remain unsettled, and the position of Christians is still difficult, caught as they are between the Moslem majority and the growing power of Communism. One of the consequences of freedom is that missions are permitted by the Indonesian government on Bali.[4]

---

[4] A statement of the situation as of 1938 is given by Dr. Henry P. Van Dusen in his *For the Healing of the Nations* (New York, Charles Scribner's Sons, 1950, pp. 222), pp. 38–47.

Renascent Non-Christian Religions

The identification of nationalism with the dominant religion of each land, the reaction against Western colonial control with a repudiation of the Christianity that was its handmaiden, and philosophical liberalism have combined to revive the religions of Southeast Asia.

This phenomenon is most notable among Buddhists in Burma, Thailand, and Cambodia. U Nu, as premier and holy man, has succeeded in revitalizing Buddhism. By calling attention to the fact that the so-called Christian nations have incited and been the primary antagonists in the last two world wars, he has claimed that Buddhism alone can bring world peace. The Buddhist holy scriptures are being retranslated, and several Buddhist world conferences have been held in Asia during the years following World War II.

Islam is the professed religion of 85 per cent of the populace in Indonesia. The political divisions of the nation and the growing strength of organized Communism have prevented Indonesia from becoming an Islamic state. The participation of certain Moslem leaders in the rebellion which started in 1958 has weakened the Moslem Masjumi, at one time the most influential among the nation's political parties. Christianity in Indonesia has suffered most from Darul Islam, under which banner many of the guerrilla groups have operated, frustrating relief attempts and preventing missionary activities in Mid-Celebes, West Java, and parts of Sumatra.

The National Churches

Thanks to the Japanese occupation, and to the independent status of the nations of Asia since the war, the Christian churches likewise have increasingly asserted their integrity as national communities.

The Protestant work in Indo-China having been a virtual monopoly of the Christian and Missionary Alliance, national church bodies now exist in independent South Viet-Nam, Cambodia, and Laos, but the missionaries of the sending society still retain considerable authority. When Church World Service began its operations in the hapless peninsula, the Vietnamese ministers were threatened with ouster if they accepted any of the aid or co-operated with the work. This situation has now changed with the Missionary Alliance taking a much more co-operative attitude toward the ecumenical operation.

The largest Evangelical church bodies in the Philippines are the Methodist, the United Church of Christ in the Philippines, and the Baptists, concentrated in Iloilo. Missionaries have been incorporated into these bodies with considerable success, and a number of missionaries hold important posts within the church organizations. Dissident groups in the Baptist area have fragmented the work. The growing co-operation between the Episcopal Church and the Aglipayan, or Philippine Independent Church, which had split from the Roman Church at the time of the Revolution in 1898–1902, has led to the latter's being drawn increasingly into the ecumenical movement in the Philippines. The extension of holy orders to the priests and the opening of the Episcopalian theological seminary to Aglipayan priests have been two of the acts by which the Episcopalians cemented this relationship.[5]

The Church of Christ in Thailand and the work under the Christian and Missionary Alliance were the two major Protestant endeavors in Thailand up to 1950. After that date the American Baptists joined with the Church of Christ in Thailand in work among the Karens who lived in Thailand. The Marburger Mission, the American Disciples of Christ, the United Church of Christ in the Philippines, and the Presbyterian Church in Korea also sent fraternal workers to the United Church. The Southern Baptists and several other missions have begun work on their own, among both the Chinese and the Thai.

The major church bodies in Malaya and Singapore in prewar days had been the Methodists, the Presbyterians, and the Anglicans. These were connected primarily with the American Methodists, the English Presbyterians, and the Anglican Church itself. Their work was among the Chinese, Indians, and Western populations. The Methodist Church in Malaya is a part of the Conference of Southeast Asia, which includes Methodist work in Sumatra and northern Borneo. It is under the authority of a bishop who is an American. The Presbyterian Church is an independent national body, but closely tied through tradition and staff with the Presbyterian Church of Great Britain. An Anglican bishop has his seat in Singapore, with respon-

---

[5] "The Independent Church in the Philippines," *The Episcopal Overseas Mission Review*, Vol. V, No. 3, Whitsuntide 1960.

sibilities in Malaya, Indonesia and Thailand, the latter two instances involve the spiritual oversight of Anglican residents. After the closure of China, the China Inland Mission sent a large staff to Singapore, organized under the name "The Overseas Missionary Fellowship." As these workers have various denominational connections, they have tended to identify themselves with the Anglican, Presbyterian, Methodist, and Baptist efforts, especially in the New Villages.

The Baptist work in Burma is organized into a national convention, with special sections for the various tribal church bodies. Two separate Methodist Churches, one started by the British and the other by the Americans, operate in geographically separate areas. An Anglican bishop has his seat in Rangoon, with responsibility for Anglican work throughout the country.

The churches in Indonesia are primarily geographical in character, and secondarily ethnic. Denominational consciousness is only tertiary. Before the Japanese occupation several of them had declared their independence or received it from the mission bodies. During the occupation they were required to go it alone. Some of them have no missionaries on their staffs to this day. The old state church in Minahasa, the Moluccas, Timor, and Java has been hardest hit by the separation from the Netherlands. Each of the thirty-two bodies which comprise the Indonesian Council of Churches is completely independent, save perhaps the Methodist, which is a part of the Conference of the Methodist Church in Southeast Asia. Approximately 500,000 additional Protestants are in groups outside the Council, in many instances separated from former parent bodies. In addition, the Christian and Missionary Alliance has work in Mid-Borneo, and the Southern Baptists, having entered in 1951, are concentrated in a few cities on Java.

Missionaries and the Churches

The years from the beginning of the Japanese occupation to the time when missionaries were able to return to their posts saw a number of significant changes:

1. The churches were required to carry on without benefit of missionary advice or subsidy. Though they suffered during this period, they also developed considerable self-reliance on the part of

the national leaders into whose hands responsibilities formerly carried by missionaries was thrust.

2. The change in the political status from colony to free nation has set an example to the churches. If the nation can be self-governing, the churches should be able to operate without benefit of missionary assistance also. The foreign policy of each nation and its attitude toward the cold war continue to condition the receptivity of missionaries from abroad.

3. The closing of China has caused heart searching among the older sending societies, making them realize that the time may come when they cannot extend assistance, and pointing up the necessity for preparing the churches to become self-sufficient as soon as possible. The result has been increased emphasis upon the three "selfs" (self-support, self-government, and self-propagation), and acceptance by the missionaries of the obligation to prepare the churches for this eventuality.

4. The closing of China and the affluence of postwar America have increased the quantity of American missionary effort by groups which previously had not been working in these lands. Save in the Philippines, there was little denominational spread in Southeast Asia, as compared with the many foreign agencies operating in Japan, China, and India, for instance. Save for the Baptists in Burma, the Presbyterians in Thailand, the Christian and Missionary Alliance work in Indo-China and parts of what is now Indonesia, and the American Methodist work in Malaya, Burma, Sumatra, and North Borneo this large area was not within the thought of the American churches.

Thanks to the accent during the American occupation of the Philippines upon preparation for self-government, the major Protestant churches early achieved independence, though large subsidies from abroad have continued. The Philippines looked forward to their liberation by MacArthur's forces and welcomed the Americans, including the missionaries, upon their return. There has been almost no limit to the number of Western workers who could be received and deployed in the Philippines. They engage in educational, medical, and evangelistic work, moving both in cities and in countryside. While the United Church and Methodist churches alike have Filipino bishops, missionaries continue to be elected to high administrative posts in the churches. Since the war, several of the larger Manila churches with American pastors have called Filipino co-pastors, or the American has stepped out. The relationship between missionaries and the national church in the Philippines is as cordial as that to be found anywhere.

The Christian and Missionary Alliance formerly worked in Indo-China. With the division of this colony into four autonomous states, the work of the church also was divided. The largest concentration of Protestants is in South Viet-Nam. No missionaries remain in the communist-dominated northern state. The Evangelical Church of South Viet-Nam is friendly to missionaries, and relations between the government and the United States are such that visas are easily obtained. Christian work in Laos and Cambodia has been much smaller scale than in Viet-Nam, in Laos because of the rugged terrain and the isolated population; in Cambodia because it is predominantly Buddhist and thus unresponsive to the Christian message. The Swiss Brethren also work in Laos, but their mission likewise is very small and the church has less than 500 members.

The Thai situation is a paradox. Whereas the nation and the church are friendly to missionaries the Buddhist character of the culture has made for slow growth. The majority of Christians are from the Laos tribe in the north, and among the Chinese residents. A customs official said to a missionary a decade ago, as he passed his freight through the port area with scarcely a look, "We welcome missionaries," and well they might because of the contributions made educationally and medically. Missionaries hold high positions in the church and in ecumenical organizations. There are no restrictions upon their entry.

The missionary participation in the life of the churches in Burma is quantitatively much less since the transfer of sovereignty than before. Burma has ruled that no foreigner can fill a post if the work could be done by a national. So while doctors, teachers, agriculturalists, and other technicians under boards of missions have been welcomed, evangelists—that is, missionaries whose major work is preaching—have been virtually excluded. Again, those missionaries already in Burma continue to enjoy the respect of the church and its Christians and are elected by the church to important positions in the Christian program.

The situation vis-à-vis the missionaries in Malaya and Singapore is quite similar to that which prevails in Thailand. Little direct work among the Malayan peoples is attempted, with the consequence that there are almost no Christian converts from among this original racial group. Missionaries, together with the church, have a free hand among the others. Missionaries are heads of institutions, preach in local churches, and are important staff members of the church bodies.

Protestant missionaries always have been relatively few in Indonesia. The European churches never attempted a blitzkrieg in the islands. The large numerical growth has been among the spirit worshipers, and other sub–races which have not embraced Islam. German missionaries among the Bataks and on Nias were reduced by the war and since 1950 have been replaced largely by a few staff members sent out by the Lutheran World Federation. A few Swiss missionaries work in Borneo, and a small number of Dutch missionaries are related to approximately half the regional and ethnic church bodies. With the return of many Dutch missionaries to their homelands, some have been replaced by Americans, Australians, New Zealanders, and Filipinos. D. T. Niles has said of Asia generally, "Missionaries are needed, they are invited, they are not wanted." With respect to Indonesia Dr. Niles might well have said, "They are needed, they are wanted, they are not invited." Because missionary visas must clear the Ministry of Religions, which is under the leadership of a Moslem, the difficulties of obtaining them have prevented many boards willing to assist from appointing personnel. The protracted civil war has forced a number of the workers from overseas to return home, or to change their locus of operation.

Missions in the Ecumenical Age

The movement toward unity and mission has been accelerated by many of the factors indicated above. Ecumenical agencies on regional and national levels have been created, and Southeast Asian Christians have rendered distinguished service in the organization of the East Asia Christian Conference.

The East Asia Christian Conference, while not born officially until 1959, was anticipated as early as 1941. In the comments concerning the Netherlands East Indies at that date, the editor of the *Interna-*

tional Review of Missions mentioned the need for a Christian Council for Southeast Asia.[6]

The unity forced by the Japanese during their occupation, the example set by the new national governments, and the movement toward unity in the western and other parts of Asia have stimulated these developments.

The Philippine Federation of Christian Churches with departments dealing with home and family life, youth, university students, audio-visual aids, industrial evangelism, etc., has been the ecumenical clearing house for these islands since its organization in 1945. (It was the successor to the Philippine Federation of Evangelical Churches organized in 1938, and reorganized in 1942 under Japanese pressures, to include all evangelical groups.)[7] This body possibly has frustrated the trend toward organic unity. The United Church of Christ in the Philippines, organized in 1948, includes the Presbyterians, Congregationalists, Evangelical United Brethren, Evangelical and Reformed, and most of the Disciples, and the Philippine Methodist Episcopal Church, which in seceding from the larger Methodist Church in 1933 had deleted four articles from its confession of faith.[8] Theological education, university-level institutions, and the Mary Johnston Hospital in Manila have brought together various groups for co-operative activities in the educational field.

The Malayan Christian Council is the center of co-operative Protestant activities in Singapore and on the peninsula. The fact that Trinity College and the Council have shared a staff member since the late 1940's illustrates how the church bodies and missions have come together functionally. The work in the New Villages has been organized and administered under this body. Together with Thailand, Singapore has been the locale of a number of ecumenical meetings. The Council has been the agency through which the church bodies have played host. The fact that the field representative of the Nanking Board of Founders has made Singapore his headquarters also has focused considerable ecumenical attention upon the area.

Thailand so long having been a single-church nation, the National Christian Council tended to be the lengthened shadow of the one church. When the Southern Baptists entered in 1949, Presbyterian

[6] *International Review of Missions*, January, 1942, p. 22.
[7] *Ibid.*, p. 218.
[8] *Ibid.*, pp. 221–222.

missionaries helped them get started. When the American Baptists made overtures for permission to work inside the Thai border, arrangements were made with the Church of Christ in Thailand. As the Christian and Missionary Alliance felt the need to follow the Laos tribes from Indo-China inside Thailand, the church conceded the area where the Indo-China mission body was to work. During the war, ministers of the Church of Christ in Thailand supplied pastoral care to congregations there. The very fact that since the war a number of new missions have entered, and that several additional churches are in process of development, has enabled the ecumenical agency to serve an increasing purpose.

The Burma Christian Council too has had but a limited purpose since the bulk of the Christian work has been Baptist in character. The secretary has been the minister of a Congregational church, an Indian by nationality. There is increasing feeling, thanks to the growth of nationalistic spirit, that this post should be held by a Burmese. The departments of literature have prepared literature in the several languages and dialects. The Audio-Visual Department utilizes a van to take motion pictures into the countryside.

The National Council of Churches in Indonesia was organized in May, 1950, almost one-half year after the transfer of sovereignty. Unlike the other national councils, the Indonesian body stated in the constitution that it was being formed to help create a single united Protestant church body that would be nation-wide. No unions have followed from its organization, but it has become the authoritative voice of the Christian bodies to the world and to the central government. A number of commissions carry out its functions. Whereas the national Christian councils had been formed of churches and missions, the missionary bodies were excluded from membership in the Indonesian Council. Instead, a Commission on Missions was organized, with a dual function, explained by the double meaning of the word "mission" in the Malay language. It is the body charged to work with the member churches for the evangelization of the nation. It also is the foreign affairs section of the Council, to relate to mission boards at the invitation of member churches. It has been the channel through which the Council has been affiliated with the International Missionary Council integrated into the World Council of Churches at New Delhi in November–December, 1961, as the Division of World Mission and Evangelism. Through its initiative, a number of non-European bodies have entered into partnership arrangements with the existing churches.

The Lutheran World Federation, at the invitation of the HKBP (Batak Church), is undergirding this, the largest church body, with personnel and funds, especially for the development of educational institutions, technical aid, and medical services. The Federation also has been invited by the Church of Nias, which like the Batak Church had developed from operations of the Rhenish Mission, to supply personnel. The Federation serves as a clearing agency only, through a field representative who has offices in the headquarters of the HKBP, channeling personnel and funds contributed by Lutheran bodies of America and Europe.

Influence of World Ecumenism upon Ecumenical Developments

The oldest of the ecumenical agencies, the Bible Society, has served as a catalyst in bringing the churches together for at least one purpose, the distribution of the scriptures. The Bible Society of the Philippines, which prints the Bible in the vernacular languages, also collected information from the churches in 1950 for the compilation of a directory, published in the periodical of the Philippine Federation of Christian Churches. The Bible Society of Malaya and of Burma has been closely integrated through staff and activities with other ecumenical developments. The Bible Society of Thailand illustrates the functional character of comity in this nation, the secretary being supplied by the Christian and Missionary Alliance. The Bible Society of Indonesia is, according to the constitution of the National Council of Churches, a member body, a relationship that does not exist elsewhere.

The existence and activities of the International Missionary Council, and since 1948 of the World Council of Churches and its departments, have stimulated the creation of ecumenical bodies in each of these lands. The United Christian Youth Movement (MPKO) was formed in Indonesia by delegates who attended the Ecumenical Youth Conference after their return from Oslo in 1947. Another Christian youth body, however, the PPKI, owes its origins to national sentiment. For most of its history, membership was restricted to Indonesian subjects. The relationship between these two organizations remains unsettled, despite all efforts to bring them together.

The activities of the Division of Inter-Church Aid and Service to Refugees of the World Council of Churches have led to the organization of relief committees in connection with most of the national councils as agencies for the receipt and distribution of relief supplies and, in the case of Indonesia, for the resettlement of refugees abroad. Home and Family Life departments have been establishd, or at least energized, as a consequence of travels of International Missionary Council staff. Departments of Occupational Evangelism have been organized in the Philippines, Indonesia, Thailand, and Malaya as the result of a conference on this subject in the Philippines under the leadership of the Reverend Henry Jones of the United States in 1957. Audio-visual departments have been strengthened and in some instances initiated as a consequence of RAVEMCCO's activities, and especially its conferences held in the area. The Literature Conference held in 1951 under the Department of Literature and Literacy of the National Council of the Churches of Christ in the U.S.A. has accelerated the production of literature. The visits of Dr. Frank Laubach, under the same auspices, over a ten-year period have stimulated the production of charts for teaching illiterates and of Christian literature for the newly literate. Subsidies from this department have multiplied the book production.

The participation of Southeast Asian churches in the organization of the East Asia Christian Conference is significant. Because of its location, each of the meetings have been held in the area: first the meeting at Bangkok in 1949, then the consultation at the same place in 1955, which led to the calling of the Conference at Prapat in 1956 and the next meeting at Kuala Lumpur in 1958. One of the factors leading to this development was the missionary activity initiated by the Asian churches as a consequence of the Bangkok meeting in 1949; by 1954 several of the churches and missions had come together at Hong Kong to organize the Asia Council on Ecumenical Mission. The consultation at Bangkok in 1955 was called jointly by the International Missionary Council and the World Council of Churches in reaction to this development, which in turn led to the holding of the Conference at Prapat the following year and to the formal organization in 1958 at Kuala Lumpur. The East Asia Christian churches and councils were well represented at each of these meetings. Dr. Enrique Sobrapeña, one of the bishops of the United Church of Christ in the Philippines, was elected president of the Asian Council on Ecumenical Mission, and then of the East Asia Christian Conference. Church bodies in the Philippines have sent personnel to Thailand, Okinawa, Indonesia, and Nigeria. When Indonesia confronted a rice shortage in 1958, Burma was second only to the churches in the United States in the amount contributed to purchase foodstuffs and medicines for the Christians of the Indonesian nation.

The enthusiasm of the churches in Southeast Asia may be attributed first to the fact that the contacts of these Christian communities with the Western sending societies were relatively limited. They saw in the East Asia Christian Conference a new source of aid. Second, Indonesia and Burma, because of their neutralist or independent foreign policies, welcome assistance which originates in Asia, rather than in the West. Third, the long history of colonialism has tended to isolate the nations save from the United States, or the colonial country, and the land from which their missionary aid originated. Within the East Asia Christian Conference they were able to enjoy commerce and community one with another. Fourth, the East Asia Christian Conference has provided them with a platform from which to speak to the older churches of the West with an authority that they would not have as isolated national church bodies. Lastly, the organization paralleled the emergence of the Asian-African bloc in the United Nations, formed by the meeting of representatives of twenty-nine nations at Bandung in April, 1955.

Indigenization of Christianity

Whereas the Asians at Madras were convinced that the Christian faith should develop indigenous forms in each land, when delegates came together in Bangkok eleven years later, in a conference predominantly Asian in character, they were equally confident that the Christian faith and its community expression in the Church must be exotic to the earth. Nevertheless, there is a growing consciousness among Asian Christians that their Christian life and institutions have been transplanted from the West. They are cognizant that if the Christian faith is to speak to more than a tiny minority in these lands, the word must be in the familiar thought forms and consistent with the several national traditions.

Christian art, architecture, music, the liturgy, and sermons tend to be imitations of those prevailing in the lands of the mother churches. A theological breakthrough has taken place in Japan; Tamil Christians sing God's praises set to Indian music; word reaches the churches of Chinese Christian accommodation to the Communist regime. Few such developments are visible in the churches of Southeast Asia.

The most dramatic evidence of cultural adaptation is found among the Bataks. The Rhenish missionaries took the position that those elements in the native culture which were not inconsistent with Christian demands, such as polygamy, would be permitted. Thus there has been a mass movement of the Toba Bataks into the HKBP. It is not necessary for a Christian convert to repudiate his own traditions and culture to become Christian, as is the case on Hindu Bali or Islamic Java. To a lesser extent this same rule is followed on Timor, where a church of approximately 300,000 has developed within sixty years. One evidence of the adaptation process in these mass movement churches is the separation of the sacraments. After a village has been baptized, the new members must complete a minimum of three years of catechetical instruction before being admitted to the Lord's table. Folk dancing, so integral a part of Philippine culture, has been taken into the church. On the School Day in Manila the Christian schools come together for a dancing fiesta, each school performing dances prepared for the event.

Several of the church bodies of Indonesia, because they are territorial or ethnic in character, have refused to identify themselves with any of the Western denominations. The Church of Mid-Java, for instance, while stemming from mission work by Gereformeerde missionaries, and adhering to a polity and theology of the same order, refuses to take any name less catholic than "Christian." Most of the church bodies of Indonesia, while definitely within the Reformed tradition, have refused to join the World Presbyterian Alliance. The Batak Church, though it includes both Reformed and Lutheran elements in its polity and theology and has joined the Lutheran World Federation, has its own Batak creed. Drawing heavily upon Western credal statements, it is still original in that it seeks to confess its faith in its own social milieu. "Here is a church that realizes the circumstances in which it has to exist with an honest effort to confront it," says Dr. G. C. Oosterhuizen.[9]

The confession was adopted by the Great Synod of the Batak Protestant Christian Church on November 28–30, 1951. It is a Batak document drafted without assistance from Western theologians. It rejects many features of tribal religion which the church regards as inadequate, such as belief in ancestral spirits, and the idea that God's power exceeds His holiness and love. It repudiates the Moslem belief that Christ is to be compared with the other prophets. The separation of Church and state is accepted on the grounds that the tasks of the two institutions differ. The animistic concept that the soul of the dead influences the living is rejected. In these and many other articles the Batak confession speaks to its circumstances. The fact that the Lutheran World Federation accepted it was an acknowledgment that the younger churches "must be invited to confess the same Christ in their locality, in their time and language."[10] While more reference to their own spiritual background, and to the *adat* (customary law) and superstitions which still live in their Christian substratum, is expected, concludes Dr. Oosterhuizen, "this is a remarkable effort, the best effort so far in any church in Asia or Africa" to develop an indigenous theological statement.[11]

The Life and Work of the Churches

The emphasis of the Madras Conference upon the nature and function of the Church, together with events immediately preceding and the Japanese occupation which followed the International Missionary Council assembly, have resulted in the emergence of a strong church consciousness among Southeast Asian Protestants. Considerable advance is registered in the subsequent years in the areas of the Church's life and work which were considered in the Tamberam reports:

THE PLACE OF WOMEN IN THE CHURCH

The denominational groups and areas have varied in the extent to which women have been enabled to make their contribution to the

[9] *Op. cit.,* p. 189.
[10] *Ibid.,* pp. 189–191.
[11] *Ibid.,* p. 191.

fulfillment of the Church's mission. Southeast Asia being predominantly rural, there has not been the drift away from the church among business and professional women reported in other areas.[12] But because these areas traditionally have been a "man's world," and because of the hierarchical structure of the churches, the tasks to which women are called in the churches have not commanded their maximum abilities and energies.[13] Despite these handicaps the Home and Family Life studies and conferences sponsored by the International Missionary Council among the churches have contributed to the elevation of women to posts in the church. A Study and Training Institute for East Asian Christian Leaders held at Chiengmai, Thailand, in 1957 stimulated the national Christian movements to help build Christian homes, train leaders in the field of family life, and educate church members for marriage, parenthood, and home building.[14]

In the Philippines a number of regional family life conferences culminated in the First National Christian Conference on Filipino Family Life, December 5–8, 1957, and the observance of the National Family Week and the Forward Movement. This emphasis by the churches has changed the status of women in Christian homes. Home surroundings and sanitary facilities have been improved and the table diet rendered more nutritious. Family discussions of problems and household devotions have been introduced. Families worship together in church. A full-time staff worker serves in the Federation of Christian Churches, and pamphlets have been produced both in English and in the major languages of the islands.[15]

The churches began to elect women as elders as early as 1930. By the end of the war they numbered more than sixty, and at the 1946 General Assembly of the United Evangelical Church one-fifth of the delegates were women. Because of the large number of wartime casualties much of the church responsibility fell upon the women members. The congregation at Linga had but three men left at the close of the war. A village congregation in Oriental Negros consisting of

---

[12] *Madras Series*, Vol. IV, *The Life of the Church* (New York, International Missionary Council, 1939), pp. 23–24.

[13] *Ibid.*, p. 24.

[14] Minutes of the Sixth Post-War Biennial Convention, Philippine Federation of Christian Churches, March 10–11, 1958 (mimeographed report), p. 44.

[15] *Ibid.*, pp. 44–52.

101 families suffered the loss of 99 male casualties. With the ending of hostilities the women began gathering the children together in Sunday Schools, kindergartens, and daily vacation Bible schools.[16]

The churches in Indonesia suffered losses of 30 per cent of their trained pastors and teachers, with women taking the leadership in local congregational activities wherever necessary. The large number of war orphans required the churches to establish orphanages, with volunteer and paid staff taking care of the homeless children. Women elders were ordained to assist in the ministry of local congregations. In 1953 the first Indonesian woman was ordained; after a period of ministry with her husband in the Moluccas she became rector of the Union Theological School at Macassar. The first functioning executive on the staff of the Indonesian National Council of Churches was Augustine Fransz, who subsequently also served on the short-lived Constitutional Assembly. A Home and Family Department of the National Council was organized with headquarters in Malang, East Java, under the leadership of an outstanding Indonesian Christian woman. The visit of Miss Irma Highbaugh to Indonesia under the auspices of the International Missionary Council resulted in increased activity among the Kaum Ibu, or women's organizations of the local congregations. Women's Christian work in Indonesia is organizationally divided into the Kaum Ibu and the PWKI, which latter is as much a patriotic as a Christian organization. The PWKI demonstrated considerable courage at the time President Sukarno took a second wife, speaking openly in opposition, on the basis not of Moslem law (which would allow him to have four wives) but of a monogamous standard, which is the product of Christian and Western influences.

The shortage of trained pastors in Thailand also has resulted in the voluntary leadership of women. Women elders as well as men take the services in the absence of an installed minister.[17] A Department of Home and Family Life has been organized in the Church of Christ in Thailand, which holds conferences and publishes literature.

The Burma Christian Council also has a Department of Home and Family Life, with a program comparable to that in Thailand.

[16] W. Reginald Wheeler, *The Crisis Decade* (New York, Board of Foreign Missions of the Presbyterian Church in the USA, 1951), pp. 112–116.
[17] *Ibid.*, p. 125.

THE INNER LIFE OF THE CHURCH—WORSHIP

Worship is the major activity of all the churches in Southeast Asia. During the war even this activity was terminated in several areas. The Japanese invaders, seeking to appeal to the religious consciousness of the dominant religious groups, brought pressure upon Christians to renounce their faith and in many instances took over churches and other Christian buildings for use as military establishments. The degree of pressure varied according to the attitudes of the commanding officer. Some native ministers were interned or imprisoned because of their former connections with the missionaries, or because they were suspected of loyalties to the displaced Western colonial power.

Freedom of worship in some formulation is guaranteed in each of the new constitutions of the national states. The example set by the American army upon the liberation of the Philippines, with many troops and officers attending church services, improved the prestige of evangelical Christianity in the islands generally. Some few instances of local village opposition to evangelism have been reported, but freedom of preaching and worship exists throughout most of the nation. The same is true in Malaya, save among the Moslems; the decade-long state of insecurity caused by rebel activity has hampered village work among the Chinese and Indians. The fact that much of the rebel activity in Indonesia during the past decade has been in Christian areas has led to some curtailment of Christian activity, with rebel and government troops capturing and recapturing villages. Darul Islam activities in Mid-Celebes have resulted in the destruction of some churches and the murder of unknown hundreds of Christian believers. The government insists that this is not an anti-Christian activity but incident to the unsettled conditions. When troops pulled Ambonese boatmen out of a worship service in 1957 and impressed them into service, the church protested that this was a violation of Christian freedom and obtained an apology from the military. The postwar zeal of the Moderator of the Church of Christ in Thailand and the consequences of nation-wide evangelistic services have led to a considerable percentage increase in church members in this nation. Despite the enhanced status of Buddhism in Burma, thanks to the renaissance sparked by the Premier, U Nu, Christians insist that their task has been made simpler rather than more difficult because of the religious ferment at work. The largest church, the Karen, together with the whole Christian movement, suffered during the days of the revolution, because of the opposition offered to the government by the Karen Christians.

The Indigenous Ministry of the Church, Ordained and Lay

The church in all Asia is inadequate to the needs of the Christian mission. The lack of status, and the inability of the churches to support a full-time ministry, has forced the laity to take a large responsibility for the ongoing church operation. A postwar effort to strengthen theological education facilities has resulted in an increase in the number of ordained ministers available. This move has been from within each of the national churches, and aided by outside agencies, including the sending societies, the Nanking Board of Founders, and the Theological Education Fund.

There are four major theological seminaries in the Philippines. Union Theological Seminary in Manila is operated jointly by the United Church of Christ and the Methodist Church. The Silliman University School of Theology is operated by the United Church of Christ. St. Andrew's Episcopal Seminary in Manila serves primarily the Aglipayan Church, which a decade ago had no theological training facilities. The Baptist Central Seminary in Iloilo trains ministers primarily for the church affiliated with the American Baptist Convention. The Bachelor of Theology degree given in the Philippines would be comparable academically to a bachelor's degree in an American church college.

During the past decade, Trinity College, Singapore, has been developed to serve as an English and Chinese language training institution serving the Methodist Church, the Anglican Church, and the Presbyterian Church. Contributions from the Nanking Board of Founders plus sizable grants from the participating mission agencies have helped make the development possible. The course extends over four years. Graduates of upper middle schools (twelve years' preparation) are eligible for matriculation. The college offers a B.Th. degree.

The leadership of the Indonesian churches traditionally had been predominantly lay rather than ordained. The 2,422 Christian village school teachers, who also ministered to the Christian community, constituted 61 per cent of the total number of all indigenous workers in 1936.[18] In the mass-movement areas it had been thought inadvisable to have two *gurus*, who would divide the local leadership. This arrangement also kept the costs to the Christian church at a minimum, since the funds for paying the school teachers came from the state. Since the end of World War II, this method of support has been less favored but remains somewhat common.

Next in the hierarchy of religious leaders were the unordained evangelists, who engaged in a full-time evangelistic ministry. The amount of training and prerequisites for entering the ministry varied from a two-year course for a person who could read and write up to three years for a grade school graduate; 1,132 of these constituted 29 per cent of the indigenous workers in 1936.[19] A number of their Bible schools remain in operation today.

In 1936 only 415, or 10 per cent, of the indigenous workers were ordained.[20] They were graduates of special schools which had three years of middle school as a prerequisite for admission. Most of the theological education remains on this level, with schools operated by the HKBP (Batak Church) at Pematang Siantur, the Church of Mid-Java at Jogjakarta, five different church bodies at Malang, the Evangelical Church of Kalimanten (Borneo) at Bandjermasin, a Union Theological Seminary of the churches of eastern Indonesia at Makassar, and the Church of the Moluccas at Ambon.

The Higher Theological School, the institution which has most affected the character of church leadership in Indonesia, was started at Depok in 1934, later moving to Bogor and thence to Batavia, now Djakarta. Since six years of middle school were required for entrance, it was at the same academic level as the university faculties. Only one class was graduated before the Japanese invasion, but this class supplied much of the leadership of the church during the period of occupation and in the years subsequent to the war. The Batak Church has established a School of Theology at Pematang Siantur in connection with Nommensen University with similar standards,

---

[18] *Madras Series, op. cit.*, p. 224.

[19] *Ibid.*

[20] *Ibid.* For an account of theological training in Indonesia before World War II, see Van Dusen, *op. cit.*, pp. 48–54.

though a select number of graduates of the lower grade theological school also are admitted.

The Theological School at Chiengmai, Thailand, was closed and its charter was relinquished shortly before the outbreak of the war. After Japan's surrender, several years of negotiation were required to obtain a new charter. During these years a maximum of seven students could be trained at one time. Since the re-establishment of the school, the enrollment and academic standards have risen, though even yet students are admitted after the equivalent of an American primary school education. The recruiting of theological candidates is difficult in Thailand even today.

The Baptists operate a divinity school at Insein, near Rangoon, which grants a B.D. degree. The requirements for entrance and the quality of the instruction are comparable to those of the Silliman University School of Theology.

In each of these lands, as Dr. G. C. Oosthuizen has stated, the church "grows faster in numbers than spiritual needs can be served by the ministry." Low salaries and lack of community status do not make the ministry attractive in Asia. Having undergone the academic discipline requisite to obtain a theological education, most graduates can earn double or triple the pastor's salary by accepting government or business employment. In Thailand in 1948 not one of the seventy-nine congregations was being served by a seminary-trained minister, though the school before closing had trained almost that number.

Thus, many of the village ministerial services in Southeast Asia are being performed, and will be performed, by laymen and laywomen. Most of the ministers on Bali support their families by farming or operating some small business. In other areas of Indonesia, local pastors earn part of their income by serving as government-paid instructors of the Christian religion in the schools. The excellent system of schools in Malaya operated by the churches makes it possible to have a preacher serving during the week as schoolmaster. The economic situation in each of these lands is such that the churches must be content with untrained lay leadership or with trained leadership subsidized by funds from abroad.

21 *Op. cit.*, p. 188.

CHRISTIAN EDUCATION

Christian educational activities in Southeast Asia range from cate-chetical classes among the newly baptized mass-movement Christians of Timor to the operation of Christian universities. At each level, the churches have been cognizant of the two questions put by the Madras Assembly: (1) "How can the Christian educational enter-prise best carry the treasure of the Gospel into the life of the na-tion?" and (2) "How can that enterprise so strengthen and enrich the life of the Church itself that it may become in its own land a strong witnessing member of the world-wide Church of which it is a part?"[22]

Many obstacles which carry over from the earlier period have stood in the way of the implementation of the ideal implied by these questions. The funds for the general education program have been in large part supplied by the mission agencies and by the national government, collected in the form of fees, or raised as contributions from the alumni. A tension thus exists between the Christian churches and the Christian educational institutions which is not easily resolved, since the economic situation generally has made the churches in the postwar period even less able to supply the needed finance. Many of the church's sons and daughters are educated in the institutions and join the staffs as teachers and administrators, so there is an interde-pendence which is salutary.

The emphasis of Protestantism upon education in Southeast Asia has been one of its major assets. Schools from kindergartens to uni-versities have been established. Whereas Japan pre-empted the field of primary school education for the state, Burma and Thailand per-mit the missions and churches to operate lower-grade educational institutions but exclude them from the field of university education. While private universities are permitted in Malaya and Singapore, no Protestant Christian effort in this field has been made.

The Association of Christian Schools and Colleges in the Philip-pines provides supervisory and co-ordination services for the many Christian educational institutions in these islands. Since education in the Philippines was a profit-making enterprise, the government levied a tax upon gross educational income. The Association, in co-opera-tion with the Catholic Educational Association and the Philippine

[22] *Madras Series, op. cit.,* pp. 56–57.

Association of Colleges and Universities in 1957 obtained the repeal of this tax after ten years of litigation. Financial problems confronted by some of the church- and mission-operated schools have resulted in the lowering of educational standards, with resulting recommendations from the Bureau of Private Schools that such be closed. Some have consolidated to reduce expenses and improve standards. Yet the church regards the schools as integral aspects of its witness. The Bible is taught daily. Were it not for the schools some of the local congregations would have collapsed. Students fill the pews, and educators have a community-wide evangelistic influence, some in hostile areas. Protestant schools in the Philippines are a definite evangelistic as well as educational influence.[23]

Education is a specialty of the Christian movement in Malaya and Singapore. Out of ninety-seven government-aided English schools, more than one-half are operated by Christian missions. Sixty per cent of English-language education for girls is under Christian auspices. The sixty-three Methodist schools enroll more than 42,000 students. While the institutions are avowedly Christian in purpose, the government pays the salary of all staff members, determines the curriculum, and matches the church-contributed dollars in erecting buildings, when they are owned by the church. Complete freedom of religious instruction makes possible the use of the Bible in the curriculum.[24] With the granting of independence, and the development of national spirit among the diffused Malayan-Chinese-Indian communities, questions are being raised over the dominance of the educational field by Christians. The schools can look forward to increasing restrictions upon their freedom as the Moslems make their voice heard in the new government.

This development already has occurred in Indonesia, where under the colonial regime the church was the major educational agency. Whereas the literate group was primarily concentrated in the Christian communities when the Japanese occupied the archipelago early in 1942, universal education under the republic has multiplied the literacy rate at least 400 per cent within fifteen years. The 1,500 Christian primary schools (some up to the fourth grade only) and the 250 Christian middle schools are now only a small proportion of the

---

[23] Minutes of the Philippine Federation, pp. 96–97.
[24] Rajah B. Manikam and Winburn T. Thomas, *The Church in Southeast Asia* (New York, Friendship Press, 1956, pp. 171), p. 61.

total educational effort. A Moslem member stated in Parliament in 1952 that, as the Christians had been favored educationally by the Dutch, they now should be penalized so that the Moslems might catch up. Legislation passed in 1953 threatened to penalize the Christian schools in the islands reaching from Bali to Timor by making state subsidies for Christian schools available only after all expenses for government-operated schools had been met. An Association of Christian Schools, which is not an official part of the National Council of Churches, represents the educational institutions in all matters of a national character. The decision of the government to demand a number of years of teaching service in government schools from all graduates of state normal colleges resulted in the establishment of two union Christian institutions of higher learning: the Christian University in Djakarta, and the Christian Normal College in Salatiga. The former is sponsored by a committee of the National Council, the latter by eleven co-operating church bodies. These have been aided by the United Board of Higher Education in Asia, mission boards, and Christian agencies of Holland, the United States, the Philippines, New Zealand, and Great Britain.

As in Malaya, Christian education has been one of Protestantism's major thrusts in Thailand. Sixteen Christian middle schools for boys and girls (mistakenly referred to as "colleges") have been restored to high academic level since World War II. While government officials patronize these institutions, the proportion of Christian graduates remains low. The non-Christian alumni exert an increasing influence upon the schools because of their financial support. Postwar efforts to establish a Christian university were frustrated, the government reasoning that, since it would be primarily an American-dominated effort, the Chinese would demand similar privileges. As the Thai government fears the Communist infiltration of Chinese-sponsored education, Christians thus have been refused the privilege of establishing and operating a university-level school.

Burma's Christian schools were an important element in the church's program. Located primarily in the Karen area, 173 primary schools, 31 middle schools, and 28 high schools were in operation shortly after the Japanese evacuation of this land. The absorption of Judson Christian College into the University of Rangoon and the refusal of the government to allow the establishment of an intermediate college were expressions of nationalistic fervor which has placed

Christian education at a disadvantage. The organization of more than 7,000 state schools has reduced the quantitative impact of Christian education.

Religious instruction is permitted or provided for in all of these lands, at least for Christian students. In Thailand all students enrolled in Christian schools are eligible to take some Bible. In Indonesia students in government schools can demand Christian instruction at state expense if they number a dozen. Christian Protestant influence through required Bible instruction, however, is being increasingly restricted because of pressure upon the governments from non-Christian religious majorities, and from non-Christian alumni.

Christian education provisions outside the churches vary considerably in the area, depending in some measure upon the mission agencies which have initiated the Christian movement in each of the lands. The American emphasis upon methodology has resulted in considerably more Sunday School and daily vacation Bible school classwork in the Philippines, Thailand, and Burma than is found in Indonesia. Such emphasis has remained unchanged during the twenty-two years, though in the American-influenced places graded curricular materials, following the American example, are used. A beginning was made in Indonesia by the visit of Dr. Elmer Homrighausen in 1955, and by the offering of limited courses in Christian education in the Makassar and Malang theological schools. A textbook based on Dr. Homrighausen's lectures was printed in the Indonesian language, but no widespread use in the local congregations has been made of the emphasis he brought.

The relative importance of Christian education has declined since the close of the war because of the expansion of government education facilities. As the Christian schools have been one means of reaching the non-Christians, this witness becomes proportionately restricted as the several governments provide educational facilities. Missionary personnel has been utilized to such an extent in educational work that in theory this development should release foreign staff for non-institutional work. In practice such has not been the case, since the churches and mission schools continue to operate at capacity. Thus the impact of Christian teaching is only relatively reduced.

Youth and student work has expanded since the war, thanks again in large measure to the American influence. The department in the

Philippine Federation of Christian Churches has sponsored voluntary organizations in many of the non-Christian universities in the islands, including a chaplaincy and student center at the University of the Philippines. The Student Christian Movement of Malaya with volunteer staff conducts a program both in schools and among students at the University of Malaya. A student hostel has been organized under the Malayan Christian Council. The Student Christian movement in Indonesia and the YMCA, which was organized after the war, conduct voluntary student programs, and the YMCA operates a number of student hostels. Student hostels have been created in Thailand too since the war by the YMCA, the YWCA, and the Church of Christ in Thailand. Facilities of the former Judson College in Burma are now used as a base for Christian work. A Christian center for the students at the University of Rangoon has been erected and is maintained co-operatively by the Student Christian Movement and the Burma Christian Council. No work is conducted by the Christian and Missionary Alliance in South Viet-Nam in the educational field save that for missionary children and ministerial training. The Menonnite Central Committee and Church World Service have sponsored work among university students in Saigon.

THE CHRISTIAN MINISTRY OF HEALTH AND HEALING

Christian medical work in Southeast Asia suffered great losses during the war, with the facilities being taken over by the Japanese armies for military purposes. Though new Christian hospitals have been created in Manila, Bangkok, Bandung, and Madiun, these do not compensate for the loss suffered during the fighting. Because of the expenses involved in maintaining medical services, continued subsidy from mission boards and/or governments has been a prerequisite for their continuance. Thus the implementation of the Madras statement "The Church must be given an effective share in Christian medical work" has been difficult.[25] There has been general recognition within the churches, and within the leadership of the Christian agencies operating the services, that "the ministry of health and healing is essentially a community service and has a wider outreach than can always be provided by the organized Church."[26]

[25] *Madras Series, op. cit.*, p. 163.
[26] *Ibid.*, p. 164.

The United Church of Christ and the Methodist Church have co-operated in the establishment of the Mary J. Johnston Hospital and School of Nursing in Manila. The Southern Baptists have erected the finest hospital in the nation at Madiun, in central Java. The Church of Christ in Thailand has constructed a hospital in Bangkok. The Seventh Day Adventists have built hospitals in Manila, Bandung, and Bangkok. Nine Christian hospitals continue in Burma, though the famed Namkam Hospital started by Dr. Gordon Seagrave is now a privately operated institution, and an appeal for funds was carried in *The New York Times* in April, 1960. Only a few of the fourteen hospitals operated by the Church of Christ in Thailand are staffed by qualified missionary or Thai doctors today, though medical work has been and continues to be one of the church's outstanding national contributions. Some of the medical staff of the Overseas Missionary Fellowship (CIM) have been allocated to these Presbyterian hospitals in Thailand.[27]

Most of the more than forty mission-church hospitals in Indonesia were taken over by the Japanese military and later surrendered to the Indonesian military. Some of them subsequently were taken over by Dutch forces, and in 1949 all were turned over to the Indonesian government. Hospitals in Bandung, Djakarta, and Tomohon were returned to the church bodies, but in 1958 the Djakarta institution was threatened again with seizure by the military. The large former Christian hospital in Jogjakarta now is managed by a private Christian organization. Relying largely upon grants from the Ministry of Health, these have had difficulties in operating as Christian hospitals. The twenty-three hospitals in the area of the Batak Church were transferred by the government to the church on condition that funds be supplied by the church to operate them over half-year periods. Inadequate mission support, and the nation's economic instability, has hampered both the church-operated and former church hospitals in serving their constituencies.

CHRISTIAN LITERATURE AND LITERACY

Though Frank Laubach first tried out his methods for teaching illiterates in Mindanao, the Philippines were slower than most of the adjacent lands to adopt his methods. Christians have joined in the

[27] For a prewar account of one of these consult Van Dusen, *op. cit.*, pp. 55–59.

Thai and Indonesian government-sponsored literacy campaigns since World War II, though the Laubach "Each One Teach One" campaigns have failed to achieve their expected results; a person who has learned to read by the Laubach method is not by that fact a qualified teacher. The combined programs by governments and the churches have raised the literacy rates of the Southeast Asian nations.

Christians have sought to provide suitable reading materials for the newly literate and others. Aided by the Department of World Literacy and Literaure of the Division of Foreign Missions, NCCCUSA, writers have been trained and publications have been subsidized in each of the lands save Indo-China. A conference sponsored by this body jointly with the International Missionary Council, at Singapore in 1951, stimulated the several national Christian communities to increase literature production and publication. Much of the new literature relates to fields already mentioned, including home and family life, Sunday-school materials, publications for university students, etc. Periodicals are published in each of the lands by either church agencies, ecumenical bodies, or both, in the vernaculars and in some instances in English.

AUDIO-VISUAL AND RADIO WORK

The end of the war has witnessed the multiplication of projected and non-projected educational and evangelistic aids. RAVEMCCO, a department of the Division of Foreign Missions, NCCCUSA, together with many of the sending agencies, has contributed subsidies to the national councils in each of the lands save Indo-China for the operation of audio-visual centers and the purchase of films, film-strips, projectors, and other equipment. Vans for taking the projected message to the rural areas have been employed intermittently or continuously in all countries but Indo-China. Audio-visual workshops have brought Christian workers together to study methods of visualizing the Christian message. Several Asian conferences have brought national leaders together. Again, everywhere except in Indo-China full- or part-time staff persons have been made available to work in this area. Films have been made in Thailand and Indonesia treating some aspects of the Christian program for use at home and abroad.

Only the Philippines has a Christian radio station, DYSR, which is operated at Silliman University. The nondenominational Far Eastern Broadcasting Company, with an even more powerful station at Manila, reaches to parts of Indonesia and as far west as Thailand. Programs are beamed in several languages and dialects. Both in the Philippines and in Indonesia use is also made of national radio facilities. Under the auspices of the Radio Department of the Philippine Federation of Christian Churches, programs such as the "American National Radio Pulpit," religious drama, and "Sunday Evening Chimes" are beamed over commercial stations. Both ecumenical and regional church bodies in Indonesia utilize state radio facilities for broadcasting Sunday worship services. Roman Catholics and Moslems in Indonesia are granted similar rights to radio time.

INDUSTRIAL EVANGELISM AND RURAL APPROACHES

The operations of the church in other lands in reaching workers has led to the development of special programs in the Philippines. A conference on this subject held in 1957 in Manila brought together delegates from other countries in Asia for a consideration of methods. A move is afoot to train staff members for each of the national councils or to serve on the church bodies. With the help of the National Christian Council and the Protestant labor unions in Indonesia, a person was sent to the United States in 1959 to study this field of operation. The fact that these lands are predominantly rural has blinded church leaders to the growing urbanization of their nations and the need for specialized approaches to the working classes.

In 1950 the Church of Christ in Thailand established a Christian village in the northern part of the country to apply industrial methods to farming. While the project has not fulfilled the high idealism expected, it has demonstrated that Christian morality and machine methods can improve the rural standards of living. The Lord's Acre Plan is being used in the Philippines. Rural self-support projects, with facilities for training Christian farmers, have been inaugurated by several church bodies in Indonesia in the last decade.

SOCIAL AND POLITICAL ACTIVITIES

Political leadership in the Philippines, Indonesia, and Burma includes a number of outstanding evangelicals. For a brief time, an Evangelical senator was the body's president in the Philippines, and Judge Bocobo has compiled the civil and criminal codes of the islands. Mrs. Ba Ma Chein, prominent church and YWCA leader, was for a time the only woman in the Burmese cabinet. Only in Indonesia is there a Protestant political party, a small group but qualitatively important. Its leader, Dr. J. Leimena, has served in every cabinet since the republic was proclaimed in 1945, save those headed by Dr. Ali Sastroamidjojo. The one-time army chief of staff is now on the staff of the Indonesian Council of Churches, and the first general secretary is serving as a cabinet minister in the present government. While no comparable Christians are found in governmental positions in Thailand and Malaya, there are many graduates of Christian schools in the government who, while not professing Christians, reflect some of the ethical precepts they acquired in the fulfillment of their responsibilities. In Southeast Asia, even as in most of the other younger church lands, Christians weigh more than they count.

Nationalism and Christianity

The nationalism produced in reaction to the colonial power continues to be significant in each of the Asian lands, though it is hampered in some degree by the continued effectiveness of regionalism. As indicated above, the identity of religion and nationalism creates a climate unfavorable to certain types of missionary activity. The white missionary, in particular, is no asset to the populace at large in neutralist Burma and Indonesia. To embrace Christianity is regarded in some quarters as close to national treason.

The fact that regional feeling remains strong in some of the areas, and the further fact that the strength of the church is in certain areas, also is a handicap at the point of nationalism. The main body of Christians in Burma have been the Karens, who for a time were in revolt against the central government. The Protestant strength in Thailand is among the Laos peoples to the north, who are far from being in accord with all that is done in their name by their near-mythical rulers in Bangkok. The Christian converts in Viet-Nam have been primarily among the Annamese who live near the mountain ranges. When the revolt of the South Moluccas was proclaimed in 1950, the Ambonese leaders took the step within the context of a religious service. The headquarters of the rebels in 1959 was in Minahasa, an area 90 per cent Christian. These events have created suspicion within the national communities as to the basic loyalty of Protestant Christians. Only in the Philippines is the spread of the Evangelical movement throughout the nation and among all classes.

Conclusion

Southeast Asia is still in revolution. Classical colonialism has been ended save in small pockets such as Portuguese Timor and Dutch New Guinea. The danger today is of Communist neo-colonialism. Thailand stages coups between rival military groups but the nation generally is placid. The Hukbalahaps have been dispersed in the Philippines; the Communist guerrillas have been defeated in Malaya so that as of July 1 the patrols and curfews will be ended; General Ne Win has sufficiently pacified Burma to allow former Premier U Nu to form a new government in Burma. But Communist guerrillas continue their activities in South Viet-Nam and Laos, and Darul Islam and Communists are competing for the control of Indonesia. Poverty remains the heritage of most of the rural peoples and many of the new city dwellers as well. And Communism feeds upon hunger, poverty, and turbulence. These young nations still have a breathing period during which their destinies will be sealed, first by internal conquests of poverty, and secondly by the international situation. Meanwhile Communist parties continue to operate in Indonesia and Malaya, and Communist-oriented leaders agitate under cover in the other lands. The growing industrial and military power of Communist China makes the several millions of Chinese residents of these lands increasingly sympathetic toward their homeland, or the land of their fathers. If the methods employed by China continue to succeed, and if China can restrain her aggressive tendencies toward geographical expansion, her influence will become paramount over this entire region. The position of the Protestant minorities would be considerably weakened by this development.

These churches must therefore be strengthened while there is yet time so that if and when they are required to stand alone they will have the inner resources and trained leadership to do so. When doors close, what then? The Church throughout the world must join together with these Christian communities to prevent their isolation, but to prepare them for the time when it may come.

CHAPTER III

The Christian Mission Since 1938:
The Pacific Islands

J. LESLIE DUNSTAN

Andover Newton Theological Seminary

Newton Centre, Massachusetts

Twenty-five years ago the islands of the Pacific were under the control of various world powers. Britain, with Australia and New Zealand, held much the largest number of the islands; France had a substantial territory; Eastern Samoa was an insular possession of the United States; the New Hebrides were governed by a condominium of Britain and France; and Japan held the Marshalls, Carolines, and Marianas, with the exception of the island of Guam, which was a United States Navy base. These arrangements had been worked out over the years, as the interests of Western nations and events in the Western world dictated. Almost from the time of their discovery the islands were caught up in the turns and twists of Western history, often with little or no regard for native life. Sometimes the value of the islands had seemed to be only strategic, as points from which moves in international struggles might be made; sometimes they had been used as sources of wealth and had been incorporated into the trade of the world; and sometimes they had been neglected and left to themselves or to the mercies of individuals who exploited them for their own gain.

Throughout the years of that earlier history, missions of the Christian churches had been at work in the area. Missionaries were sent out by the London Missionary Society, the Methodist Church of Australasia, the German Lutheran Missionary Society, the Evangelical Mission Society of Paris, the Melanesian Mission, the American

Board of Commissioners for Foreign Missions, and others. These men had worked on the various islands, sometimes opposed by traders and settlers from their own nations, sometimes supported by their governments, but often left to their own devices to carry out their purposes as best they could. They taught the island peoples, organized churches, advised on matters of government, set up codes of moral law, and interpreted as seemed to them correct the meaning of the Christian faith for the people.

Through this history, secular and sacred, the lives of the island people had been molded. For good or ill, and to a greater or lesser degree, the people had been influenced by Western ways. On the smaller islands, those of little or no economic or strategic consequence, many of the earlier native patterns remained; on the larger islands the impact of the West was much greater. On some of the islands there were communities of Westerners who had gone there to live for one reason or another; and here and there were more transient foreigners who left their mark on native life. And always, everywhere, there were the church and the missionaries.

The basic issue for the people of the Pacific islands up to this time, although they could not have stated the matter as an issue and the Westerners would have expressed themselves in varying ways, turned on the relationship between the islands and the rest of the world. Western traders and businessmen, whether individuals or large corporations, had incorporated the islands into Western economy on Western terms. The results of those efforts varied. Islands that had no resources of any consequence were left untouched or relatively untouched. But where valuable resources existed, communities of Westerners were established, a minimum form of Western-ordered life was imposed on the native peoples, and in some cases natives were forced to work for the Westerners under some plan of indentured labor. Generally speaking, in those situations native life was badly disrupted. That, however, is only one side of the picture. The other side is that through the work of the traders and exploiters the islands were drawn into a closer relationship with the world. Shipping lines made movement between the islands and from the islands to lands beyond readily possible. And with the establishment of trade a new type of economy was introduced.

Western governments had taken control of the islands. Sometimes governments acted to protect and assist their own nationals, sometimes to gain points of strategic importance in the ever threatening international struggle, and sometimes simply to forestall an action by some other power. In some places Western government imposed upon native peoples a simplified form of Western law and order; in other places government was content to let native life go on as it was as long as peace was maintained and Western enterprises were unhindered. Generally speaking, Western government was not interested in the problems created by the impact of its people upon the islanders. Nevertheless, government was another factor contributing to the basic issue facing the islands.

Christian missions were primarily concerned with the spiritual well-being of the people. Missionaries had a fairly clear idea of the evidences of that well-being; they knew it involved a commitment to a divine power and a manner of living consonant therewith. On the one side they were sure that infanticide, intertribal warfare, cannibalism, loose sex practices, jealousy, and individual pride were not ways of Christian behavior; on the other side they were equally sure that orderly days, thoughtful provision for family needs, the ability to read and write, the knowledge and obedience of law, and the worship of God were essential ways of serving God. They set about putting their certainties into actuality, by instruction, persuasion, and on occasion the exercise of authority. That some of them were led into economic and government affairs was inevitable with their understanding of their task, but such apparent diversions were actually in complete harmony with their basic purpose. Wherever they worked, missionaries brought churches into existence and created organizations for them. On many of the islands a native church leadership was chosen and was given a measure of training.

The missionary enterprise thus became another factor in the creation of the fundamental issue created for the islanders. Yet the extent to which missions drew the people into the Western world varied. On some islands this occurred to a considerable degree, but on others the pre-Christian native organization was simply transformed into the church structure. Everywhere missionaries went there was a measure of transformation of native ways: that much is certain. But evidence suggests, as a general principle, that where other Western influences were at work, as well as the church, the incorporation of native life into the West was substantial; where other Western enterprises were lacking, the modification of native life was minor.

At the time our survey begins two developments were of particular importance. First, there was the role Japan had come to play in the Pacific. After the First World War the Marshalls, Carolines, and Marianas, which had been German possessions, were made a Japanese mandate under the League of Nations. By 1935 Japan had closed those islands to people of other nations, had put them under the control of a South Seas government, and had begun to turn them into an integral part of the Japanese empire. The resources of the islands were exploited for Japanese trade, the islanders were taught Japanese ways, and some of the native leaders were taken back to Japan for further education. Pastors from Japanese Protestant churches were put in charge of mission enterprises, and a government subsidy was provided for religious work. A few German *Liebenzeller* missionaries were allowed to return to the area in the late 1920's, and on one island Americans continued to conduct a school. With those minor exceptions, the Pacific Ocean north of the equator became a Japanese sea and the people of the islands related to the Japanese nation.

From the islands, the Japanese began to reach out into other areas of the Pacific. Their fishing boats sailed south to the neighborhood of New Guinea, one of their companies opened an iron mining enterprise on New Caledonia, traders entered the market for the nickel ore found on that island, and Japanese people moved there to become storekeepers and the operators of service enterprises for members of their own race. Across the Pacific, which had formerly been a kind of preserve for Western nations, the influence of the Orient began to spread.

At the same time, partly as a consequence of that first development and partly out of an increased concern for the state of humanity everywhere, there came signs of a growing interest on the part of Western nations in the welfare of the island people. Whereas earlier the West had seen the islands only as places to be used by it, a marked change in policy appeared. The advent of the airplane (the first transpacific commercial flight occurred in 1937) opened the whole area to the public gaze in a manner not earlier possible. The Rockefeller Institute gave its support to efforts in behalf of native health. Trained anthropologists were made available to government authorities to advise as to the best means of helping the island people as they sought, through all the influences that had been and were playing upon them, to work out an ordered life for themselves. And here and there attempts were made to bring the islanders more into the government of their affairs.

Any attempt to summarize the impact of the West upon the people of the Pacific is fraught with difficulty. The islands themselves and their resources have been brought under the control of the West for the benefit of the West. And the patterns of living of the island people have been influenced to a greater or lesser extent. But whether or not native life has achieved an organized form and center of its own, with an inner power enabling it to manage itself, is a matter that allows of no clear answer. Up to 1935 little thought had been given to it.

When the war began in 1939 it seemed to people in the Pacific a somewhat distant affair. Yet it was not long before its pressure was felt. English colonists and businessmen became members of defense organizations; the government of French Oceania was seriously split by the fall of the homeland and the establishment of the Free French movement; shipping was badly disrupted and the changing demands for goods altered the economic enterprises in the islands and caused much hardship; the internment of the members of the German Lutheran mission on New Guinea by the government forced the native people to assume responsibility for the work of the churches; Port Moresby was fortified and troops were stationed on Papua; and German warships sank a few vessels traveling between the islands. Yet in spite of these events and changes, life remained substantially as it had been.

Then in 1941 the Japanese launched their wide-sweeping campaign of conquest across the Pacific. Within a short space of time they took over the government of some of the islands, imprisoned the people of Allied countries, turned the natural resources to their own use, and brought the native people under their control. As soon as possible an Allied effort to recapture the areas taken by the Japanese and to clear the Pacific of the enemy was under way. Some of the islands became the scenes of devastating battles: New Guinea, Papua, the Solomons, the Admiralties, the Gilberts, the Marshalls, the Marianas, and the Carolines. The native people were not always involved in the sanguinary struggles that took place, but many were killed and all were made clearly aware of the behavior of the civilized world. Other islands became supporting bases, both for Allied and for Axis forces; the New Hebrides, Fiji, Tonga, and Eastern Samoa became troop garrison centers, and their life was submerged by the military. New Caledonia, because of the need for nickel by the Allied forces, became the scene of governmental squabbles over control and almost continuous labor unrest. Hardly an area of the Pacific, with the exception of French Oceania, went through the war without being drastically involved. The islands of the ocean were completely drawn into the enterprise of the world.

Inevitably, the churches of the islands felt the full force of the war. During the Japanese occupation some missionaries were killed and others were imprisoned; where the fighting took place, churches, schools, and other mission property was destroyed; and as native people were moved into areas needing human labor or left their homes to escape the conflict, church organizations were disrupted. Yet Dr. Van Dusen was able to write a book with the descriptive title *They Found the Church There*, based on the experiences which servicemen in the islands reported to him; and other Westerners learned of the dedication and faithfulness of the Christian islanders. Through the war, the people were introduced to forms of behavior and ways of living that were different in many respects from what they had previously known. Men who came among them and claimed to be Christians acted as they had understood Christians did not act. And they were made to see a side of Western civilization which had not earlier been clear. The effect of the war was felt deeply in practically all of the religious groups of the islands.

When the war ended, a few readjustments among the governing powers of the islands took place. The United States forces occupied the Marshalls, Carolines, and Marianas, from which they had driven the Japanese. The Japanese government officials and economic administrators had been repatriated and the navy stepped into the tasks which those men had been carrying. An area government was set up and the immediate needs of the island people were met. In 1947 the United Nations became the trustee for the islands with the United States as the administering power. In 1951 the authority over affairs in the area was transferred by the United States from the

Commander in Chief of the Pacific Fleet to the Department of the Interior. The Department continues to work through a High Commissioner and his associated officers in the direction of island affairs.

Australia and New Zealand had long thought of the South Pacific as of strategic importance to them; the war made that undefined idea startlingly clear. The Anzac Pact of 1944 put this into words. The two governments had control of certain islands. By an administrative act in 1945, Australia combined the mandated territory of New Guinea and the protectorate of Papua under a single government. Britain and France retained the islands over which they had authority. The United States closed the navy base in Eastern Samoa, causing a temporary disturbance in the economy, but retained its possession of the islands. New Zealand turned its mandate over Western Samoa into a trusteeship.

Shortly after the close of the war, the governments of Australia and New Zealand proposed a meeting of representatives of powers with interest in the Pacific to consider the welfare of the islands. In 1948 the first meeting of the South Pacific Commission was held. Representatives of six governing powers and fifteen non-self-governing groups were present. The purpose of the Commission was "to encourage and strengthen international cooperation in promoting the economic and social welfare and advancement of the peoples of the non-self-governing territories in the South Pacific" (from the preamble to the agreement creating the Commission). The Commission was designed to be an advisory and research agency with no authority of its own; but by its origin and its government relationships it has the possibility of markedly affecting the lives of the island peoples. At its first meeting the Commission considered matters of health, education, agriculture, and economic affairs. The churches were represented through the International Missionary Council, the Missionary Councils of Australia and New Zealand, and the Roman Catholic orders. Headquarters for the Commission were set up at Nouméa, New Caledonia, and a staff of experts was engaged. There have been two further meetings of the Commission since its formation, at four-year intervals.

After the war a large number of people were discovered living in the mountains of New Guinea who had had no previous experiences with the outside world. Rather than allow inexperienced individuals or impersonal enterprises to go into these untouched areas, perchance at the cost of life and surely at ill-considered effect on native life, the Australian government ruled that no unauthorized persons could enter the area until effective control had been initiated.

Some of the first people to return to the islands after the war were the businessmen and commercial operators. They were anxious to re-establish and extend their enterprises. Moreover, the war had uncovered the existence of raw materials in the islands which had not previously been known, and which would provide additional possibilities for commercial exploitation. And clearly these non–native people were essential to the welfare of the islands, for their efforts would provide the economic base for the further advancement of the native people. But after the war the controlling governments ordered the end of all indentured labor; this forced the operators to change their methods of mining and shipping. Fundamentally a kind of three-way competition began to appear: between the island people, who began to sense their own rights and to express their demands for freedom; the commercial Westerners who were in the islands for purposes of profit, which was difficult enough to gain under the most favorable of circumstances, and made even more so by the new policies of the government, and the governments who were responsible for both the protection and the advancement of the natives, and for the security of their own citizens. In some islands, such as New Guinea and Fiji, this triangular relationship threatened to break into overt struggle, although nothing lastingly serious has resulted. In Micronesia, the United States naval administration organized the U.S. Commercial Company and made it responsible for the restoration of the economy of the area. This was soon changed to the Island Trading Company. Generally speaking, it was assumed that these agencies would operate at a profit, or at least with a balanced budget. Experience indicated the difficulty of achieving such a goal. Subsequently, the economic enterprises of the islands were put into the hands of residents, some of whom are Westerners and all of whom had lived there a long time.

The situation in Micronesia illustrates clearly the basic problem facing the peoples of the Pacific and the governments having authority over them. The island people have been drawn out of their own ways of life, ways which were simple, involving limited social organization and scarcely more than a self-subsistence economy. They have been brought into direct and fairly long-time contact with the

world as a whole and have seen the patterns of living of other nations. But if they are ever to become an integral part of the life of
all humanity they must not only learn new habits of thought and
behavior and accept a new center of faith and trust but also possess
sufficient economic resources to undergird the inevitable changes.
An individual may achieve a considerable measure of freedom and
selfhood while living on a low level of economic existence—probably
the limit beyond which he cannot go in his development is not clear;
but if he is to continue to advance in personal growth, he must have
an economy that will enable him to do so. Man may express his
aesthetic sense in crude carvings on the sides of caves or on the
beams of some tribal house, but if that sense is to flower into all the
richness of art and sculpture and poetry, a wealth of available resources is needed. Man may retain the history of his people in memory and transmit that memory generation after generation, but his
people cannot be very great in number or involved in many contacts
with others; if he is to remember the history of humanity he must
acquire certain processes and techniques and skills, which demand
substantial wealth. The problem of the Pacific is how far into an
understanding of and share in the stress of world life the people of
the islands can be led, given the resources available to them. As
Coulter (*The Pacific Dependencies*, page 373) points out: "Out-
board motors are not necessary for many Ponapeans who have them;
it would have been much better for them to spend their money in
improving their elementary homes. It is no service to the natives to
help them acquire tastes that they have no means of satisfying with
their present or prospective incomes." While there is no reason why
the native peoples cannot be guided to achieve a fairly high measure
of civilization, the process must go forward slowly so that the whole
life of the people may grow in completeness.

The Christian church and Christian mission have been at work
through the changing circumstances of the years. They have had
to face all the difficulties of the quarter-century, and now they move
into the future with the realization that the church which was, no
longer exists. Probably that is not quite the correct way to state the
case. The church which grew out of the work of the early missionaries is being swept away and a new church must appear which is
relevant to the new day. Yet the process must be one of evolution.

The older people have their understanding of the Christian faith and their ways of expressing that faith; they are clear as to the order, the beliefs, and the practices which are its outward embodiment. But that understanding of the faith will no longer serve among people who have seen much of the world, both its good and its evil. All the changes in living that have come about have their effect upon the new generation of island people now coming to places of leadership, and they will respond only to a church that has meaning for them.

The truth to which this gives rise has already appeared on many of the islands as younger people question the authority of the older ones and their formulation of the Christian faith. Conflict and discussion ensue and the younger people leave the church to relate themselves to government leadership or to work out lives for themselves. The churches become little eddies of past ways within a stream of living that increasingly leaves them behind. The church survived the war years. It was greatly tested, especially in those areas directly affected by the fighting. Because in some cases the missionary leadership was removed and in all cases was much involved in the conflict, responsibility for the churches was put on the native leaders. They worked in accordance with ways they knew, practices they had been taught, and beliefs they held. They made such adjustments as were necessitated by the exigencies of the time and carried on their work with faithfulness. All the while, however, church members and nonchurch island peoples were learning new ways and coming to a new understanding of life's possibilities. Thus the church faced, and today continues to face, the task of transforming itself to meet the situation which has developed. Once the church was the center of existence, the motivating, directing institution, binding all customs and practices into a united whole. The problem is whether it can hold this position in the future. The older natives' leaders would maintain the structures of life that were; the younger feel that such a procedure will not be adequate.

This problem is complicated by the indefiniteness of the place the islands hold in the total development of the world. There is the possibility that the islands may be forced to live on their own resources, if there is a gradual removal of Western subsidies which have more recently sustained life; alternately there is the possibility that the Western powers, either for strategic purposes or out of a sense of personal responsibility, will continue to support the lives of island peoples and thus make it possible to integrate them into Western civilization and order. It is not clear at this time which of these two possibilities will be followed. But certainly the future will be determined by the decision which is taken. The fact that the destiny of the island people is not wholly in their hands will have a marked influence upon the work and the role of the church.

Yet, if the future of the island people is to be determined in part by the controlling Western powers, there has been a definite effort by missionary agencies to put the control and direction of church affairs into the hands of the people. The feeling has been that only if the church is fully an institution of the islanders can it come into a place of effectiveness in whatever developments may occur. To this end, the past years have seen an increase in the number of ordinations of natives to the Christian ministry. Indians on the island of Fiji were ordained for the first time in 1941. The New Hebrides, the Solomons, Micronesia, and other places have similarly been the scene of native ordination. Gradually a native clergy comes into existence. On some islands where new areas for evangelization have been opened, native leaders have been put in charge of the groups that have gathered. And in New Britain an organization known as the Melanesian Brotherhood has been formed, largely a lay group, which has carried considerable responsibility for work at the centers formed by the Anglican missions. The Brotherhood is now extending its efforts into New Guinea.

This increase in the number and importance of native leaders has emphasized the importance of theological education. In Micronesia a central Pastor's Training School was opened after the war on the island of Ponape, designed to serve the Marshalls and the eastern Carolines. In 1952 the proposal was made to open a theological college in Fiji. Schools which had been established in the South Pacific before the war have continued their work, raising their standards as they were able, and other schools have been started. A pastor's school was conducted at Papeete for the Society Islands. Lawes College in Papua reported in 1958 the largest number of students in its history. The school in Samoa has maintained its effectiveness. Students have been sent from the islands to other parts of the world—the Philippines, the United States, and Australia—for advanced study.

In 1949 a survey of theological education was proposed by some of the mission boards. The responsibility for this was put into the hands of the New Zealand Missionary Council. Two years later the Council, as a means of reporting informally on its work, began the publication of a series of newsletters to be distributed to all the theological training institutes in the area. These letters were to spread a knowledge of the work the schools were doing and to be media for the sharing of ideas. The survey itself concentrated on the New Hebrides at the outset.

This part of the work of the church involves a number of difficult problems. The native people who are to be pastors and leaders of the churches ought to have some training for their work. The training ought to give them knowledge of the essential possessions of the church and some understanding of the experiences of their people. Yet this knowledge and this understanding ought not to be in Western terms but in terms applicable to contemporary island life. Nevertheless, the task of training native leaders at the present time falls almost of necessity on Western missionaries. There is the matter of language too. Throughout the ocean area there are many native languages; and up to the present there is no single language used and understood widely—and so there is no one language which can serve in theological education. Again, there are wide differences in the development of the peoples of the various islands, from those who are now in the early Stone Age life to those who have advanced to a simple form of modern urban existence; over the entire area some of these differences must remain because of the limited resources of some islands. This condition makes practically impossible one single, unified pattern of theological education for the entire area. Missions and churches realize clearly the necessity for a trained leadership, but the way to carry on that training is not so easily created.

A number of times during past years a proposal for a single theological school serving the South Pacific has been made. In the North Pacific a Central Training School for Pastors and Teachers is conducted on the island of Ponape but it illustrates the problems noted in the preceding paragraph. Instruction must be in English since the students coming from various islands speak various languages; the standard of work is at about high school level, which is the extent of the academic achievement of most of the students; and plans to raise that standard depend upon the preparation of the students and bring up the question of their usefulness after graduation. Moreover, the Training School does not meet the needs of all the churches throughout the Trust Territory, for distances are too great and islands are too widely separated. The training of native leaders in the western Carolines is being handled separately in that area.

In the South Pacific there have been two divergent developments. On the one hand, certain of the training institutions have been made more effective, by raising standards and making adjustments to meet the conditions of the churches; these institutions have drawn students from increasingly wider areas. On the other hand, new training institutions have been opened. Both trends together show the increased interest in making sure that leader training be of a higher type and be more readily available. But nothing has come as yet of the proposal for a single institution for the entire area. Echoes continue to be heard. At a conference of Anglican bishops, clergy, and laymen of New Guinea held in 1957, stress was placed on the need for a central theological college for the South Pacific.

Paralleling this increased interest in the training of church leaders and the provision of increased opportunity for training have been a number of actions putting the responsibility for the churches into the hands of the island people. This has been done by the transfer of authority from missionaries and mission agencies to organizations of the churches, either in a single island group or over a wider area. In 1951 an autonomous field organization for the Lutheran work on New Guinea was worked out and submitted for approval to the home boards. The approval was given, a constitution was drawn up, and the Lutheran Church of New Guinea came into being. In 1952 a General Synod of the Churches in the Loyalty Islands met at Nouméa, with the island leaders and members in control. At the same time a plan was evolved for the Church of the New Hebrides. These two developments came in the area for which the Evangelical Missionary Society of Paris is responsible. In 1954 the Bishop of Melanesia was consecrated, after his nomination by the clergy of the diocese, both native and European meeting together. It was the first time such a consecration had taken place in the islands and thus was an indication of the increased responsibility being placed upon the churches. In 1956 the churches in French Oceania were given their own constitution putting the conduct of their affairs in the hands of the people. And in 1958 a House of Laity was added to the Synod in the Diocese of Melanesia, to be composed of representatives from the churches of the various islands.

All the while, those who have been involved in the mission work in the South Pacific have had in their minds the idea of a United Church of the Pacific Islands. The idea was voiced before the war at a meeting of missionary leaders held at Melbourne, Australia, in 1938 to consider matters of common interest. At that time the proposed United Church of the Pacific Islands was thought of as a kind of federation rather than a union of existing enterprises. A year later the National Missionary Council of Australia appointed a committee to arrange for a conference on the same subject to be held in the early 1940's. Interest in the possibility of uniting the work in the Pacific had been aroused by the proposal made at the Madras meeting of the International Missionary Council that a permanent consultative organization for the Pacific be established. After the war, a South Pacific Missionary Conference was held at which the idea was broached again. In 1950 a plan was worked out for bringing regional churches together. But there are many obstacles in the way. And it well may be that the idea itself is not applicable to the island conditions, being nothing more than a Western predilection. The circumstances on the various islands are different, and the possibilities for development of the people on the islands are different, so that to form an organizational structure to include all the needs and the varied work of the area would entail a considerable effort. While there might be some advantage to a unified approach to all the islands, one wonders whether the gain would warrant the energy needed to bring about the intended end. Moreover, there is the question of how the islanders would come to think of themselves, whether as rooted in their own linguistic and cultural groups or in some larger and more undefined complex of Pacific island people. It is doubtful whether in the immediate future such an effort is wise. Yet because there are basic similarities between the islands and a rather general sameness of circumstance and need throughout the entire area, the idea of one united church will continue to live. And if the churches are drawn more and more closely into the life of the whole world, the day may come when it should be made reality.

The missionary agencies at work in the Pacific have conducted, ever since their entrance on the field, educational programs and in-

stitutions for the people. This work was accepted as part of the
Christian responsibility of those who sought the conversion and welfare of the islanders. For years the governments which had authority
over parts of the area were content to allow the missions to carry
this responsibility. There were a few minor exceptions such as the
case of the Japanese, who provided a minimum education for a few
natives in the North Pacific islands in order to begin the process of
integrating the population into the Japanese world. In the main,
however, education was conducted by the missions. Village schools
were established and supervised; teachers were trained and appointed; and in some centers boarding schools on a somewhat higher
academic level were maintained. Generally speaking, the education
provided was fairly elementary for most of the students, with a few
advancing to a rather more advanced achievement.

One of the important results was that church and school became
integral parts of village life. The local church was a uniting force
among the people, and the school a responsibility of the people.
Thus education became an element within the structure of village
activity, something which belonged to the total unity of existence.

Before the war, as governments came to feel an increasing obligation toward the people in the islands, a few changes were made.
New Zealand took responsibility for elementary education in Western Samoa; the government proposed a scheme for teacher training
in the Gilberts; and the French authorities changed the program of
school examinations, which action, while it left the schools in the
hands of the church, necessitated the raising of standards. But aside
from a few instances such as these, governments did little to alter
the existing arrangements.

After the war, however, government interest increased markedly,
partly because the attention of the world had focused on the islands,
partly because of the trustee agreements under which Western nations held some of the islands, and partly out of concern for the
welfare of the island people. In the North Pacific the United States
Commissioner set up an area-wide system of education, with local
island schools, district higher schools, and teacher training schools.
Medical and technical education was also made available to selected
individuals. Probably one of the reasons why such a complete and
area-wide program was launched was that during the Japanese re-

gime the mission schools had disappeared, and with the evacuation of the Japanese authorities no education of any kind remained. In Fiji the government took over the work of training teachers; and in the Cook, Ellice, and Gilbert Islands the elementary schools became government schools. Under the Papua-New Guinea Act passed by the Australian government in 1949 proposals were included for the advancement of education. Subsequently the elementary schools were organized under a government system.

Governments showed interest also in vocational education. Native people needed to learn more effective agricultural methods so as to make the best use of available land; the introduction of machinery and of new materials for building created the need for trained artisons and machinists; the putting of trade into the hands of the island people made it essential that some of them learn the elementary processes of the business world; and the desire on the part of the people to be free from disease called for the training of medical practitioners and health supervisors. The medical school which had been established in Suva before the war became, through the aid of the government and the Rockefeller interests, the Central Medical School for the Southern Islands after the war, while for the northern islands a school of similar character was established on Guam. Vocational schools were also organized under government auspices, one in Fiji for the southern islands and one of much more limited character on Guam for the northern islands.

Yet the work of the governments did not begin to fulfill the needs of the area, so a great deal of educational work remains in the hands of the churches. In 1955 the London Missionary Society was conducting over 250 schools with nearly 15,000 students enrolled. In the New Hebrides all educational work was in the hands of the mission; the Australian Presbyterian missionaries prepared a new syllabus for the schools and wrote new textbooks in 1954; a boys' high school was opened with courses in agriculture and technical subjects as well as the usual academic disciplines; and a teacher training institute was established. In the Solomons the government urged the missions to expand and further develop their educational program.

The advance of government into education appeared to be slow indeed. The church authorities openly urged that responsibility upon government but at the same time continued their enterprises and developed them as conditions seemed to demand. Yet as the transition from church to government took place certain serious problems began to appear.

Government schools do not provide any religious education. On the contrary, they are conducted on the secular principles common to the Western world and reflect the secular spirit of the age. In some places time has been provided in the school day when the local clergymen can instruct the children belonging to their church groups. Furthermore, when the government takes over the schools the integrated structure of native life which combined church and school into a complete village existence is broken. Thus the life of the people, which was unified, is disturbed and an alien element has been introduced. That this element is secular is only part of the problem; more basic is the effect it has upon the lives of the people. On the one hand, then, the churches have felt that government should relieve them of the educational responsibility, but on the other hand they have been aware of the result which may well follow from the transfer.

Then there is the matter of language. Governments are concerned to provide for the island peoples a common tongue which can be used and understood by all. The proposal is to use English as the lingua franca, the exception being in the area controlled by France. And in view of the need to create some kind of unity among the peoples of all the islands and the necessity of their dealing with the outside world, the government proposal seems highly desirable. Yet missionaries know that native life is rooted in native relationships, and those relationships are expressed in particular vernaculars. Language is far more than a means of communication; it is a group possession, an outpouring in form of a group spirit. Thus the loss of the ability to know, to appreciate, and to use the vernacular may damage the structure of tribal life irreparably.

In general, the missionary agencies fear that the government will think of education in Western terms and organize it on Western patterns, whereas the issue turns on the usefulness of such education for the native peoples. There can be little question but that tribal life is tied up with the vernacular tongues, and that the continued health of that life depends upon the maintenance of the island languages, but the island people also need to be able to enter into the ongoing life of the world. This may require a gradual breaking of tribal life and the growth of a unity among people on a much wider basis.

Government and mission are not leaving this matter to chance. The meetings of the South Pacific Commission and the work of the research staff may give much guidance to the authorities involved as the work goes on. Already consultations have been arranged and held, as, for example, that between missionaries and government officials in New Guinea. The proposal of the moment is that an effort be made to give the island peoples two languages: their own and English.

Two conditions have militated against the work of the churches. One is the continued recurrence, throughout the period of time under review, of outbreaks of pagan ways. Sometimes these outbreaks have taken the form of old magical, spiritualistic practices; sometimes they have been in the form of organized groups gathered by a retelling and reinterpretation of tribal myths. Heathenism appeared in active form when the Japanese came to the islands in 1941. Later on, after the war was over, Messianic cults appeared: in New Hebrides and New Britain in 1948, and in New Guinea in 1952. These centered around an ancient story which promised the coming of material prosperity without the trouble of working for it. While the outbreaks of heathenism seemed to be no more than a drift back into ancient ways in response to the pressure toward a more civilized, orderly existence, the Cargo cults arose because of strong opposition to Western leadership and disappointment with the results of Western guidance.

The other troublesome element has been the entrance into the area of religious groups that are divisive in spirit and result. Representatives of Jehovah's Witnesses, the Assemblies of God, the Seventh Day Adventists, and other sects have come to the area, either as civilian workers or as missionaries. They have started work without regard to the churches and missions already established and have created division and conflict among the people. The fears and emotions of a people confused and disturbed by forces already at work among them have been put into organized, conscious forms. Since the doctrine of human rights prevails these things must be, even though for the time being they appear to be deleterious to the welfare of the people.

On one occasion a split occurred in the churches of French Oceania. The European community divided into antagonistic groups because of the relationship of the people to affairs in France, and the islanders separated with their European friends. It was a simple illustration of the continued influence of Western affairs on island life. The breach was subsequently healed.

The National Missionary Council of Australia is responsible for the Christian Literature Society, which undertakes to provide printed materials for the churches of the islands. The task is difficult because of the number of different languages used by the people. A printed volume has, for that reason, only a limited distribution. Nevertheless, through the years the Society has continued to publish works needed and desired by the people. *Pilgrim's Progress* has appeared in a number of languages; simple theological books, volumes on home and family life, and copies of the four Gospels separately have been printed in various languages. A magazine, *Pacific Island World,* was launched, using the English language, and through the years has gained an increasingly wider distribution. In the North Pacific the American Board has arranged for some printing of materials. Volumes that had been worn out through the years, such as hymnbooks, have been reprinted and the needs of Sunday Schools and youth societies have been met. For a time a team of language experts were in the area reviewing and revising earlier translations. These efforts indicate the clear sense of those related to the church work that the possession of printed material and the ability to make use of it are essential adjuncts to the Christian enterprise.

The churches and missions of the area continue to face a fairly extensive evangelistic task. At a conference in the South Pacific in 1949 the delegates agreed that French Oceania, Eastern and Western Samoa, Tonga, Cook, and Nauru islands were, generally speaking, wholly evangelized so that they might be termed Christian islands. Yet such areas do not stay that way, and the work of presenting the Christian Gospel to each succeeding generation, and of reminding backsliders of their Christian commitment, remains. Other islands are far from having responded to the Gospel. Large sections of the Solomons, New Caledonia, and the New Hebrides are non-Christian; and New Guinea may quite correctly be considered one of the large unevangelized areas of the world. During the 1950's large numbers of people were found, previously unknown, living hidden away in valleys that had remained unexplored. The government has established careful plans for approaching these people and dealing with them constructively. In such places the Christian forces have their place and are working with the government in launching their enterprises.

People on various islands have moved for economic reasons, and so have presented the church with another task. Oil was discovered in New Guinea in 1941 and workers' camps were built near the wells. Some of the men who moved to the camps were church members who, in their new circumstances, needed the care of the church; others needed to hear the Christian claim. A nickel factory was opened on Nouméa in 1952; the church responded by establishing a Christian center for the workers who moved there. Nickel mines were opened on New Caledonia with people going from Tahiti to do the work. Pastors were sent with them. A phosphate works was opened on Makatea in 1958 to which more than 1,500 people went. People were moved from the Phoenix Islands to the Gilberts in order to give them opportunity for better life. And in the North Pacific some islands were vacated to make possible the testing of atomic devices, the inhabitants being settled on other islands. All such changes involve a disruption of organized life and necessitate special care by the church.

On the island of Fiji there is a large Indian population; Rabaul has a Chinese community and a number of Malayans; on Tahiti there are a considerable number of Chinese. Not many among these races have yet been challenged by the Christian faith so they continue to be part of the continuing task of evangelism.

One of the problems with which the churches of the islands must deal is that of finding opportunities for missionary service beyond their own limits. There are difficulties of language, and resources, and training when considering sending Christians from the islands to other parts of the world. Yet some such efforts have been made. Samoans have gone to Papua and New Guinea, Fijians to New Guinea and the aborigines of Australia, and Solomon Islanders to New Guinea. All who are connected with the Christian enterprise realize that more possibilities must be opened for the wider outreach of the people.

The churches of the Pacific have passed through days of severe testing. And the membership has shown a dedication and commitment that have been surprisingly firm. The testing is far from over. For until the relationship of the islands to the rest of the world and the place of the population in humanity are settled, island affairs are likely to be unsettled and uncertain in direction. The churches will go forward into the future dealing with conditions as they may change. In the total interest of Christian people, the islanders must not be forgotten, but must be ever reminded, by the presence among them of representatives of other lands, that they belong within the universal people of God, called into being by His grace and sustained by His power.

CHAPTER IV

The Christian Mission Since 1938: Africa South of the Sahara

WILBER C. HARR

President, 1958–1960

National Association of Professors

  of Missions

Evangelical Theological Seminary

Naperville, Ill.

1. Introduction

Only a daring soul, and perhaps a foolish one, would claim competence for telling the story of the Christian mission since 1938 in Africa south of the Sahara. It is a lengthy, difficult, and complex story and any set of generalizations help pave the way to genuine frustration. No two writers will tell the same tale or make the same emphases. It will take time for Western minds and hearts to focus and only then will the living panorama of Africa, her people, the mission of the Church, and the emerging of the Church speak to most of us. Obviously this focusing must not take too long. The gradualism with which many would approach Africa, saying "Maybe tomorrow," finds an echo coming back: "Today."

THE LATOURETTE REVIEW

These chapters were planned as a tribute to Dr. Kenneth Scott Latourette and supposedly begin where his volumes *The Expansion of Christianity* end. His review of the Christian mission in Africa emphasized a number of points. He thought the penetration of Western culture in the three decades following 1914 most significant. He believed that this impact meant the progressive and rapid disintegration of old forms of African life and that Christianity and the Christian missionary were placed in this milieu. As late as 1945 Dr. Latourette felt compelled to study Africa area by area, and he veered from speaking of "the African" and "Africa." He deemed it necessary to speak of the meanings of two world wars as they contributed to unrest in Africa and to the world mission of the Church in particular. Near the end of his study on Africa he approximated generalization, stating that what was happening in the mid-thirties was largely a continuation and accentuation of what had been going on three decades earlier. He concluded by stating how favorably he was impressed with the way Christianity was spreading and taking root.[1]

This analysis provides a kind of starting point from which to work as student minds roam over the material relating to the expansion of Christian faith in Africa.

POSSIBLE GENERALIZATIONS RELEVANT TO LATOURETTE'S POSITION

The story of the last twenty years is a fascinating one as statistics are hurled somewhat randomly at unprepared peoples. Africa's total population as given in one set of figures in 1938 was 148,412,000.[2] A comparable figure for 1957 was 223,000,000.[3] The same set of 1938 figures listed the Christian Protestant community as 4,918,366.[4] The 1957 figures for Protestantism south of the Sahara were 9,355,044.[5] For all of Africa it was listed as 12,625,198.[6] Accurate comparisons may not be statistically possible and certainly have only limited relevance. The foregoing figures may be about as close as one can come to accuracy.

One more general comparison may have illustrative importance for present-day perusal. The 1938 survey gave Fourah Bay, Free-

[1] K. S. Latourette, *A History of the Expansion of Christianity,* Vol. VII, *Advance Through Storm* (New York and London, Harper & Brothers, 1945), pp. 216–254.
[2] Joseph I. Parker (ed.), *Interpretative Statistical Survey of the Christian World Mission* (New York, International Missionary Council, 1938), article by Alexander MacLeish, "Unoccupied Areas," pp. 265–266.
[3] *World Christian Handbook* (New York, International Missionary Council, 1957), p. 170.
[4] Parker, *op. cit.,* p. 20.
[5] *World Christian Handbook,* p. 170.
[6] *Ibid.*

town, Sierra Leone, as the only institution of university standing south of the Sahara geared to the training of African constituency.[7] C. P. Groves writing in 1958 mentioned a number of other institutions.[8] A popularly written study book of 1959 listed seven universities established in the last decade: University College, Salisbury; University College, Makerere; Lovanium, Leopoldville; University College, Ibadan; University College of Ghana; University of Liberia; and University of Dakar.[9]

These few illustrative statistics highlight the conclusions of Dr. Latourette as given approximately twenty years ago, and also establish a framework into which the last twenty years of mission and church activity must be placed.

LIMITATIONS FOR THE GENERALIZATIONS

Statistics are usually vulnerable in one way or another, and when applied to Africa they may be especially so. For instance, the reliability of any census taken in an African area is open to question, and there is a wide range of variation in general population statistics and on Protestant figures. Moreover, the unevenness of the Christian spread and the reasons for that unevenness are not revealed by the figures. Nor do such statistics speak of forces which may be increasingly competitive to the Christian witness. To illustrate, one questions the figures of claimed Islamic strength in Nigeria. Between the northern emirates and the southern section of Nigeria is the land referred to as the "Middle Belt League." In this belt will be peoples dominated by Moslem native administration: Islam will claim the land, yet the majority of the people may be non-Moslem.

Indeed, it is a comparatively new experience to find men and women of Africa who identify themselves with the whole of Africa. There have been, and are, solid regional differences. A mixture of traditional tribalism and politics may enter legitimately into a number of the current African problems. Edwin Smith made a point of this problem of identification in writing the life story of James Aggrey. Aggrey of Africa was unusual in that he identified himself with all of Africa as early as forty years ago.[10] Such identification

[7] Parker, *op. cit.*, p. 297.

[8] C. P. Groves, *The Planting of Christianity in Africa*, Vol. IV (London, Lutterworth Press, 1958), p. 277.

[9] E. Ross, *Africa Disturbed* (New York, Friendship Press, 1959), p. 4.

[10] E. Smith, *Aggrey of Africa* (New York, Richard R. Smith, 1931).

would not be so unusual now and only very reactionary souls can believe that it will not increase.

2. *Christian Mission and the New Climate*

To tell the story of mission and church organization on the African scene is not enough. If there is any area on earth where questionable "secular" and "sacred" factors stand in important relationships it is Africa. From within Africa have emerged forces which have affected and are affecting the Christian mission, and these have been most marked since 1938.

A historian of missions in Africa has analyzed three periods of missionary relationships in Africa. First, he saw missionaries going to areas where tribal authority was in full control. Next came partition of the continent to European overlordship and a kind of balance on that jittery, unsteady apparatus. He now sees the obvious stage of developing African peoples asserting independence, not in isolation but as active world citizens.[11]

This third stage looms large for any mission which would witness to Christ on the African scene. To search out situations going back to the old stages may be a possibility but begs the issue. Concentrating on them would mean that Christian mission is either unwilling or unable to cope with dynamic new situations.

CHRISTIAN MISSION AND THE SHIFT IN WELFARE AGENCY

There was a day when Christian missions claimed a near monopoly as welfare agency. It may have been an overclaim, but that is not to be discussed here. The point is that there is a radical departure from the old on this very score.

Emory Ross produced a study book for North American mission interests in 1936—the first of three he has prepared in recent years.[12] In that particular study he pointed out that the first schools in almost every part of Africa were mission schools, staffed and supported by mission agencies from Europe and America. His statements went

---

[11] Groves, *op. cit.*, p. 272.
[12] E. Ross, *Out of Africa* (New York, Friendship Press, 1936); *African Heritage* (New York, Friendship Press, 1952); *Africa Disturbed* (New York, Friendship Press, 1959).

farther, insisting that the Protestant mission movement was in the vanguard, and that Roman Catholic mission activity had lagged behind.[13]

Dr. Ross made a related statement publicly in Evanston, Illinois, in August of 1958 in an interpretative lecture on the mission in Africa. He said there were few recognized leaders of the new Africa who had not had beginnings in a mission school or in a school sponsored by a mission. He stated the case very strongly—perhaps too strongly.

According to George Carpenter, the chief organized means of cultural mediation has been the Christian school. He maintains that governments are giving it a high priority in most areas and that graduates from secondary schools and universities are in great demand.[14]

In this connection, there is considerable mission activity which conceives its task as "preaching the Gospel" and subsequently sees the educational thrust, historically and at present, as peripheral. Time does not allow or invite a look into the crystal ball or its missionary equivalent to predict the extent to which that point of view may turn out to be right or wrong, but some developments must be considered.

A brief study tour we made in Nigeria in 1957 was surprising and revealing, particularly since eighteen years had passed since we had served as part of the Protestant staff in that area. In 1939 the only schools in the Adamawa area of Northern Nigeria were mission schools with the exception of a few small Koranic centers. If there were others they were very few. We knew of none. As of that date even the mission schools were half empty and the season of the year dictated largely whether or not anyone would be in attendance. In 1957 the mission schools were crowded to the doors and unable to take all of those who desired to enter. More important than the increase in attendance, however, was the attitude of government. The Emir at Jalingo pointed out that the government was entering the field of education, and that schools were already in towns which twenty years before had had none. In a few cases both government and mission primary schools existed side by side. The need for educa-

[13] Ross, *Out of Africa.*
[14] G. Carpenter, *The Way in Africa* (New York, Friendship Press, 1959), p. 38.

tional facilities was too great to accuse the schools of overlapping, but the Emir made it clear that the government would be involved in education more and more.

A similar pattern prevailed in Sierra Leone. The mission of the Evangelical United Brethren Church has been in Sierra Leone for over one hundred years. At one time it sponsored (one might almost say owned) scores of little elementary schools. Unless the same church wants to operate competitively with the government, or unless it wishes to build a case for parochial education, it is only a matter of time until the mission is completely out of elementary education in Sierra Leone. Indeed, to all practical purposes, the mission is already operating only in very indirect ways in that field of activity. One rightly asks, Why not? The inference is very clear: the government is taking over the function of educating the children. If there is to be educational service rendered today, the mission had better shift its emphasis to the Bunumbu Teacher Training Center. But such a shift is more than an organizational matter, in that for many years North American church personnel have developed a mind-set relative to the little mission bush school. Emotional adjustment of the North American Christian constituency may be much more difficult than the legal and administrative factors which will be a part of the present change. The evidence seems to show clearly that education is moving, and will continue to move, into non-mission hands.

Similar developments appear in other mission-related service activities. One of the last to see the change is the medical dimension of mission activity. In many ways the missionary medical personnel have been the "aristocrats" of the missionary enterprise. Their training is expensive, and the working out of the medical missionary task puts an odium on mediocrity. But even here the handwriting is on the wall, and African men and women are qualifying splendidly. There is no need for regret on this score.

Christian missions are having to meet the involvements of this changing climate. As they do, they are discovering the necessity of studying themselves and the resources which bring them into being as well as studying Africa. Many an American churchman would still prefer to think of the old Africa and find a certain kind of paternalistic comfort in primitiveness.

CHRISTIAN MISSION IN RELATION TO THE POLITICAL SCENE

From inside Africa a new climate appears, putting a premium on political involvement, and this affects the Christian witness. We have already called attention to the high incidence of African leaders who began in schools related to the missions. Many of these leaders are no longer in the organizational life of the mission or the church. Many of the stronger young personalities are finding their fulfillment in the political arena rather than religious vocations.

The Western world knows little of Chief Luthuli, Zulu and Christian leader who in the last few years has had his name splashed across American headlines. His ancestral home was near Durban on the coast of Natal, and he was educated at various mission schools. Subsequently he became a teacher, joining the staff at Adams College in South Africa. He was a delegate to the Tambaram Conference of the International Missionary Council in 1938. In 1936 Luthuli left Adams College and went to Groutville as chief, plunging into the field of politics, where he has been ever since, even though poor health has seriously handicapped him. One significant point in his story relates to his motivation. He seems to have come to politics through an ideal fostered by his religion rather than by way of any strong personal ambition. Many years ago a glimpse of the freedom found and fostered in the Gospel set his feet in a new direction.[15]

John Karefa-Smart is from Sierra Leone. With his wife he developed a splendid mission study book in 1959 under the title *The Halting Kingdom.* This book was beamed largely at Western youth groups and was disturbing to many.[16] John Karefa-Smart is an ordained Protestant minister and has been splendidly prepared in modern medicine and public health. Much of his early education was received in mission schools of Sierra Leone, and then in Western colleges. He would be one of the first to say that the educational opportunity which came his way was due to missionary personnel and church relationships. At present he is serving in one of the most important ministries of the government of this newer African state.

[15] N. Gordimer, "Chief Luthuli," *Atlantic Monthly,* Vol. 203 (April, 1959), pp. 34–39.
[16] John and Rena Karefa-Smart, *The Halting Kingdom* (New York, Friendship Press, 1959).

He and his wife, writing as a unit, maintain that a Christian attitude toward life involves an acceptance of personal responsibility.[17] The acceptance of this personal responsibility appears to be leading him in a direction somewhat removed from what his training dictates, but after talking with him few would be inclined to pass a negative judgment on his decision.

Dr. B. Malinowski stated on occasion that the new internal African climate affects non-Christian as well as Christian leaders, which is another way of saying that the Christians need not claim all the glory. He espoused this position in the foreword for Jomo Kenyatta's book *Facing Mount Kenya*. Malinowski supports the proposition that African intellectuals are catalyzing African public opinion, and not all the intellectuals are Christian.[18]

Chester Bowles wrote an informative article on Africa for *Collier's* magazine, in which he posited the idea that the Bible was the most explosive political force in Africa and that the mission movement is largely responsible for Africa's modern revolution.[19]

NEW CLIMATE AND APARTHEID

The word "apartheid" has been so much with us in recent years that few concern themselves with its history. We are reminded of a sentence written in 1949: "The year 1948 will probably go down in history as the one in which South Africa felt the impact of the release of the word and idea of *Apartheid*."[20]

Although the word is discussed only briefly in this chapter, its importance for the mission of the Church cannot be denied. It has come into usage swiftly. The 1938 interpretative statistical articles do not carry this word, nor do they say much about problems which would bring it into being. Now communication is such that its meanings are known all over Africa and across the world. Writers of the last twenty years disturb us by questioning whether the voice of the Church has been prophetic in this matter.[21] Whether the

---

[17] *Ibid.*, pp. 39–40.

[18] J. Kenyatta, *Facing Mount Kenya* (London, Secker and Warburg, 1956), p. x.

[19] Chester Bowles, "Africa," *Collier's*, June 10, 1955, pp. 40, 42, 44.

[20] S. M. Mokitimi, *International Review of Missions*, Vol. 38 (July, 1949), p. 276.

[21] Note popular sources like T. Huddleston, *Naught for Your Comfort*

Church is at fault or not, it has been made clear that entrenched racial privilege is at present a little but potent tornado in the African climate.[22]

SELF-EXPRESSION

The organization of people in terms of self-expression has speeded up in the years under consideration. It is difficult to keep an African map up to date. Many new flags began flying in Africa in 1960.[23] We were reminded of this change when Dr. William Fitzjohn, recently representing Sierra Leone in Washington, D.C., spoke of the scramble for embassy properties in that city.

Revolution is a part of this climate and needs to be noted. Revolution is not necessarily the bloody overthrow of established authority. In some cases, revolution in Africa may involve only the transformation of social beliefs. Instances are on record where it represents an escape mechanism for frustrated groups. Elsewhere a kind of industrial revolution is taking place. Huge water projects like those at Kariba and Inga exemplify this change. The humming cities are rather surprising. Kano, in Northern Nigeria, may be known to the tourist trade as an old city with miles of crumbling adobe walls pushing the intruder away. But just outside the walls is a buzzing new city which has processing plants equipped for handling the huge pyramids of peanuts standing close by.

Professor Leo Silberman's report is relevant to the African revolution. He has pointed out a number of items. (1) An old notion is starting to crack, namely, that modern development and the presence of Europeans are necessary partners. Silberman calls attention to the old idea that only Europeans could develop the country—an idea held as late as 1929 when Field Marshal Smuts delivered the Rhodes Lectures. All this led Africans to hesitate before committing themselves to a market economy when settlers were complaining and crying eternally for subsidies of all kinds. (2) But in the current African climate the new is being seen. Extensive literature of which

(Garden City, Doubleday and Company, 1956), or A. Paton, *Cry the Beloved Country* (New York, Charles Scribner's Sons, 1951).

[22] Groves, *op. cit.*, pp. 150–166.

[23] Units we have in mind are Mauritania, Senegal, Ivory Coast, Togo, Dahomey, Nigeria, Cameroun, Gabon, Congo (French), Congo, Malagasy, Somalia, Central African Republic, Chad, Niger, Upper Volta, Mali Republic. *Time*, Vol. LXXVI (December 5, 1960), p. 23.

the Fagan report is an illustration indicates that 400,000 African miners are being recruited annually in South Africa, and thus being generally recruited away from their homes and families. New drama is unfolding. The Dalgliesh report shows how African men may upgrade themselves in industry. The Sudan has nationalized the foreign Cotton Syndicate. Egypt followed by doing the same with the Suez Canal and other national enterprises. Trading has been a favorite development for African folk, who now face something new: the creation of economic diversification and problems of imbalance.[24]

This self-expression has been related to the mission. It reflects itself in a number of ways: An instance is found in the mission and structure of new churches. Mission boards are facing the fact that external control is not a part of the new day. It may be only a surmise, but my personal observations in Africa in 1957 seemed to indicate that religious self-expression accompanies self-expression in other fields. Our later reference to the emergence of the Church in Africa will amplify this brief statement (see p. 105).

Also, the self-expression has led to a kind of erratic set of relationships which continue to have a major bearing on missionary work. It will be recalled that delegates from Africa asked the International Missionary Council in session at Tambaram, 1938, to study the problem of "separatism," which has fostered the proliferation of sects and dissident Christian congregations. Thus the problem is not completely new. But it is a continuing and a growing problem. Professor Sundkler's comprehensive study completed in 1948 is exceedingly formidable. The second appendix by itself is staggering, for he lists hundreds of groups found in South Africa which would be classified as separatist.[25] More recently, in an interpretative lecture on Africa at Evanston, Illinois, Emory Ross ventured the opinion that the number of such groups on the African scene would pass one thousand. Professor Sundkler enunciates reasons for these movements: (1) Separatism is a kind of mechanism for meeting in circumstances when nonreligious meeting is impossible. (2) Separatism develops from racism. (3) Differences in church discipline and lack

[24] Leo Silberman, "African Economic Developments and Ourselves," *Christian Responsibility in the Emerging World Economic Situation.* Papers for a seminar, the University of Chicago, Center for the Study of the Christian World Mission, March 9–12, 1959, pp. 1–7.

[25] B. Sundkler, *Bantu Prophets in South Africa* (London, Lutterworth Press, 1948).

of agreement on problems like witchcraft and polygamy set up situations for separatism. (4) Separatism emerges occasionally to aid economic development. (5) Missionaries may have failed to settle grievances satisfactorily. (6) Quarrels between people give rise to new movements. As Sundkler concludes his study he maintains that two reasons are basic: In the first place, racism is a reason for separatism, and secondly, excessive denominationalism brings many separatist groups into being.[26] Few would believe that the twin problems just mentioned have been erased. Nor would one be wise to say that racism and excessive denominationalism are unrelated to problems within the structure of Christian mission.

Yet again, self-expression may set the stage for organized forces which compete with the Christian witness. Even incipient nationalism may claim men's attention to such an extent that it is almost worshiped.[27] But we would speak of only two such alternatives.

The first of these is Communism. Let us be clear at this point. The evidence seems to indicate that African revolution has not been caused by Communism. It may be that Communism will exploit the revolution. Civil and social disorder may be a breeding ground. Mr. Silberman has commented on this.

> It goes without saying that the industrial revolution and the setting up of higher social security standards are accompanied by strikes and sometimes riots. . . . If there were in the Belgian Congo 4½ times the number of buildings erected in 1953 than in 1947, then with the relaxation of this boom there must be temporary unemployment. If freight shipping to the French Cameroons trebles as compared with the highest pre-war figure, then the nascent bourgeoisie there demands control over the port, customs, inland transport.[28]

Communism may catch hold in Africa, in spite of the fact that most African societies have been fundamentally religious, in spite of the fact that few African leaders seem to want it, and in spite of the fact that seldom does one find Communist parties of strength. Communism occasionally shows signs of vitality. When this has happened, it has been for one of a number of reasons. In some cases, some say they would like it because it is the bane of the West. Other times it

---

[26] *Ibid.*, p. 295.
[27] An illustration would be A. A. N. Orizu, *Without Bitterness* (New York, Creative Age Press, Inc., 1944).
[28] Silberman, *op. cit.*, p. 6.

catches on because under self-expression things do not work out as planned and in the disappointment there is a chance for Communism to develop. In still other cases, a lively party in a colonial power has carried over into Africa.

Little more than mention has been made of Islam. It is unsatisfactory to try to check its statistics of a generation ago, but figures are available now. A conservative figure for followers of the Prophet has been given as 52,226,120.[29] It may be that Islamic advance should not be classified as part of the internal climate, on the assumption that Islam comes from the outside, and because even now one finds a high incidence of missionaries from Asia, particularly from Pakistan. Mosques and reading centers are to be found in many new areas.

But the Moslem renewal should not be ignored in this internal climate. Much of the African mind accepts it as being indigenous. More often than not, the proselytizing will be done by African lay folk in the marts and byways. In the Sudanic belt much of the political control is in the hands of Moslem leaders. That could, and does, make a difference.

Emory Ross's study books on Africa have been noted.[30] One searches in vain for serious consideration of the Moslem advance in the first study. It is occasionally woven into the third.

CONCLUDING MISCELLANEOUS MATTERS

We have taken much time to deal with the climate in which the new mission moves. Let us mention in passing just a few more aspects of the new climate which are important but not easy to document. In the new African climate there is often violent criticism of the areas from which the mission has traditionally come; at the same time there seems to be a will to imitate the area under criticism. There is an explosive question of land; all over the continent in one way or another problems of land rise up to plague and harass. There is the general upheaval of African society. The speed of change may be as important as the change itself. It should not be surprising to hear a father say "I do not understand my son" while he repairs a roof for his little circular house along the rocky ledges of a Nigerian

[29] *World Christian Handbook*, 1957, p. 175. John Gunther, *Inside Africa* (New York, Harper & Brothers, 1955), p. 63, gives the figure as 60,359,000.
[30] See footnote 12.

hillside. Within twenty-four hours you may meet the son, dressed in Western garb, serving as the proprietor of a bookshop, and hear him say with complete honesty, "I don't understand my father."

It is in this climate that the Christian mission works its way.

3. External Factors and the Mission

We have spoken of the climate in Africa itself. Let us examine briefly some of the forces which have more recently worked from outside and affected the mission within Africa.

CHRISTIAN MISSION AND THE WAR

Certainly one of the first factors to be named is World War II. Some of the delegates had barely returned to Africa from the Tambaram Conference before the war clouds released their storm. The war and its effect cannot be dismissed from the post-1938 pattern of mission.[31]

First of all, preparation for war affected missions before the conflict began. Germany provides an illustration. In 1933 the Nazi regime instituted a plan for winter relief geared to keeping certain funds at home which would normally be used for overseas work. A year later German Exchange limited the transfer of funds overseas. They could be used to maintain German missionaries only.

Secondly, a number of European powers became involved. While Germany had no territory in Africa she had gradually built back missionary force and prestige to standards of which she was justly proud. Her missionaries and funds were bound to suffer with war. France was involved quickly because of her collapse before the German armies. The setting up of Vichy France divided Africa. French West Africa was under Vichy. French Equatorial Africa was related to De Gaulle and Free France. Italy became part of the problem when Mussolini, at an opportune moment in his estimation, staked his empire on the side of Germany. The Belgian Congo was cut off by Belgian occupation. Other parts of Africa gained importance in the war effort when the Mediterranean became an impossible transport lane for Allied forces and material. A network of airfields was

---

[31] See *International Review of Missions*, Vol. 41 (1940), and Survey Article which always appears in January issue, Vols. 29 and 30. Also Groves, *op. cit.*, gives a whole chapter to this problem, pp. 238 ff.

laid out south of the Sahara providing service across Africa. This was a new feature and its facilities can still be seen in the areas where these fields were constructed. It should be noted that about this time Field Marshal Smuts returned to power in South Africa, and while his country was precariously balanced in its interests, it entered the war on the side of the Allies.

Missions faced myriad problems.[32] There were missionaries south of the Sahara from Finland, Norway, Sweden, Denmark, Belgium, France, and Holland. In addition there were great influential societies like the Basel Mission Society and the Paris Mission Society.

On the one hand there were the problems occasioned by Germany, centering on German missionaries. They were found in many areas, particularly in Tanganyika, which had been a pre-World War I center for German mission interest. Policy here generally called for internment. In Tanganyika alone 110 German men (without their wives) and 50 single women workers were interned.

The reaction in Germany was significant. There were conflicting voices. Some said that the German missionary was obeying his call to preach the Gospel and this should not be bound up with the nation. Conversely, there was a note of rejoicing that the identity of the mission with the life of the nation was recognized by the fact of internment. More specifically, there was a real discussion in Germany about the matter of parole, and information reached the International Missionary Council through neutral sources that the German government saw no objection to allowing parole. Yet the organ of the so-called SS, *Das Schwarze Korps*, ferociously attacked one German mission of which it was known that the majority of the missionaries had been given parole. It accused them of treasonable action. A number of German missionaries refused to accept parole; they might have had no subversive intentions but feared consequences to themselves or relatives.[33]

The other problem was occasioned by the overrun countries. Here were missionaries who loved their work but were up against tremendous odds in terms of support and morale. One of the great chapters of modern missions was written here through the use of "orphan missions." Training centers, personal support, and a simple

[32] *International Review of Missions,* Vol. 29 (January, 1940), p. 111.
[33] *Ibid.,* Vol. 30 (January, 1941), p. 105.

surrounding with the arms of Christian love were a part of the orphan mission pattern.

One might say, without blessing the war, that some good came out of it all.[34] Protestants were drawn into joint counsel and the poignant call of suffering showed the strength of Christian fellowship.

Africans became a part of all this; it wasn't only a matter of missions and governments. Africans knew something of what to expect. Older people remembered World War I. More recently, Italian exploits in Ethiopia had taken place. This time numbers of African men were used. As many as 300,000 King's African Rifles moved from East Africa. There were 125,000 non-Europeans from South Africa. Stories were told me personally in 1957 from West Africa of involvement of those men, men fresh from the bush.

Some positive aspects appeared which affected the mission of the church. One was the understanding men had of one another. Organizations such as the Springbok Legion of Ex-Servicemen and the National War Memorial Health Foundation came to life. These carried no color bar and were aimed at peacetime co-operation. Another was the simple fact that the men were generally fairly well cared for. Many of them lived under better conditions than they had ever experienced. The Army Education Corps carried out large-scale services. These men also learned how to go after something they wanted.

Negatively, there was relaxation of moral standards, and emotional points of view which were created then have never been discarded. People were forced to move, sometimes out of fear, other times to help the war effort.

A last word centers on the relation of the Atlantic Charter and Africa. The memory of the Atlantic Charter and the four freedoms caught hold of many Africans and of folk interested in Africa. There is in existence a document which shows how people thought and planned on this matter.[35] The fact that it seemed to be shunted aside should not obscure what is also fact. The study of this document

---

[34] Groves, *op. cit.*, p. 247.

[35] "The Atlantic Charter and Africa from an American Standpoint," a study by the Committee on Africa, the War, and Peace Aims, New York, 1942.

helped establish a number of significant conferences involving the Christian mission in Africa.

OUTSIDE SECULAR INVOLVEMENT

The interest and concern of outside agencies in Africa's secular involvement have not disappeared since 1938. While such involvement may not appear on a normal map it has taken several forms and includes governments, foundations, companies, and other agencies. We intend to introduce the problem through illustrations.

1. There has been Portuguese involvement. In 1936, almost the date for this study's beginning, Portugal began what she called her development in African territories. She has not radically changed her policy since then, even though it has been slowed at times. This policy, from the outside, was geared to private enterprise according to Portuguese record. It fostered a single industrial pattern as concerning the homeland and Portuguese land in Africa. There was hope for economic solidarity. It was bluntly stated in 1951 by Portuguese government authority that Portugal would like to see progressive abandonment of traditional agricultural exploration by "natives." This was to be abandoned in favor of operation of land duly registered in perpetual title.[36]

2. The Belgian Congo was also affected from the outside. Since 1938 technical assistance programs have become part and parcel of the economy. There was a solid attempt made to break the exodus from rural area to urban, through government intervention outside as well as from inside. Prior to World War II Leopoldville's population had not exceeded 35,000. By 1951 it had reached 220,000 and was still growing.[37] Developments in this area during the year 1960 are still so freshly upon us that the implications can hardly be weighed objectively. The whole world knows the travail of the Congo as her hopes and dreams for independence and self-respect have run headlong into power struggles and problems involving at times others than the people of the Congo themselves.

3. The Federation in Southeast Africa, involving Nyasaland and the Rhodesias, has its points of tension. Nyasaland could not pay her

---

[36] "Africa Is Here," Report of the North American Assembly on African Affairs, Wittenberg College, Springfield, Ohio, 1952, p. 44, José Nunes de Oliveira, Inspector General for Overseas Administration for Portugal.
[37] *Ibid.*, pp. 48 ff.

own way until 1948. As late as 1939 her annual revenue was £1,000,-000. This ballooned to £4,000,000 in 1951 with corresponding improvements in public and social services. Much of this help came from outside. By the way, her population was the largest and her territory the smallest of the three members of the Federation. The result has been large-scale migration.

Northern Rhodesia had a public revenue well under £1,000,000 in 1937. She also had about 13,000 Europeans. Her 1951 revenue exceeded £15,000,000 and the number of Europeans 36,000. The European population has been increasing from six to seven thousand annually. Copper mining is still the dominant feature and has brought tragedies, opportunities, semi-sophistication, and political consciousness. How much depends on considerations from outside Rhodesia is a legitimate question. A review of the way the copper industry sets up its interests is a world study all by itself. (We commend it to you.)

Southern Rhodesia had a European population thirty years ago of 35,000 and its public revenue was almost exclusively in mining, about £1,500,000. By 1951 secondary industry, such as agriculture, was the largest economic activity. Revenue had quadrupled. European population had gone up to 128,000 and was increasing 12,000 annually. One could add that there was also a sizable increase in African population (1,340,000 to 1,960,000).[38]

4. Three territories, Uganda, Tanganyika, and Kenya, are often grouped in East Africa. Such grouping may be an oversimplification, but it can be used. Living here were 53,000 Europeans, many of them second- and third-generation people. Here was the sixth largest coffee production in the world. Forty-five per cent of all sisal is produced here and almost all the pyrethrum used in insecticides. Most of the cash crop in Kenya has been and is grown by Europeans. There have been inadequate resources for Africans who wished to buy machines, little government subsidy, and little training for proper land utilization. One needs to understand that there has been a little experimentation in Tanganyika and Uganda by African farmers, which indicates that coffee can be successfully raised by others than Europeans.[39]

The traditional lines which have been suggested in preceding par-

[38] *Ibid.*, p. 23.
[39] *Ibid.*, p. 29.

agraphs clearly show past alliance largely born of the colonial era. Popular material is inviting our attention in new ways.

Clarence Randall of the Inland Steel Company was sent to Africa in November, 1957, as a special representative of the President of the United States. He was to direct a study on the barriers to international travel. He speaks of the developing cities, the incredible mineral resources which he thinks exists, and what he considers the greatest of all African resources—power. He seems overwhelmed by this. Some of his illustrations approach hyperbole. (He says that Inga, near Leopoldville, when fully developed will produce one-fifth as much power as all the electricity now being developed in the United States.)[40] Thus African relationship to a world culture known as secular is just in the beginning stages.

CHRISTIAN MISSION AND SOCIAL WELFARE RELATIONSHIPS

In this technological world into which Africa has suddenly been catapulted one must get behind the scenes. It seems fairly reasonable that when communities are partially uneducated in a Western sense there is comparatively low productivity. Low productivity is accompanied by poverty. Poverty keeps one from preparation, and poor preparation may prevent the adequate assumption of responsibility.

1. It is a truism to boast of the near monopoly Christian missions historically have had in the welfare field, and we have written of it in this chapter. Motivation for such might have been modest in certain cases, but it was there. One needs to be careful now not to overclaim, yet at the same time we realize the tremendous continuing force in the missions.

2. Others have been at work. As early as 1930 Lord Passfield said without equivocation that African interests needed first attention.[41] From Belgium came approximately the same word, stated in 1931 by M. Pierre Rychmans before the United Nations Organizations.[42] Let us understand clearly here that the setting forth of such a position does not mean complete implementation of it.

3. Subsequently, mission organizations have moved swiftly. United Missions in the Copper Belt, formed in 1936, consisted of six missions

[40] Popularly treated in *Saturday Evening Post*, August 2, 1958, "I Saw the New Africa," by Clarence B. Randall, p. 63.

[41] Memorandum on Native Policy in East Africa, Cmd, 3573, 1930.

[42] Groves, *op. cit.*, p. 160.

co-operating to alleviate the disequilibrium in that area.[43] Similarly the International Missionary Council, through its Department of Social and Industrial Research, had a good experience in 1935 as it explored its opportunities for service in South Africa.[44]

4. But there has been continuing interest on the part of outside agencies. Much of what missions did thirty years ago is now conceived of as being government responsibility. The British Parliament passed the Colonial Development and Welfare Act in July, 1940. By 1945 it had approved over 500 plans and had received grants in excess of £ 12,000,000.[45] Similarly a Belgian Welfare Agency was established in 1947.[46]

Where does all this point? It indicates a future of partnership. Recently, yet before present involvements, a most attractive publication was released from Belgium, obviously in the interest of promotion and public relations. It was entitled "Family Album" and stressed the importance of partnership between Belgium and the Congo.[47]

The meaning of genuine partnership is significant here. In the first place, partners commit themselves in trust to one another. Secondly, partners are mutually liable, which can be costly. Thirdly, partners mutually accept the benefits from the partnership.

Commenting on this, Bruce Greaves stated in 1951 that if Christian community was to be a part of the partnership, he envisioned three things. First, Christians would have to demonstrate the possibility of a multiracial community. Next, they must do all in their power to close the gaps which yawn so widely as to make partnership unreal. Finally, Christian community is in a good position to assist in defining "partnership" and making its implications clear. Partnership finds prospective partners planning together; proposals coming from one side alone are generally unacceptable psychologically. Let it also be said that there are many in Africa and outside who believe there is no hope for partnership in the state if it cannot be patterned on the Christian community.[48]

[43] *Ibid.*, p. 172.
[44] *Ibid.*, p. 160.
[45] *Ibid.*, p. 274.
[46] *Ibid.*, p. 279.
[47] "Family Album," Information Service of the Gouvernement General, 1957.
[48] B. Greaves, "Africa Is Here," Report of the North American Assembly on African Affairs, Wittenberg College, Springfield, Ohio, 1952, p. 27.

THE MISSIONS

Christian missions have continued as organizations in Africa since 1938. They represent outside agency largely, even when a South African white goes to West Africa. Before moving to the last aspect of this study a glance at missions as an outside agency may be helpful.

The day of the mission organization has not disappeared. A comparison of the 1938 *Interpretative Statistical Survey* and the subsequent *World Christian Handbooks* reveals missionary organizations from overseas still in Africa. There are in fact more, rather than less, if one pauses to count. In North America at last four agencies are at present attempting to establish a kind of co-operative unity for boards desiring to work in Africa, believing they can do certain things better together than separately. Harold Lindsell calls attention to these in another paper in this collection. We refer here to the Division of Foreign Missions of the National Council of Churches of Christ in America, the Evangelical Foreign Missions Association, the Interdenominational Foreign Missions Association, and the Associated Missions of the International Council of Christian Churches. All have units in Africa.

The continuing presence of missions can be seen in the existence of the conferences since 1938. Conferences have been held at Whitby, Ontario (1947), Willingen, Germany (1952), and Accra, Ghana (1958). Allow the matter to be brought closer to us. Protestant missionaries from North America to Africa alone have increased fourfold in the last thirty years.[49] The largest number of North American missionaries going anywhere is to Africa south of the Sahara, and we are informed that this area gets slightly more than 29 per cent.[50] Pierce Beaver writing in 1954 and speaking of missionary expansion since 1945 mentioned fourteen new agencies as having started work in Africa during that interim.[51] The Sudan Interior Mission has one of the largest rosters of missionaries (1,024) of any missionary organization and its work is entirely in Africa.[52]

In spite of correct statements that the going in Africa is heavy,

[49] *Occasional Bulletin*, Missionary Research Library, Vol. 7, No. 9, Price and Moyer, "A Study of American Protestant Foreign Mission in 1956."
[50] *Ibid.*, p. 1.
[51] *Ibid.*, Vol. 5, No. 7, Pierce Beaver, p. 4.
[52] *Ibid.*, Vol. 7, No. 9, Price and Moyer, p. 2.

illustration after illustration indicates that Africa can use, and will welcome, competent missionaries from outside. We recall the almost undue pressure put upon a missionary doctor in Northern Nigeria to oversee government dispensaries. His competence made him desirable in spite of the fact that he was already doing more than could be expected of any man. We remember also an agricultural man in Sierra Leone who was constantly being solicited by government centers to experiment. He was able to achieve co-operation with certain communities when no one else could.

A haunting fear captures us at a last point. To what extent is there the possibility that a kind of Christian colonialism has been holding on in Africa since 1938? We do not mean here what Paul may have meant in his letter to the Philippian Church when he said, "Our commonwealth is in heaven" (Philippians 3:20). Commentators have found much diversion in working with that verse, and there is no claim to New Testament competence here.

What is meant when men say the word "colony"?[53] There may be many definitions, but two key words, "emigration" and "domination," are essential to a partial understanding of the term, for both appear in a colonial situation.

Emigration means occupation and not always is it physical conquest. It is a phenomenon involving contact. Emigration as used in describing a colonial situation is often seen through two word pictures. On the one hand you see colonizers coming from afar, wanting to bestow on new areas the development of their traditions. On the other is something else: early occupiers are reduced to a kind of legal or actual tutelage.

Under emigration may appear one or another of two kinds of colonies. There is the habitable one—like home. Again, there is the skeleton colony for exploitation purposes. Occasionally this skeleton colony becomes a habitable one.

"Domination" is the second key word. This is the legal, or approximately legal, side. As domination becomes a part of the colony idea two things generally appear. They may not appear simultaneously, but they are generally at hand. One is domination without a legal core. This is imposition, which makes rejection very difficult for the

---

[53] There are many summarizations of the colonial idea. The following one may be found helpful: R. Maunier, *The Sociology of Colonies* (London, Routledge and Kegan Paul, Ltd., 1949), Vols. I and II.

"early occupiers" because it may not be based on altogether legal grounds. The other is legal domination. The "emigrators" may remain in a strict relationship to the area from which they have come, preserving rights and duties toward it. This is a kind of dependence. Similarly, there is dependence for the indigene. The symbol to which he gives himself may be a flag or a governor.

The disturbing thought is that one can remove political implications of the preceding paragraphs and apply mission considerations. There are thousands of missionaries in Africa from Europe and North America. In a sense they represent the "emigration." The development of their traditions is often present. Likewise there are many African people who are the recipients of this thrust and who feel themselves under a kind of foreign spiritual tutelage. It still follows that "emigration," even of missionaries, will not be colonization unless "dominance" is related to the experience.

But that has happened in Africa too. It still happens, we believe, in many areas. In a personal diary, written in 1957, is an account of a conversation with friends in Northern Nigeria. These were African men. Speaking of a vote which had been taken in a church gathering, these Africans affirmed that had the vote been taken when originally announced instead of later they would have voted differently and that a hasty adjournment had given time for missionary pressure to be exerted. The next morning, the Africans had voted in a way which represented regression in the life of the church as far as they were concerned. They had neither forgotten nor forgiven this.

It ill behooves any of us to criticize another's Christian witness or pass judgment on it. However, the writer of this chapter hopes that mission boards will study African mission policy to see if there are aspects of this new kind of "colonialism" present. This, in our estimation, will run very deeply into our missionary structure, and maybe even the structure of the Church. For instance, will the insistence on a world confessional pattern of Western denominations be a missionary illustration of what we have been discussing?

This is part of the story of today and only suggests that the mission may still be an exterior force, carrying problems and privileges. In view of what has happened in Africa in the last twenty years the mission of the Western church may need to do an honest self-analysis.

4. The Church

The thrilling climax to the expansion of Christianity is the emergence of the Church. It is so across the world and no less in Africa. Not always is the story one of triumph, but even in the occasional defeats the account is a positive one. To tell the story we present illustrations of churches of different types, knowing as we do this that the whole account has not been told. In at least one of these cases the story of the Church has been very well written.[54]

THE CHURCH IN BUGANDA

To understand the church in Buganda demands an understanding of mission history which reaches back to the time of Henry Stanley. In 1875 King Mutesa asked Mr. Stanley, "What tidings can you bring me from above?"[55] Subsequent experience was dramatic, although not always as promising as it appeared it might be in those early days as missionaries responded to Mutesa's invitation.

The major reason for the inclusion of this church is not its long history. There are other reasons. This, on the one hand, is a church which came into being because of mission activity and thus pays it a compliment in some ways. It is also a church which has had its period of disengagement, and times in more recent history when folk have wondered about the effort expended to create it. Further, it was one of the churches chosen by the Missions Studies Department of the International Missionary Council and the World Council of Churches for study,[56] in which the answers to certain questions were sought: What does it mean for individual Christians or local churches to stand at a given point of time in a given situation? How do Christians respond to different factors in their environment and what influences and determines that response? What does it mean to be in the Church at this time?

Keep in mind that this church was the result of an Anglican mission.

Buganda is statistically a Christian country according to the study.

[54] J. Taylor, *The Growth of the Church in Buganda* (London, Student Christian Movement Press, Ltd., 1958).
[55] F. P. Noble, *The Redemption of Africa* (New York, Fleming H. Revell Company, 1899), Vol. I, p. 247.
[56] Taylor, *op. cit.*

It is figured that 537,000, or 41 per cent, are Roman Catholics. About 311,000, or 24 per cent, are in the Church of Buganda. There are other, smaller groups. Old religious forms claim 27 per cent, and Islam over 7 per cent.

In giving these statistics it should be stated clearly that for many church membership means little. Present-day studies have proved that as the Buganda kingdom has suffered social disruption, it has proved the reality of a great church.

This church may come alive to us through introduction of three phases of its current experience.

First, it is facing adaptation problems which the fathers never knew. These are often problems which would relate the church to the community. Fragmentation and soil exhaustion are relentlessly opposing progressive development.[57] People are moving so one may find areas where as low as 30 per cent are Baganda.[58] Integration of immigrants is not complete. Changes in the way of making a living are taking place. Imported machine-made goods have caused village crafts to decline. In agriculture the old peasant cultivation has given way to coffee and cotton growing. Both of these are money crops, and there is no assurance that money will be used for what the Baganda have always considered essentials. More than this, there is the ephemeral nature of political groups. The old Bataka organization was conservative, with a long history, and was the main agency for dispensing propaganda. This gave way to the Uganda National Congress, and by 1956 enthusiasm for the latter was disappearing.[59] Periodic riots in Buganda have been bothersome.

Second, the church has wrestled with its own organization. Church attendance has been dropping, not always for religious reasons. The traditional long afternoon services are dying out. The serving of a midday meal has become almost a universal custom, and few are prepared to wait for it until five or six o'clock.[60] Trends in this church are more the result of internal life than external; that is, the lack of a thorough pastoral ministry is part of the problem.[61] Take a good catechist away and the work sags. Catechists have been inclined, according to report, to be indifferent and censorious. Vil-

[57] *Ibid.*, p. 113.
[58] *Ibid.*
[59] *Ibid.*, p. 120.
[60] *Ibid.*, p. 131.
[61] *Ibid.*, p. 139.

lagers admit that these two signs may be related to other problems, such as discouragement and economic insecurity. This church has a problem with its stewardship, not because the people are stingy, but because of a conventional state of mind which finds them traditionally giving on personal grounds and to present needs.[62]

There are answers to these problems. They may rest, believes this church, in the following, and the world Christian community has tried to be helpful at these points. There must be new attention given to the ministry. It must be better qualified—and there are dangers in this too. African concepts of leadership and authority will have to be considered. The Buganda societies will also have to recognize that they treat young men unfairly if they insist on their working in an outmoded ministerial hierarchy and with poor educational opportunity.[63] On this ministerial matter it should be added that laymen are coming forward, and they too are being given preparation which may have a good new word for the day ahead.

Third, the church has had a reputation for good usage of the Bible. It almost lost it; Bible study and expository preaching had become decidedly frothy, in spite of the fact that splendid work in Bible translation had been done by Protestant and Roman alike. The church now seems to move three ways. It endeavors to provide a continuous process of Bible training for different levels—and wants it to be good training. It desires to remove paralysis in the production of Christian literature. Lastly, it is trying to reawaken its constituency to that tradition of solid interpretation of the Word in a preaching ministry.

Finally, the church's use of the sacraments of baptism and holy Communion are present explosion points. The essential problem here seems to be not in the acceptance of the validity or efficacy of the sacraments but in the massing of detail and meanings around them.[64]

THE ASSOCIATION OF CHURCHES OF CHRIST IN THE SUDAN

In the territory south of the Sahara, largely but not completely contained in Nigeria, is the present Association of Churches of Christ in the Sudan. The translation from Hausa may not be quite literal.

[62] *Ibid.*, p. 135.
[63] S. Neill, *Survey of the Training of the Ministry in Africa* (New York, International Missionary Council, 1950), Part I, pp. 10–11, 21–22, 38–39.
[64] Taylor, *op. cit.*, p. 245.

The Hausa name is Tarayyar Ekklesiya Kristi a Sudan. The use of the word "Sudan" is not in reference to a nation but to the grasslands stretching across Africa south of the Sahara. This church, if it be a church, cannot be called a national church for it does not cover all of Nigeria and reaches too into other new nations.

A number of propositions may help us to understand it.

First, it came into existence because of a variety of mission approaches. To trace its history prior to 1937 would involve checking a number of missions. Respectively involved here would be (a) the British Branch, (b) the South African Branch, (c) the American Christian Reformed Church Branch, (d) the Canadian Branch, (e) the Danish Branch, (f) the Norwegian Branch, and (g) the Swiss Branch, (h) The Mission of the Evangelical United Brethren Church. These "branches" come together in a kind of co-operative unit known as the Sudan United Mission.[65] To mention the branches is to oversimplify the situation. Certain of the branches secure missionary personnel from across denominations while others are served by personnel from within the structure of the denomination. Again, some of the units show a minimum of co-operation with contemporary ecumenical interests; others are completely committed to such contemporary ecumenical co-operation as may be found, for instance, in working with the International Missionary Council and the World Council of Churches.

Secondly, the background material for the life of the church is to be found in a number of missionary conferences. As early as 1923, in isolated spots in Northern Nigeria, missionaries would gather to talk over their hopes. There eventually grew the conviction that from their evangelistic effort the "People of God" would emerge. The missionaries felt such emergence to be the Church. In those early conferences they even talked about a constitution for that Church.

An intermission conference was held in 1926 at Miango in Northern Nigeria where the missionaries had gathered to talk about problems of African marriage (across the years this has seemed to be a perennial problem to missionaries). They ended by drafting a trial constitution for a church which might be presented to mission agency and to Africans.

---

[65] J. L. Maxwell, *Half a Century of Grace* (London, Sudan United Mission). See map No. 2 between pp. 6 and 7.

In 1929 missionaries met in conference again. This time African churchmen were beginning to appear at least as consultants. A measure of apparent regression took place here. The question as to whether a church was feasible was raised. Would it not be better to move towad a federation of missions?

Third, in the years following, as African and missionary worked together, premises were worked out, and these premises were presented at the Tambaram Conference in 1938.[66] This Nigerian community was convinced that the Church emerges under the grace and goodness of God; it is related to the witness and labor of missionaries; and it emerges wherever there is Christian community. Also, as the Church emerges she is one. If she is divided it is by man. This premise made missionaries in particular immediately conscious of their responsibility. If God wills unity and then men divide, men are engaged in sinful activity. This same premise made young African churchmen conscious of their oneness.

There is no intent here to defend or reject this interpretation of the nature of the Church. A personal word cannot be avoided. There may be readers who will disagree with the interpretations and conclusions stated here. Reasons for such disagreement will be apparent after the next few paragraphs. It was a thrilling experience to be a part of this whole experiment in 1938 as a missionary of the Evangelical United Brethren Church. If there is gross misinterpretation, then there comes opportunity for dialogue between us. The description as given is certainly the way some of us saw the situation.

Fourth, from 1938 to the present a number of things have happened. (a) There has been a trend toward an ordained ministry. The first ordinands into the Church in the Sudan as it was then called came late in 1938.[67] You will note that the word "united" does not appear in the early name. The reason tenaciously held to was that inasmuch as the church had never been divided, no word which would suggest division was suitable. (b) There was a continuous drawing of nationals and missionaries into experiences of churchmanship. Problems of polity, self-support, status, and Christian literature are samples.

Fifth, the variation of background and opportunity offers an

---

[66] *The Madras Series*, Vol. IV, *The Life of the Church* (New York, International Missionary Council, 1939), p. 406.
[67] Maxwell, *op. cit.*, p. 217.

almost unbelievable panorama. The original evangelistic thrust, and
a still continuing one, was provided by the Sudan United Mission
with general headquarters in London. It is "interdenominational,"
and not necessarily completely "nondenominational." The Sudan
United Mission is the federation we have previously mentioned as
being in the thinking of missionaries gathered in conference. At
present the Association of Churches of Christ in the Sudan is the
approximation of "church" growing from this mission activity. It
would probably have to be classified as a numerically small church,
with perhaps not more than 25,000 members in communicant relationship. Statistics are hard to gather. It reaches across political lines,
existing in Chad and Cameroun as well as in Nigeria. Statistics are
misleading because almost any unit in the mission federation may
have comity rights on sizable populations. Generally, the Association
of Churches of Christ in the Sudan has the same general boundaries
for its units as do the missions in the federation. Personal observation
in 1957 was made in the one area where there were hardly 1,000
communicants. Yet the unit at work here had comity rights for
approximately 300,000 people.

Sixth, the present story is filled with mixed blessing. On the positive side, the church has continued to grow. A theological training
center was established in 1937 and continued until 1959, when a
seminary was initiated at Bukuru, just outside Jos in Northern Nigeria. All the original missions plus additional units are at present
giving blessing to this new venture. So also is the young church,
which has continued to ordain men across these last twenty years.
It should be noted that training centers for Christian lay leadership
have been established. Their comprehensive approach to Christian
community has been well validated. Gindiri Training Center looms
as one of the finest training centers for Christian leadership in all of
Northern Nigeria. Its scope of training is very comprehensive.

A negative aspect has developed. Because it has so much of what
might involve the future in other places, we wish to share it as we
saw it. Eventually, and more specifically after World War II, missionaries working through the mission units backing the young
church seemed to feel that Western denominationalism was not
getting just recognition.

This problem should be more kindly stated. There were missionaries so convinced of the rightness of their own confessional denom-

inational base that they were restless unless it show in the life of the church. Some missionaries advocated a movement away from the Church in the Sudan to what has finally come to be the Association of Churches of Christ in the Sudan. Some will refute this statement saying churchmen themselves voted this change. That is true. We stand ready to be convinced that it was at the initiative of African churchmen that this took place. Extended conversations with African lay leadership and pastors have not been reassuring on this point. The missionary argument was that the original concept was premature. Let operations work through co-operative unity first, and then organic unity will follow. They were saying, in essence, let the church be divided first, then allow it to get together instead of encouraging it to stay together. Some missionaries bluntly told the writer of this chapter that they did not trust the African church to guide its own destiny. What they were actually saying, I believe, was that the church would stray from the moorings initiated by the missionary. (Frankly, I think it *would* have strayed from such limits.) A rather rugged correspondence, too personal to share here, has taken place between missionary leaders. At least one of the most able executives of the Sudan United Mission definitely stated that he felt that movement from "Church" to "Association of Churches" is a loss and entirely out of line with the wave of the future. African church leaders told me without being solicited that "they were sick of it." There are Nigerian churchmen who believe a kind of missionary colonialism was used and they don't like it.

The story of the Association of Churches of Christ in the Sudan is certainly not ended, and at some not too distant day there will be new chapters waiting to be read and studied. As of now, much in the life of this body sets the mind and mood of the relationships between Christian missions and emergent churches as developed in the twenty years following 1938.

The reality of the emergent Church in Africa is perhaps the most significant fact of the years since 1938. Granted that there was some such emergence prior to the period under consideration, it was but a minor movement compared to what has happened since. Other illustrations could have been chosen; variations of program and pattern would appear; yet the reality of a dynamic Church in Africa would always be before us.[68]

[68] A very heart-warming illustration would be the story of American Pres-

A WHISPER WHICH IS BECOMING AUDIBLE

Perhaps the most important word that can be said along the lines of the thought of these pages is that an All-Africa Conference was held in January, 1958, at Ibadan, Nigeria. The five major themes show the direction of the churches and of churchmen: "The Church, Youth and the Family"; "The Church and Economic Life"; "The Church and Citizenship"; "The Church and Culture"; and "The Growing Church."[69]

The information sessions of this conference showed the real movement of the church. Here discussion and plans relating to Christian literature took place and a literacy and writing center has since been established near Kitwe in the Northern Rhodesian area (also the location of one of the newer ecumenical training centers). In these sessions, not without some trepidation, plans were made for the moving together of the International Missionary Council, the World Council of Churches, and the African churches. (This is not to discount the conference held just prior to this one, at Accra, a conference of the International Missionary Council.) Young-church studies, even the one used in this chapter made by John Taylor, were presented. The surveys relating to the training of the ministry which had been done in three stages between 1950 and 1954 were reviewed. Since then the implementing of these surveys organizationally and financially leads us to conclude that a new day is at hand for the training of the African churchman.

Perhaps the most important note of the conference is one which is not completely reflected in its report. Kyaw Than reported on the East Asia Christian Conference, a body for maintaining cooperation among the churches and Christian councils in East Asia.[70] Its charter clearly states that as churches they too are involved in mission and stand under the conviction that Western missionary activity in the area should be related to the existent churches.

Why should a report of the East Asia Christian Conference be important? At Ibadan the African church found its voice. At previ-

---

byterianism turning over its activities, program, and missionaries to the Presbyterian Church of Cameroun. *Christian Century*, Vol. LXXIV (December 25, 1957), p. 1533.

[69] Report of All-Africa Conference, *The Church in Changing Africa* (New York, International Missionary Council, 1958).

[70] *Ibid.*, p. 98.

ous conferences the missionaries had been speaking to the world as interpreters of the Christian movement in Africa. At this conference African churchmen and churchwomen moved forward handling issues capably and with confidence. A resolution passed is much like the early findings of the conferences which were the foundation for the East Asia Christian Conference:

> RESOLVED, That this Conference name a committee here to consult with the Christian Councils of Africa, church bodies and other agencies concerned with the witness for Christ in Africa, in order to give consideration to the implementation of the report of this Conference and particularly as to the appointment of a Continuation Committee and/or a regional secretary. It is suggested that the General Chairman of this Conference and the Chairman of the Steering Committee be members of the committee.[71]

This resolution was adopted by the conference, the committee was named, and it has been functioning. One cannot help concluding that a step so responsibly taken, when coupled with the factors as outlined in this chapter, will speak significantly to issues in Christian witness in the days ahead.

5. Conclusion

This study has intentionally avoided doing certain things which under other circumstances would be worthy objectives. Only a casual mention, and certainly no analysis, has been given to Roman Catholicism, which has experienced rapid growth and has pioneered in many ways in the practice of mission since 1938. But often her concerns have been the same as the concerns of Protestantism. Nor has there been any discussion of institutions and organizations. Avoidance of the growing "faith" missions does not mean they are unimportant. The consideration of their concept of the nature and work of the Church is exceedingly relevant, and has been specially treated in this *Festschrift*. But they cannot escape the general outline of these pages, and if the internal and external climate is as described such missions must find their place not outside but inside the picture. It would have been possible to chart Christian mission chronologically since 1938, but such strict adherence to the years has

[71] *Ibid.*, p. 17.

been somewhat carelessly thrust aside in favor of capturing a new direction.

The mind and mood of Africa since 1938 is the important issue, and that has already partially shaped the missionary enterprise. Acceptance of the direction carries promise for more complete realization of Christian mission; conversely, an ignoring of this mood and mind may be exceedingly costly. From inside Africa has come new power which will affect mission in the days ahead, from outside come influences leading to stress and strain, and in the midst of it all is a new emphasis on world community. Dynamically, somewhat erratically, and yet always with the certainty of the ages stands the reality of the Church.

CHAPTER V

A Study in the Self-Propagating Church: Madagascar

CHARLES W. FORMAN

Yale Divinity School

New Haven, Connecticut

In our day the churches of America and Europe are increasingly convinced that their mission to the rest of the world should be carried on in partnership with the churches which exist in the rest of the world. "Our calling is to make personnel and funds available to churches for *their* use in *their* missionary and evangelistic outreach under *their* own administration," said one of the principal American mission board secretaries in a keynote address at the 1959 Divisional Assemblies of the National Council of Churches. It is self-evident that the Christian mission can be carried on in this way only if the churches of Asia, Africa, and Latin America are aware of their missionary calling and are engaged in "*their* missionary and evangelistic outreach." As Christian missions move into this new era, then, it becomes more and more important to learn just how far and in what ways the younger churches have been aware of and have carried out their missionary calling.

The church from which there would seem to be the most to learn is the church of Madagascar. None of the younger churches has been so consistently devoted to its mission or has carried on so much missionary and evangelistic outreach as has the church of that great island. It is true that the churches of Polynesia have sent out missionaries over greater distances but the number of their workers has been far fewer,[1] as has been the number sent out by the churches of Asia.

---

[1] The London Missionary Society has had the principal relationship to both areas and at the end of the nineteenth century when Polynesian missions were still flourishing the Madagascar churches could boast ten times as many church

The Malagasy church was from its very beginnings a self-prop-
agating church. The fact that the missionaries had to be withdrawn
from the island shortly after the start of their work because of
the hostility of Queen Ranavalona I forced the early band of converts to take on responsibility for whatever preaching there was.
Ranavalona I's reign lasted from 1828 to 1861. There could have
been no more difficult time for a group of untried and uninstructed
Christians to undertake the maintenance and propagation of the
church. The Queen was ready to use any means to destroy the faith.
The persecutions and martyrdoms which those early converts endured are famous. Yet their very martyrdoms proved an effective
form of preaching. Their patience and joy in the face of death won
them the respect of many of their contemporaries and increased interest in the new faith which could produce such people. There
must also have been a great deal of secret evangelism going on, for
many people became ready to declare themselves Christians as soon
as there was freedom to do so. The number of Christians increased
many fold during the years of persecution. At the beginning of the
period there were between one and two thousand. Some two hundred of these were killed and many more were taken away as slaves.
Yet at the end of the persecutions the number had grown to between
seven and ten thousand.[2] In the town of Ilafy, for example, not far
from the capital, at the beginning of the period of persecutions there
was a small church of thirty-eight members. Of these, four were put
to death, three died in prison, six went through the poison ordeal
(two of them dying in the process), and a number of Christians fled
from the area. Yet at the end of the reign of Ranavalona this same
church reported a membership of 260. True, the influx of new members may have come immediately upon the cessation of the persecutions rather than while they were in progress. The Ilafy report
was made shortly after freedom was re-established. Yet the evangelistic work which resulted in such a great growth was obviously
done while the persecutions were going on.[3]

---

workers as were found in the LMS sections of Polynesia. Norman Goodall,
History of the London Missionary Society, 1895–1945 (London, Oxford University Press, 1954), p. 334.

[2] Andrew Burgess in his book, *Zanahary in South Madagascar* (Minneapolis,
1932), p. 120, puts the number at 7,000; James Sibree in *The Madagascar Mission* (London, 1907), p. 41, reports a tenfold increase.

[3] H. Rusillon, *Un Petit Continent Madagascar* (Paris, Société des Missions

Most of the secret spread of Christianity took place in and around the capital in the central province of Imerina. It was here that the missionaries had done all of their work and here that Christianity really took root. But the faith also spread beyond that province. The Merina people, commonly called Hova although Hova is strictly speaking a class designation rather than an ethnic term, were the most advanced and civilized people of the island and had since the late eighteenth century established their rule more or less effectively throughout the whole of Madagascar. The government was strongest in its home territory, and therefore it was only natural that Christians fleeing from the persecutions should leave Imerina for the more distant areas where the Queen's authority was not so universally recognized. Thus it was that the same process which led to the secret spread of Christianity within Imerina led to its expansion to other parts, even as during the persecution which followed upon the death of Stephen "those who were scattered went about preaching the Word."[4]

The most noted area in which the Gospel spread in this way was the province of Betsileo. There, far to the south of Imerina, the Hova rule had been established over the comparatively slow and backward Betsileo people. Large numbers of Christians fled to that province and found safety in its forests and hill towns. When the persecuting Queen died and the people were free to make their Christianity known, considerable numbers of Christians suddenly appeared, particularly in the Betsileo capital of Fianarantsoa. William Ellis, who had been sent out from London to survey the situation after Ranavalona's death, took word of the Betsileo development to England, and the London Missionary Society determined to send four missionaries to work in the province.[5] But quite apart from the missionaries and before they were able to start their work, the Betsileo church proceeded to grow. The first church was established in Fianarantsoa in 1863. A year later a second one had to be built. Shortly after, a third was added. By the time the first missionaries

---

Évangéliques, 1933), p. 380; cf. also G. Mondain, *Un Siècle de Mission Protestante à Madagascar* (Paris, Société des Missions Évangéliques, 1920), pp. 224–225. Mondain relates that the first two martyrs from Vonizongo were taken when on a missionary trip to the Sakalava.

4 Acts 8:4.
5 *The Chronicle*, March, 1872, p. 48.

arrived in 1869 there were already seventy-nine churches and sixty-three Christian schools in Betsileo.[6]

The Official Evangelists

By this time the situation had changed completely in Imerina with consequent changes for the method of carrying on indigenous missions. No longer was the secret testimony of fleeing Christians, or the public testimony of martyrs, the way by which the self-propagation of the church was accomplished. The death of the persecuting Queen was followed by two brief reigns during which Christianity was given full freedom although the monarchs remained non-Christian. Then in 1868 Ranavalona II began her long reign. There was some apprehension among the Christians when she chose the name of the persecutor, but she turned out to be quite the opposite of her predecessor. She early declared an intention to "rest my kingdom upon God." And after a period of instruction from Malagasy pastors she and her Prime Minister were both baptized. In 1869 she ordered the burning of the royal idols since they no longer represented the religious convictions upon which her government was based. Apparently the government had seen that even its most severe penalties could not stop the spread of the new religion and consequently it decided to join forces with the growing power. The immediate result was the most rapid self-propagation of the church in the whole history of Madagascar. Although the Queen stated clearly that everyone was free to attend church or not, she did insist that all burn their idols[7] and there was a general assumption on the part of the people that they would follow the example of their Queen in becoming Christian. Throughout Imerina churches were quickly constructed and the natural leaders of the communities were chosen as pastors. Before the burning of the idols in 1869 there were 37,000 Christians in the country; at the end of 1870 there were 250,000.[8] The number of native pastors increased during 1870 from a little

---

[6] Mondain, *op. cit.*, p. 269. One church in Fianarantsoa claims to have been established in 1859.

[7] Adrien Boudou, *Les Jésuites à Madagascar au XIXe Siècle* (Paris, Gabriel Beauchesne, 1950), Vol. II, p. 41. Mondain, *op. cit.*, p. 267.

[8] Sibree, *op. cit.*, p. 46.

over a thousand to 10,405.[9] This was a national movement leaving little room for personal decisions and quite beyond the control of the missionaries. Some of them complained vigorously about the lack of freedom in this type of church growth. "The State Church in Madagascar is less tolerant than that of Turkey, Spain, or England," said one. "I have often thought," wrote another, "that we are expected to preach not the Gospel of Jesus Christ according to the New Testament, but the Gospel according to the Prime Minister."[10] Yet technically the church was not a state church. It had no position in the constitution. There was official freedom of religion and there was not meant to be any discrimination against non-Christians in public functions.[11]

What government participation there was in the work of evangelism and church growth came largely through the Palace Church. This was a unique institution. It met the traditional Malagasy expectation of a religious connection for government and yet left the church at large free from official control. It was a congregation made up of the highest nobility of the country and was under the control of the queen and the Prime Minister in a way in which the Protestant churches generally, with their English independent traditions, would not be. It was technically just one congregation, a member like any other of the Congregational Union of Imerina.[12] It was housed in an impressive and graceful building in the palace grounds, a building which, though now overgrown with weeds and bolted shut, still stands as a monument to the religious convictions of the later Malagasy monarchy. Its dedication was an occasion for national celebration when special services were held in the church for fourteen successive days with no public business carried on during the period. On some days there were as many as eight services and the Queen and Prime Minister were present at every one.[13]

The Palace Church provided a way somewhat within the free church tradition by which the government could enter directly into the task of evangelism and choose its own evangelistic workers. At the time of the burning of the idols the government had already

[9] London Missionary Society, *Report for the Year 1871*, p. 119.
[10] Boudou, *op. cit.*, II, pp. 46–47.
[11] Henri Rahamefy, "L'Église du Palais à Madagascar," *Le Monde non-Chrétien*, Vol. XXXII (October–December, 1959), pp. 411–413.
[12] *Ibid.*, pp. 415–420.
[13] Goodall, *op. cit.*, p. 346.

shown its desire to help in the work of evangelizing the more distant
parts of Imerina by conferring with the missionaries on the subject
and by freeing the teachers and evangelists whom the mission sent
out from the onerous demands of the *fanompoana* or feudal labor
service.[14] Once the Palace Church was established its chief concern
became the instruction and Christianizing of the people.[15] In October,
1869, the Prime Minister, Rainilaiarivony, held a meeting of the
preachers and teachers at his residence where it was decided that col-
lections would be taken up in the Palace Church and other churches
for the purpose of sending evangelists throughout the island. The
selection of the evangelists was apparently made initially by the
churches to which they belonged and then confirmed by the government. Two months after the initial meeting it was announced by
the missionary chairman of the Congregational Union that 126 evangelists had been selected, commissioned, and sent out by the Queen.[16]
The Union, quick to preserve the autonomy of the churches, voted
that these men were not to appoint pastors or make themselves pastors over churches. The evangelists were accompanied by an official
escort,[17] and each one carried an official authorization and instruction for labors from the Queen. Their work has often been attacked
by hostile critics, especially by Jesuits, who have written of them as
possessing "a zeal worthy of the English heresy combined with bar-
barism."[18] And it is true, as we shall see later, that many criticisms
can be directed at some of the high-handed methods of work of
Palace Church evangelists. Yet a reading of the instructions which
were given to the first group as they started out[19] shows that in the
original conception of their work and in their actual dispatch there
was a praiseworthy concern for a true preaching of the Gospel and
a real desire to help the people to whom they were sent. And there
is no doubt that their services were badly needed in a time when

[14] Friends' Foreign Mission Association, *Review of the Work of the Friends'
Foreign Mission Association in Madagascar from 1867–1880* (Antananarivo,
1880), p. 33.
[15] Rahamefy, *op. cit.*, pp. 421–422.
[16] Boudou, *op. cit.*, II, pp. 38 and 45. London Missionary Society (hereafter
cited as L.M.S.), *Report, 1871*, p. 58.
[17] George E. Burton, *The Waiting Isle: Madagascar and Its Church* (London,
Livingstone Press, 1953), p. 56.
[18] Père de la Vaissière, *Histoire de Madagascar, ses Habitants et ses Missionnaires* (Paris, Libraire Victor Lecoffre, 1889), Vol. II, p. 46.
[19] See Appendix to this chapter.

churches were going up on every hand but there was no one to preach the Gospel. Furthermore, some of them presumably went beyond the borders of Imerina where churches were being established and inaugurated mission stations in the more distant parts of the island, principally along the east coast and in the southwest.[20]

This first group of evangelists had had no regular training and could have had only the most rudimentary knowledge of Christianity. Yet the government is hardly to be blamed for using such workers since the missionaries had already been sending out Malagasy evangelists who could not have been much better prepared.[21] More fully trained workers were being developed and the Palace Church was quick to make use of them as soon as they were available. The missionaries had established a training college in 1869, and when the first group of students was about to complete its course in 1873 the government announced suddenly that the ten men of highest rank in the student body were to be employed as emissaries of the Palace Church. Again it was the Prime Minister, Rainilaiarivony, who was responsible for the action. The men selected for the service were all nobles and therefore liable to unpaid service of the Queen under the feudal system. All were of a rank of at least ten honors, fifteen honors being the highest rank in the kingdom. Those students who were not of noble rank were left free to take up regular appointments in the churches.[22] The missionaries were dismayed at the loss of their best workers, on whose leadership they had counted. However, there was some consolation in the fact that their work was not to be strictly a feudal service; they were to receive a salary of eight dollars per month to be paid from the Palace Church. The men were sent to the ten major cities of Imerina where they were to look after the advancement of the church work.[23] A solemn farewell service was organized by the Prime Minister for their departure in April, 1874, and they were given a kind of official accredi-

[20] A map published in 1880 as the frontispiece in Friends' Foreign Mission Association, *op. cit.* (hereafter cited as FFMA), shows some 32 stations, beyond Imerina and the area of the foreign missions and exclusive of the station of the Native Missionary Society, the IEB, manned by native evangelists. It is hard to see who these could be except those sent out by the Palace Church.

[21] *Ibid.*, p. 50.

[22] LMS, *Report, 1875*, pp. 40–42.

[23] FFMA, p. 32. M. G. S. Chapus in *L'Église du Palais* (Tananarive, 1937), lists eight places to which Palace Church representatives went.

tation to the authorities of the regions into which they went.[24] There was considerable uncertainty as to how their work would fit in with the already established work of missions and churches in the provincial cities. Fortunately they were all men of ability and had been well trained by the missionaries, so they worked effectively and amicably with others in the common task. For example, the man who was placed in Arivonimamo, a nobleman named Ralambotsirofo, holding twelve honors and therefore having great influence among the people, was reported by those in his area to have done good work, to have shown a fine character and noble bearing, to have worked well with the missionaries, consulting them on every important step, and to have been a great help to the growth of the church in that region.[25] Shortly after these ten were dispatched a second group of ten young men from the training school for teachers was selected by the Palace Church and sent out to assist the first group in the establishment of schools.[26] After a five-year period the first ten were recalled to Tananarive, where they were given high positions in government service, and their places were taken by men of not such high standing, who often proved unequal to the task before them.[27] From time to time in the reports sent by the missionaries to London there appeared complaints against church workers who were recalcitrant or even immoral but who could not be put out of their positions because they were in the employ of the Palace Church and had powerful protectors in the capital.[28] There were stories of people being "thrashed to church" and on occasion Palace Church evangelists were known to order the policemen to bring people to church. One evangelist ruled his district with an iron hand and, in the missionary's opinion, ruined it. Naturally when evangelists had such prestige, it was not unknown for rogues to pose as emissaries of the Palace Church in order to secure the best hospitality of a village for a week end or a period of weeks. T. T. Matthews, who worked just beyond the borders of Imerina in the province of Vonizongo, tells of one such impostor. When he was called upon to give a sermon he announced that he would preach from the fortieth

---

[24] Mondain, *op. cit.*, p. 277.
[25] FFMA, p. 51.
[26] *Ibid.*, p. 32.
[27] Mondain, *op. cit.*, p. 277.
[28] M. G. S. Chapus, quoted in Boudou, *op. cit.*, p. 39.

chapter of Matthew. When the local people expostulated with him that there were not forty chapters in Matthew he disdainfully replied, "I don't know anything about your village Bibles. I'm going by the capital Bibles."[29]

The Evangelistic Officials

The growth of the church was fostered not only by the official evangelists sent out from the Palace Church but also by the evangelistically-minded officials representing the government in different parts of the country. Although the Queen had said clearly that there was to be freedom to pray or to stay at home, zealous officials wanting to prove their loyalty often brought pressure upon their subjects to follow the Queen's example.[30] In Imerina itself the general acceptance of Christianity was carried out fairly rapidly after the Queen became Christian and ordered all idols burned. In the rest of the island the Merina people who had moved out of their homeland in connection with trade or government soon followed the same example. But among the other peoples over whom the Hova ruled there was no such immediate and general acceptance of Christianity. Accordingly the chief efforts made by evangelistically-minded officials took place in the territories outside Imerina where there were large populations still untouched by the Church. Sometimes the governors sent out to the provinces were seriously Christian and did their best to lead the people rather than drive them in the direction of Christianity. For example, Rainiseheno, who was appointed governor of Betsileo in 1869, as much, it was said, for his goodness and piety as for his intelligence and ability, had a great desire to advance the kingdom of Christ among the Betsileo. He frequently preached in town or in the countryside and took general oversight over all of the churches in the neighborhood of Fianarantsoa. One Christian remarked about him, "Each of our town churches has a pastor and the governor is father and mother to us all." Under his tutelage the Hova Christians who had shown complete apathy with regard to the conversion of the Betsileo changed radically and came to feel that

[29] T. T. Matthews, *Thirty Years in Madagascar* (London, Religious Tract Society, 1904), pp. 119–120, 105.

[30] James Sibree, *Fifty Years in Madagascar* (London, Allen and Unwin, 1924), p. 81.

their "heart's desire and prayer to God," as they put it, was that
their fellow men who were still heathen "might be saved." Under
him a majority of the church members in Fianarantsoa came to be
Betsileo, though with Hova leadership.[31]

Yet even such a governor as Rainiseheno carried the policy of requiring church attendance "to an extreme that is absolutely cruel;
constraining the Betsileo to come extraordinary distances to worship
at Fianarantsoa." As one of the missionaries working in the area
wrote: The government's "unwise policy of forcing attendance because it cannot distinguish between things sacred and secular believing that those who will not worship as it does are rebellious
prejudices the ignorant against Christianity."[32] The Betsileo were
often forced to help build churches and marched to church in troops
by their chiefs.[33] Some took church attendance as another form of
required labor, *fanompoana*, under the feudal system.[34] It is not surprising under these conditions that when the Hova rule was replaced
by the French the Betsileo very largely fell away from these long-
established churches in their territory.[35]

A similar story comes from the area inhabited by the Tanosy tribe
in the extreme south of the island. Hova rule did not extend very
effectively far outside of the headquarters of that territory, Fort
Dauphin, but within the area they ruled the Hovas required Christianity. A church was established when two evangelists arrived in
1880. Church attendance was obligatory and after attendance for
six Sundays a person was baptized. If services were missed the of-
fender would have to stand with a heavy rice bowl or Bible on his
head as the congregation filed past him. In one government church
of the area it was the practice to give out gin to enliven the singing.
For a time there was an unscrupulous governor in Fort Dauphin
who, though he went to church regularly and required the people
to go also, helped himself to jewels from the royal tombs. He committed suicide when an investigation was begun. He was followed
by a more serious-minded Christian, Andriamarovony. The first

[31] Report by C. Jukes, *The Chronicle*, August, 1870, p. 167.
[32] *The Chronicle*, March, 1872, pp. 49–52.
[33] Boudou, *op. cit.*, II, p. 47.
[34] De la Vaissière, *op. cit.*, II, p. 49.
[35] W. S. Houghton *et al.*, *Report of Deputation to Madagascar, July–October, 1913, including joint report of London Missionary Society, Friends' Foreign Mission Association and Paris Missionary Society* (London, 1913), p. 115.

mission work of the Norwegian Missionary Society in this area was begun under his rule in 1888. There developed a real partnership in mission between Andriamarovony and J. B. Hogstadt, the missionary. The governor gave Hogstadt the care of the official church and gave official credentials and instructions to the teachers whom the missionary trained and sent out to the villages. He told them to teach the people "to read and write so that they may develop in the right way and learn how to worship the true God as they should." An officer was sent with each teacher to install him, and each year the pupils were called in to take examinations and the governor gave out prizes. When the Tanosy people proved distrustful of the missionary and his representatives because of their link with the hated Hova rule, the governor ordered them to assemble in Fort Dauphin (1891) and tried to make clear to them that it was for their own good that the government and the missionary were providing education for them. He also distributed gifts among the parents to win their favor. Yet the Hova rule proved so oppressive that when the French government came in the Tanosy quickly dropped out of both schools and churches. Only gradually was it possible to build up the Christian community again, on a voluntary basis.[36]

The action of the governors of Betsileo and Antanosy can be taken as fairly typical of those of the Hova governors wherever they were found. The same attitudes and demands are reported from the east coast and elsewhere.[37] However, the statement that the governors received orders from the Palace Church to convert the people under their jurisdiction would hardly seem to be supported by the evidence. Quite the contrary is stated by one who lived in Madagascar all through this period.[38] Sometimes the people, without any pressure from the governors, built chapels (which were sometimes used only as cow sheds) or, in full assembly, offered to burn all their idols, simply out of fear of the Hova power.[39]

[36] Mrs. P. C. Halvorson, *Lo-ha-ra-no* (Minneapolis, Augsburg Publishing House, 1948), pp. 128–134; Rolf A. Syrdal, *Mission in Madagascar and the Beginnings of the Malagasy Lutheran Church* (Minneapolis, 1957), pp. 32–36.
[37] Alfred Peyrot, "Action Missionnaire de l'Église Malgache," *Journal des Missions Évangéliques*, March–April, 1946, p. 54.
[38] Sibree, *Fifty Years in Madagascar*, pp. 81 ff.
[39] *The Chronicle*, December, 1888, p. 530, reports such chapels among the Bezanozano; and Boudou, *op. cit.*, II, p. 43, tells of the Sakalava offering to turn over their idols and amulets for burning.

The combination of evangelistic officials and official evangelists was a thoroughly indigenous form of missionary activity of the Merina Christians, expressing something of the traditional unity which they had known between religion and every phase of community life. There was nothing about the system which was copied from the missionaries. In fact the missionaries were in a peculiar position in relation to this type of evangelism. They found themselves opposed to such methods in principle. They might easily have broken with the whole system and have attacked it, bringing a fatal division among the Christian forces. But there had been growing up among them a policy favoring the development of the indigenous church of the country rather than the copying of Western Christianity, a policy which had found expression in the Liverpool Conference of 1860,[40] and they wisely refrained from any sharp break with the expressions of the church life of the land. Rather, they worked within the system and through brotherly exhortation tried to Christianize it as much as possible.

The same kind of policy was adopted with regard to slavery, an institution which it can well be imagined was extremely painful to these men who stood in the tradition which had led the antislavery fight in Britain and America. Yet they continued year in and year out to limit themselves simply to urging the Malagasy Christians to search their consciences on slavery. In relation to evangelism they likewise continually tried to teach the church leaders—including the Queen and Prime Minister and nobles of the court—that Christ's kingdom was a spiritual kingdom and thus to modify the natural tendency of the Malagasy to make it a form of political kingdom. On the whole they were favorably impressed with the extent to which the leaders of the people came to understand this distinction.

But though they may have understood it in theory, when it came to practice the distinction was easily blurred. Though the Queen seemed to take seriously the demands of her faith, the Prime Minister was always more concerned for political advantage. He had divorced his wife, the mother of his sixteen children, at the time of his baptism because the Queen with her new convictions would not accept him as her husband according to traditional usage as long as

[40] J. T. Hardyman, *Madagascar on the Move* (London, Livingstone Press, 1950), p. 149.

he had another wife. He was to proceed to marry her successor when she died. It is not surprising that his action in 1873 in choosing his own evangelists for the Palace Church and sending them out under his own orders seemed to link evangelism with his political power. Far more did the officials who lived at a distance from the capital, where there were none to supervise them, fall back on traditional methods of influencing people.

The compromises in evangelism proved highly damaging in the long run to the acceptance of the Gospel among the non-Merina peoples of the island. They all looked upon Christianity as a part of the Hova power and when the Hova were overthrown they regarded themselves as free of the necessity of being Christians. Even in our own day non-Merina pagans sometimes refer to Christianity as taboo for them because it is a Merina religion.[41] The Tsimihety people are reported to have claimed that the name Jehovah is proof that the religion is only for the Hova. And as recently as a generation ago a member of the Antankarana tribe in the extreme north of the island, when thinking of becoming a Christian, was told by his fellow tribesmen: "Do you not know that the Christian religion is the religion of the Hova, who formerly took our country, reduced us to slavery, and for years stole our harvest? And you go to pray with them; you betray us."[42] The type of indigenous missions adopted by the Hova government, though it proved tremendously effective in bringing the Merina into the church, can only be regarded as fruitless and unfortunate when it comes to its outreach to the other people of the island of Madagascar.

Evangelism of the Tananarive Churches

At a time when the government and its officials were showing such zeal for the propagation of the faith, it could be expected that the churches themselves would evidence a strong interest in evangelism. The early days of unpersecuted Christianity in the Malagasy kingdom were indeed days of enormous enthusiasm and zeal. Organized

[41] Ray Arnold, "An Approach to the Presentation of the Doctrine of Christian Hope in Theological Training in Madagascar," unpublished paper, p. 19.
[42] Burton, *op. cit.*, p. 57; Robert Becker, *Dao, l'Antankarana: Vie d'un Évangéliste Malgache* (Paris, 1932), p. 7.

church life really began when missionaries returned after the persecutions. Before that time Christians had met in small groups in
homes and in the fields after dark and had prayed and sung and read
the Bible together, but there had not been any real church organization. With the return of the missionaries, contributions from Britain
made possible the erection of some large and impressive church
buildings in the capital in memory of various martyrs, and soon
there were six and later ten great churches which dominated the
different parts of Antananarivo, as the capital was then called. They
also dominated the church life of the country. Each congregation
took responsibility for a wedge of territory fanning out from the
city to the borders of Imerina and for this area it attempted to provide evangelists and pastors. There was usually a missionary attached
to the church. Sometimes with him and sometimes without him the
preachers and laymen of the church would undertake tours through
the church's district. The churches of Tananarive were thus recognized as mother churches organizing and supervising the ecclesiastical life of Imerina.[43]

Once the Queen became Christian and ordered all idols burned,
the responsibilities of the churches of the capital were more pastoral
than evangelistic. The village churches which were so quickly organized all over the province had to have Christian instruction and
some guidance in the development of regular church life, for which
they were completely unprepared. Many a time they would simply
meet in their newly erected building, and since they had no one to
preach to them or to lead them in prayer, they would, after a decent
interval, go home again "without a service but with a clear con-
science."[44] Under such conditions the pastoral care by the mother
churches was hardly distinguishable from pioneer evangelism. At one
period young men of the capital who had been given permission to
preach organized a society for the purpose of supplying volunteer
preachers to the villages around the city to see to it that as far as
possible inability of a mother church to care for its district did not
prevent each village from having a preacher on Sunday morning.
Starting with three members in October, 1885, the society grew

[43] Rusillon, *op. cit.*, p. 381.
[44] Burton, *op. cit.*, p. 56.

within a year to a membership of over seventy. The group even managed to send out one evangelist in the first year and a second shortly afterward to work in the more distant parts among the heathen tribes.[45]

The work of the mother churches also included not a little evangelism among non-Christian populations. In the outlying parts of Imerina were districts as heathen as any in the country and the workers sent by the churches into these areas faced a taxing evangelistic task. For example, in 1870 the Ambohipotsy church, located on the south end of the great ridge of Tananarive by the spot where the first martyr was speared, sent a man and his wife to evangelize Sambaina, one of the most remote villages of its district, three days' march from the capital. There was great opposition from the village people, who broke into the evangelist's house and threatened him and his wife with death. The mother church could not maintain contact with them and finally the contributions for their work completely dried up. But they stayed on, earning their own living, and finally the opposition melted. Sixteen years later when a foreign missionary was traveling through the countryside, he found a flourishing church with some seven hundred in attendance making fine use of Bible and hymnbook, all because of the effort of this one couple still in their midst. This type of pioneer evangelistic work was continued well into the twentieth century in districts attached to some of the city churches, and in all of them the sense of responsibility for a particular piece of the countryside has been maintained even to the present day.[46]

Some of the metropolitan churches extended their districts even beyond the borders of Imerina, reaching out to the completely heathen tribes of the adjacent provinces. To the west this was wellnigh impossible because a wide uninhabited belt lay between Imerina and the Sakalava people, who covered most of the western part of the island. A member of the Ambatonakanga church, himself a Sakalava slave, did go with his brothers in 1864 to his home village and

[45] LMS, *Report, 1886*, p. 138; *1887*, p. 161; Mondain, *op. cit.*, p. 285.
[46] LMS, *Report, 1886*, p. 143; *The Chronicle*, September, 1913, p. 203. For other examples of the outreach of the churches of the capital see LMS, *Report, 1887*, p. 72; *The Chronicle*, February, 1870, p. 62; February, 1873, p. 39; Goodall, *op. cit.*, p. 349.

taught the people there, but no organized work was undertaken in that direction.[47]

To the east and northeast more orderly work was possible. The Faravohitra church, whose territory stretched eastward from the city, moved right across the inner forest belt which runs along the eastern side of the island and reached the comparatively small and backward tribe of the Bezanozano. The congregation supported several evangelists and teachers for this tribe for many years, with as many as fifteen workers maintained at one time. For some years there were no satisfactory results because the teachers were inefficient and even immoral. In 1880 there was a reorganization. The foreign missionary who was then put in charge improved the work and substantial advances began. Occasionally the church sent out delegations to visit the work and to bring back reports to stimulate contributions and get young men to volunteer for service. Volunteers were sought not only in Faravohitra itself but also in its daughter churches. One village family was particularly noted for providing a large portion of the workers.[48]

The Andohalo church, whose district adjoined that of Faravohitra, carried out the most important missionary enterprise of any of the metropolitan churches. Shortly after its organization in 1864 the foreign missionary who was pastor of that church received an appeal for a teacher from the Hova soldiers stationed in the province of Antsihanaka, the fertile and beautiful land of the Sihanaka around Lake Alaotra, five days' march northeast of the capital. The church already had a missionary spirit and on the suggestion of its pastor readily agreed to send a man. It chose an educated slave named Rabe, whose freedom was purchased. He was given an unusually high salary and promised regular support. Rabe, henceforth called Rabesihanaka because of the work with which he was associated, stayed three years and was the first recognized Malagasy missionary to his heathen fellow countrymen. He organized a number of churches, primarily among the Hova soldiery and officialdom who wanted to please their queen, but also including many Sihanaka. He reported a great improvement in the morality and the cleanliness of the native people, noted for their debauchery and for their dirtiness, which latter characteristic was particularly offensive to the Hova.

[47] Mondain, *op. cit.*, p. 226.
[48] LMS, *Report, 1888*, pp. 171–172; *The Chronicle*, December, 1888, p. 534.

Following his period of service, the Andohalo church kept about a dozen workers in the territory raising $400 a year for their support. The keeping of the Sabbath became general and the people chose pastors for themselves and paid teachers for their children. But after the early achievements there came a decline, and in 1875 for the first time a foreign missionary was sent by the London Missionary Society to develop the work.[49]

In some respects the missionary effort of the Tananarive churches may appear to be nothing more than the kind of effort which was common in many parts of Asia and Africa—evangelism carried on under the control and initiative of foreign missionaries using the interest and service of local personnel. But such appearance is deceptive. To be sure, the foreign missionaries occupied the leading positions in church life far into the twentieth century, and their suggestion and example had much to do with the successes achieved. But on the whole it would seem that the missionaries were giving seriously needed continuity and supervision to what was essentially a national movement of evangelism and church development rather than being themselves responsible for an evangelistic effort in which they used native assistance. This is what made Madagascar different from the majority of nineteenth-century mission fields. This was most certainly the way things worked in regard to the major Malagasy missionary organization, the Isan Enim Bolana, to which we turn.

The Isan Enim Bolana: Beginnings of Its Mission

No Protestant body outside Europe and North America has carried on missions as long and as steadily as the Isan Enim Bolana. The name means "every six months," or six-monthly meeting. It is the

---

[49] Sibree, *Fifty Years in Madagascar*, p. 124; Joseph Mullens, *Twelve Months in Madagascar* (London, 1875), p. 265; Mondain, *op. cit.*, pp. 226–227. Mondain, reporting on p. 273 the introduction of a foreign missionary in 1875, says that by that time the native work had dwindled so that there were only two or three lifeless churches left. Mullens' report, published in 1875, says there were thirty-one flourishing churches with locally employed pastors and teachers, but this figure was derived from brief conversations during a tour and J. T. Handyman has stated in a letter to the present writer that he regards it as much too high. Mondain, he feels, is closer to the truth though unnecessarily low.

great semiannual gathering of the churches of Imerina. Nearly every traveler to Madagascar has been impressed by its huge concourses and has described with enthusiasm the impressive occasion when thousands of people in their traditional white lambas gather in Tananarive for two days of preaching and prayer, simultaneously filling the four largest churches of the capital, the men in one, the women in another, and youth in others. But just as important as these impressive displays are the missions which this body has maintained and which have been its real working purpose.

The meetings were begun in December, 1868, when the most rapid growth of the church was commencing. They soon became a kind of church assembly for the land, reminiscent of the great *kabarys* when the kings gathered together all the people to hear new laws and to elicit support. Although without specific authority over the local congregations, the decisions of this body were from the first regarded as normative. Two lay delegates from each Imerina church together with the pastors and foreign missionaries have traditionally constituted the body. The first meeting set up the arrangement by which city churches took responsibility for country districts and thus it involved a certain missionary interest. But missions were not a conscious concern of the meetings until 1873. In that year some soldiers returning from travels across the island reported to the Isan Enim Bolana planning committee on what they had seen. In consequence the missionary responsibility of the churches was chosen as a question to be considered in the next assembly.

In 1875 missionary activity was formally incorporated into the life of the organization. From then on the missionary aspect loomed steadily larger in its activities and discussions. The small committee which handled most IEB business was given the responsibility of choosing and sending out missionaries, and each of the churches was to collect funds for the work. It was arranged that on the second day of each assembly the mother churches of the city would entertain the delegates from their daughter churches at a great meal, four or five hundred people being fed in each church. At that time the delegates from the daughter churches normally presented their missionary offerings. In these ways mission was incorporated into the very center of the life of the church rather than being a specialized interest of a separate society, as it was in nearly all European churches at that time.[50] In fact, in the opinion of some observers, the circumference was too much the center. The churches became interested in the external work of missions to the extent of neglecting their own internal life and faith and this was a continuing problem in their existence.[51]

The actual missionary work began inauspiciously. Two men, Rainisoamanana and Rainimboazafy, were chosen to go out, the first Malagasy missionaries representing the church as a whole. In January, 1876, a valedictory service was held for them with the Queen and the Prime Minister taking a leading part. They were to go to the country of the Bara, a wild and warlike tribe immediately south of the Betsileo. Some Bara chiefs were present to affirm the readiness of their people to accept the two envoys. But the Bara were still largely independent and like all other tribes they hated and feared the Hova. After six months the position of the evangelists became untenable and they had to return to Imerina.[52]

A second attempt was made, this time among a somewhat more receptive people. A group of Tanosy had migrated from their home in the Fort Dauphin area up to the neighborhood of the Hova stronghold of Ihosy not far from the scene of the Bara work. One of the chiefs of this group, Radodo, proved friendly and two evangelists were sent to him in July, 1877. But the other Tanosy chiefs became jealous of Radodo's consequent new prestige, and also apprehensive for their tribal traditions. They unitedly remonstrated with him, telling him he was but a younger brother and should not try to be first. They said these Hova were spies. When he insisted that he had pledged his word to the Queen that he would protect them they started to attack his land. Simultaneously, the Bara began to take advantage of the situation to seize back Radodo's capital and

---

[50] *Journal des Missions Évangéliques* (hereafter *JME*), 1902, part 2, pp. 465–466; Sibree, *Fifty Years in Madagascar*, p. 168. The first account here speaks of 1876 as the year when missionary responsibility was first taken on, but all other sources declare that it was 1875. Mondain, *op. cit.*, p. 274, states that in 1872 a committee of seven missionaries and twelve Malagasy was formed to examine what the churches should do to evangelize the non-Christian areas. This may be the Native Missionary Society sometimes referred to in connection with the missionary activities of the church. Goodall, *op. cit.*, p. 348, says that this society was established and incorporated in the IEB in 1875.

[51] *The Chronicle*, July, 1888, p. 331.

[52] Mondain, *op. cit.*, p. 274; *JME*, 1902, part 2, p. 466.

other towns he had taken from them. Enemies came up to his very walls at night and shots were fired into the town. Frequently at night the two evangelists standing near the walls were greeted with cries and threats from prowling foes. Radodo's own people began to desert in fear to his opponents. Finally he had to return the evangelists by a secret path to Imerina. He said that he and his people would plan to go back to their homeland where, under the protection of the Hova rulers of Fort Dauphin, they could learn the new wisdom. Such an exodus of Tanosy actually did take place though it is not recorded that any considerable number were brought into the church as a result.[53]

After two such failures in successive years, it might be thought that the missionary zeal of Imerina would have been somewhat dimmed. On the contrary enthusiasm grew stronger than ever. In the very next year, 1878, a larger contingent, this time of five men, was ready to be sent out. The Palace Church promised to provide half the support of these and any other evangelists whom the IEB might send. The LMS and the English Friends, who had been working for ten years as a sister mission with the LMS, offered to give $150 and $50 a year respectively, and the Imerina churches contributed $1,400 for beginning the work. These were large amounts for that day, when four cents was a day's wages. A valedictory meeting was again held with the Prime Minister presiding.[54] Since the earlier missions had been frustrated because of the hostility against the Hova, a decision was made to send workers in the future only to areas where the Hova power was firmly established "rather than to

[53] *The Chronicle*, November, 1878, pp. 245–247; Mondain, *op. cit.*, pp. 274–275, shows no knowledge of this story and attributes the failure of the mission and the exodus of the Tanosy to the common resentment against Hova rule. This would appear on the surface to be a more realistic explanation, the above story being a more pleasant one circulated at the time. However, if discontent rather than interest in Christianity were the real reason, it would not seem likely that the Tanosy would have moved into the neighborhood of Fort Dauphin, which was another Hova stronghold, as both accounts agree that they did. Therefore the apparently more fanciful account may have a great weight of evidence as well as a greater antiquity.

[54] LMS, *Ten Years Review of Mission Work in Madagascar, 1870–1880*, p. 155; FFMA, p. 33; Mondain, *op. cit.*, p. 275; *JME*, 1902, part 2, p. 466. For the sake of comparison the amounts given in the sources in pounds and francs have been converted into dollars at the rate of five Malagasy dollars to the pound, which coincides with the rate others have used (cf. Fletcher, *The Sign of the Cross in Madagascar*, p. 269, and Goodall, *op. cit.*, p. 348), and four francs to the dollar.

disaffected parts of the island which are not subject to the Queen's authority."[55] This proved to be a fateful decision for all the future work. It meant that all of the evangelists whom the IEB sent out from this time on for the purpose of working with the non-Christian peoples of the island were in fact stationed in centers of Hova power where a small group of Hova Christians had already been gathered. Inevitably, the ministry to this small group of Christians, who were badly in need of instruction in the faith, consumed most of the time of the evangelists so that the workers who were sent out very specifically for evangelism among non-Christians tended to be lost to the work of church development among Christians.

Of the new contingent of five sent out in 1878, one went to the northeast coast but the other four went as a group to the coast southeast of Betsileo where there were a number of strong garrison towns of the Hova among the Taimoro and Taisaka people. A foreign missionary started to accompany them in order to get them properly established but he was struck down with fever and had to return. One of the four also had an attack of fever and died soon after reaching the coast. But three were able to establish themselves in the main centers and took the place of the governors in the area as heads of the churches. They found some preachers already there and to these they gave direction and advice. They were able rapidly to build up the churches and also to establish schools in the outlying villages despite great reluctance on the part of the villagers to send their children to a school which might involve some Hova plot. They were men of integrity and complete dedication—one named Rainimboazafy may well have been the leader in the first mission two years earlier—and they were able to achieve results that were regarded as marvelous.

The LMS missionaries in Imerina took a lively interest in their progress and after a year sent a representative to examine their work. He was received by singing bands of villagers in place after place. At one of the main centers there was an official reception in the square before the lofty government house. Unfortunately the work which began so encouragingly was allowed to fall into decay owing to a failure to keep up the number of workers. In 1887 an effort was made by the IEB to retrieve the situation by commissioning evan-

[55] *The Chronicle*, November, 1878, p. 245.

gelists to three of the towns where work had been begun, and a foreign missionary was also stationed in the area. But by this time it was beginning to appear that the IEB should turn its attention more to the north of the island and its southern commitments were gradually dropped.[56]

The Betsileo Isan Kerin Taona

The reason for the IEB shift of locale was that a new missionary force was appearing on the horizon and it seemed that the work in the south should be entrusted to it.[57] The Betsileo churches, inspired by the example of Imerina, had started a six-monthly meeting, later changed to an annual meeting or Isan Kerin Taona, in 1876. In the late 1880's this body was showing ever increasing life and pushing out missionaries of its own in several parts of the south. It sent workers among the Bara whom the IEB had first approached and then among the Taimoro on the east coast, who had been the object of the third IEB missionary expedition. It also reached some of the great Betsimisaraka group, who stretched as far along the east coast as did the Sakalava along the west, and started to penetrate the fastnesses of the Tanala, in the great forest that divided Betsileo from the sea. For a time there was also work among the Sakalava. In 1888 this body had eighteen preachers and evangelists supported entirely from funds of the association, which was twice as many workers as the IEB could put in the field.[58]

In spite of such promising beginnings, the Betsileo effort had its lapses. Its home area was one of secondary concern for the LMS so that when retrenchment was required it was the Betsileo province that suffered. Many a time the LMS considered turning the area over to other missionaries such as the Norwegians, who were coming in and building up a strong Lutheran church for South Madagascar, but the local church members were adamant against transfer. The end of Hova rule when it came had a crippling effect on the

[56] *Ibid.*, February, 1880, pp. 28–34; July, 1887, pp. 314–315; November, 1888, p. 505. Peyrot, *op. cit.*, p. 56.

[57] *The Chronicle*, September, 1913, p. 203.

[58] L.M.S., *Report, 1888*, pp. 114, 117; *L.M.S., Ten Years Review of Mission Work in Madagascar, 1870–1880*, p. 156; *The Chronicle*, December, 1889, p. 398; *JME*, 1905, part 2, p. 448.

churches which were dominated by the Hova. Under these circumstances their missionary effort practically disappeared for a time.

But renewal came after the First World War. In 1920 the Betsileo churches held a centenary meeting commemorating the introduction of the Gospel to Madagascar. Before a crowded assembly consisting mainly of Betsileo but with a good number of Hova, various proposals were advanced for a permanent memorial to the occasion. None elicited enthusiasm until a poor Betsileo woman stood up and suggested that even as the Hova had brought the Gospel of Christ to the Betsileo, the Betsileo should take the Gospel to the Tanala, the forest dwellers who had been an object of concern in the earlier period. The proposal met with deep silence, followed by some low rumbling in the body of the church, ending in a crescendo of agreement. "That is it; that is it. We Betsileo will evangelize the Tanala." An assessment was made on every church member and the work was started in the Ibongo area of the forest under the direction of a committee of the Isan Kerin Taona.

Progress was slow because the staff was small (only three for a period of years) and because of the fear and superstition of the forest people. Six churches were established in the first three years. By 1947, however, the number of churches had grown to ninety and several elementary schools had been established. Self-support was encouraged and a limited amount was achieved, financial help continuing to come from the Betsileo church with contributions also from the LMS. Catastrophe came in 1947 when the revolt which swept Madagascar established its focus in this forest area and every visible feature of the mission work was destroyed. Recovery fortunately was rapid and in the space of a dozen years seventy churches were again in operation. Nearly all of the workers continued to be Betsileo or Hova since the educational facilities available to Tanala were not sufficient to allow them to enter the training center for church workers in Fianarantsoa. But though the leaders came from outside, the Tanala church was established as a distinct organization using outside help as it (or its foreign missionary head) saw fit.[59]

[59] Information on the Betsileo mission work is taken from a letter of May 11, 1961, from T. E. Buck, an LMS worker in the area for many years, and a letter of May 15, 1961, from J. T. Hardyman. The cessation of the work during the early part of this century is evidenced by the fact that the 1913 deputation of Houghton *et al.* in its *Report*, pp. 117 and 134, spoke of the need for self-exten-

Isan Enim Bolana: Its Development

Meanwhile the Isan Enim Bolana developed its interest in the north of the island.[60] Between 1880 and 1890 twenty-three young men were commissioned for the opening of hitherto untouched fields and $15,000 was raised from the churches for their support.[61] On the whole money came in more easily than recruits could be found. During this period the practice developed of alternating the chairmanship of the IEB year by year between Malagasy and foreign missionary, a practice which continued till 1959.[62] The missionaries continued to have great influence in the meetings and frequently spoke, inspiring the Malagasy to more missionary concern or challenging the new graduates of the theological college to volunteer for missionary service.[63] A good proportion of the graduates[64] did volunteer and at the time the French conquest of 1895 swept across the land there were ten to twelve "native missionaries," as they were called, scattered all across the island north of Tananarive. The practice also grew up of having these emissaries report back to the IEB assemblies and speak in the various churches of Imerina when they returned for their five-yearly furloughs.[65]

These beginnings of steady work came to a dramatic halt with the French invasion. A multiple disaster struck the Imerina missions at that time: first the French conquest itself, which overthrew the ruling Hova power; then a wild and disorganized pagan rebellion against everything foreign, which swept across the country for a short time killing and destroying; and finally the calculated attacks of the Jesuits, who greatly increased their power with the advent of the French. As the representative of the achievements of Hova nationalism and Protestant Christianity, the missions of the IEB were

sion in Betsileo and described the Isan Kerin Taona with never a reference to any missionary work being done by it.

[60] One worker had gone north at the same time that the Taimoro mission of four set out in 1878. The second worker was placed in the north in 1880, being sent to the edge of the Sakalava territory at Ankavandra. FFMA, pp. 33–34.

[61] Fletcher, *op. cit.*, p. 269.

[62] Sibree, *The Madagascar Mission*, p. 32. The first Malagasy chairman took office in 1884.

[63] *The Chronicle*, July, 1887, p. 314.

[64] In the 1888 class it was two out of nine. LMS, *Report, 1888*, p. 152.

[65] *The Chronicle*, April, 1884, p. 115; LMS, *Report, 1911*, pp. 250–251; *JME*, 1902, part 2, p. 466.

subject to attack from all these directions. The rebellion proved the worst; from every one of their posts the IEB workers had to flee before this scourge. Most of them lost all their possessions in flight; some were closely chased by the marauders and died from the fatigue and privations they suffered. The work was brought to a complete stop. The immediate danger from the rebellion soon ceased but the churches were facing too many difficulties and uncertainties with the new government and the Jesuits for them to be able to give much attention to the resumption of their evangelistic responsibilities. Not until 1898 was it possible to start any of the missionary work again. From then on there was a gradual rebuilding of the structure so that by 1907 the level of 1895 had again been reached with eleven missionaries in the field.[66] But difficulties continued. As long as French rule lasted there were laws against open-air preaching and strict requirements governing the establishment of new churches. The anticlerical policies of Governor Augagneur made for additional hardships until near the time of the First World War. In one way the difficulties made the IEB workers more important since they had more natural access to homes than foreigners had, and home visitation had to be the chief method of starting new churches.

The IEB again scattered its missionaries very widely over the northern regions: at Tamatave and Anosibe on the east coast and Majunga on the west coast, at Mavetanana on the way to Majunga, and at Mandritsara in the north center. But there was one area of concentration which marked a real change from the past. About half the working force was placed in the one province of Antsihanaka. Here was an area where Imerina missions had been responsible for the initiation of the work in 1864 and where the foreign missionaries had not come until later. The advent of the French had made the position of English missionaries impossible in the region and therefore the LMS withdrew and turned the entire province over to the IEB. This was a natural area for concentrated work, something which the IEB had thus far sadly failed to achieve, and a good area in which to test the effectiveness of Malagasy missions. Some of the reports which the IEB missionaries gave of conditions upon their arrival in the field shocked the Imerina Christians—a church deacon practicing polygamy, a preacher who kept rum on the pulpit to help his preaching—but the Sihanaka people had already shown them-

[66] *JME*, 1902, part 2, p. 466; Sibree, *The Madagascar Mission*, p. 53.

selves receptive, there had been strong beginnings under the earlier
native missionaries, and there was every reason to expect a fruitful
work.[67]

In 1913 the first intermissionary conference for Madagascar was
held, and the Isan Enim Bolana was one of the missions involved in
its deliberations. The Edinburgh missionary conference of 1910 had
launched a new spirit of missionary co-operation, and missionary
conferences began to be held in country after country around the
world. The main tasks before these meetings were to map out the
area of each mission's operations in order to prevent overlapping and
duplication in the work and to establish some continuing organ of
missionary co-operation. The Madagascar meeting accomplished
both tasks. It mapped out the main areas of mission responsibility
in a way which has served as a basis of work plans ever since, and
it inaugurated a continuing series of intermissionary conferences and
an established intermissionary committee which has recently become
a national council of churches. The unique thing about the Madagascar conference was that it included the Isan Enim Bolana in its
planning. While in other countries the division of territorial responsibilities was considered only among the foreign missions, Madagascar
was one place where native missions had a recognized part to play.
By this time the IEB had thirteen missionaries at work—at least one-
tenth the missionary force in the northern half of the island and the
only missionary force of any size in the north outside Imerina.[68]
Thus it appeared that the IEB was very important for the approach
to a huge region with half a million inhabitants. The other missions
recognized that they had paid far too little attention to this region
and agreed to take responsibility for both western and eastern sides
of the area. At the same time they felt that the IEB had spread itself
far too widely and needed to take up a definite district and work it
systematically. So a long strip up the center of the island was set
out as the area for which the IEB was to be responsible. The strip
started with the narrow northward-stretching province of Antsihanaka, to which the IEB clearly had the best title, and reached be-

[67] *JME*, 1902, part 2, p. 464; 1906, part 2, pp. 370–371. *The Chronicle*, July,
1903, p. 176; September, 1913, p. 203. Sibree, *Fifty Years in Madagascar*, pp.
141–142.

[68] Edinburgh World Missionary Conference, 1910, Vol. I, p. 240; Houghton
et al., op. cit., p. 31. It may be assumed that at least one-fourth of the 160
missionaries reported in the country were located in the south.

yond to the next people, the Tsimihety, who extended almost to the tip of the island and whose chief center was Mandritsara, which had also been an IEB center for some time. To the west of the Tsimihety was a slight bulge as far as the coast to include Analalava, where an IEB station had been set up not long before. This was the official IEB territory. Any IEB workers who continued in the areas assigned to other missions were to be supervised by foreign missionaries.[69]

The years following 1913 saw the attempt to meet the responsibilities assigned by the intermissionary conference. They were important years with respect to the question: Could the indigenous church take its place alongside the foreign missions in prosecuting the common task with full responsibility for its own area? The answer to that question was not reassuring. The IEB increased its efforts notably. In six years the number of workers went up from thirteen to sixteen, the financial support by 25 per cent.[70] Of the two areas which made up the IEB territory, the greater effort was concentrated in Antsihanaka. Here there were seven evangelists and thirty-one churches. At the same time in the Tsimihety country the IEB stationed its ablest workers, though they were but two in number. One was among the southern Tsimihety at Mandritsara with twelve churches in his district. Then among the northern Tsimihety at Befandriana, with nine churches round about, was a man named Rakotojaona, himself a member of the Tsimihety people, who had devoted his efforts unstintingly since 1903 to the building of the church in his area.

Yet despite all this work it was clear by the time of the second intermissionary conference in 1920 that the church in these two regions was not prospering. Nearly half the IEB workers were still scattered in other areas, so effective concentration of resources had not been achieved. The number of churches in Antsihanaka had grown little. The larger churches were badly divided by party strife. The Sihanaka themselves were less in evidence than they had been in earlier years, though this was not so much the fault of the missionaries as of the population shift which was taking place as the

[69] Houghton, *et al., op. cit.,* pp. 53–55; *The Chronicle,* May, 1917, p. 75; E. O. McMahon, *Christian Missions in Madagascar* (London, SPG, 1919), p. 79.
[70] Robert Griffith, *Madagascar, A Century of Adventure* (London, London Missionary Society, 1919), p. 69; H. E. Lewis, Robert Griffith, and F. H. Hawkins, *London Missionary Society Madagascar Mission Report of the Deputation, 1920* (London, 1921), p. 71.

less aggressive Sihanaka withdrew before the influx of Merina moving out of their crowded homeland. The churches in Tsimihety territory remained, except for the two in the main centers, backward and undeveloped. Rakotojaona himself made a memorable plea in Tananarive for foreign missionaries to come and help in the task.

Apparently there were many who came to the conclusion, expressed in a later LMS secretarial report, that the Malagasy missionaries on the whole did not have the persistence and drive necessary to carry through the effective establishment of a new church among non-Christian people. They tended to grow slack, and since they were scattered and unsupervised there was nothing that would hold them to the mark. A general agreement developed that foreign workers were needed to give leadership and direction. Furthermore, foreign missionaries could represent the church as more than a Merina institution and under their leadership the talents of the Merina might be effectively employed without alienating the other tribes.[71]

With such considerations and experience in mind it was agreed in 1920, with the unanimous approval of the IEB committee, that LMS missionaries should move into the Sihanaka and Tsimihety lands and take charge of the work. There were some in the French mission who bemoaned this signalization of failure by the indigenous mission, and the LMS recognized the danger of removing the sense of responsibility from the Imerina churches. But the IEB committee which faced these drawbacks felt that they were outweighed by the advantages. It may be regretted that the possibility of sending European workers to strengthen and to work alongside the Malagasy without being put in charge of them was not considered. But the patterns of the time were such that it was assumed that if the Europeans went in they would be in control. The LMS missionaries were given full charge of the evangelists' work though the salaries still came from the IEB. At the same time the French mission moved in with a similar arrangement for the Analalava area, the small western extension from Tsimihety which the IEB had operated along the coast. The IEB was left with no full responsibility for any territory. Perhaps to assuage feelings, a declaration was made at the intermissionary conference that the IEB now carried ultimate responsibility

[71] Lewis *et al.*, *op. cit.*, pp. 34–38, 45; A. M. Chirgwin, *Report After a Secretarial Visit to Madagascar* (London, London Missionary Society, 1931), p. 23; cf. *JME*, 1902, part 2, p. 466.

for the evangelization of all north Madagascar and that at its request the various foreign missionary societies came to supervise and to assist in its task. The whole of the north was now to be open to its workers, though they would all be placed in consultation with foreign societies and they would all be under the supervision of foreign personnel.[72]

It would not be surprising if these decisions had been followed by some increased efficiency in the work since that was their purpose, but it could hardly be expected that they would also be followed by a larger outpouring of personnel and funds for the mission. Yet both results followed. The number of evangelists increased so that for the three decades after 1925 it stood usually between twenty-five and forty-five whereas in the three decades before it had usually stood between six and sixteen. In addition to the evangelists, who were theologically trained and ordained men, responsible for the growth and full development of the church, there came to be an increasing number of teachers who worked each in a village school under the evangelists' supervision and who received some financial help from the IEB though they were primarily on government salary. The number of these teachers was three or four times that of the evangelists. Contributions increased even more impressively: francs 16,000 in 1921; francs 40,000 in 1926; francs 80,000 in 1930. By the late 1940's over a quarter of a million francs were contributed every six months for the IEB work and in the late 1950's that figure passed the million mark. Even when allowance is made for increased prices and inflation, the gain is tremendous. The workers spread all over north Madagascar. By 1930 the Sihanaka, Tsimihety, Marafotsy, Sakalava, Betsimisaraka, and Boina areas had all been entered and had three to ten stations each. Certain locations were recognized by the foreign missionary societies as IEB stations where the IEB would be responsible for the staffing, though their staff remained under the supervision of the foreign worker responsible for a wider area. The March, 1958, report of the IEB showed thirty-six stations for which the organization was responsible, spread out among all the northern people. Connected with these stations there were (in 1955) some 400 churches with 4,300 members and 1,000 catechumens. These churches have themselves been giving close to a hundred thousand francs a

[72] Lewis *et al.*, *op. cit.*, pp. 44–45, 68–69.

year to the IEB and some have been helping to pay the salaries of their evangelists.[73]

One of the most important gains of this later period was the appointment in 1950 of a full-time secretary, Andrianony. He has given a coherence and direction to the work it did not have before. He has traveled about encouraging the workers and providing some of the leadership and direction the absence of which caused the early work to falter. More recently the IEB has even provided a district superintendent for the French mission, to take the place of one of the foreign missionaries who formerly had charge of the IEB evangelists. The chief objection to this latest move is that it used IEB personnel more for church management than for evangelism, which is the real purpose of the work. An even further departure from the evangelistic center seems to be implied in the project begun in the late 1950's to erect a fine Christian high school in Tananarive. The school is to be named in honor of Rasalama, the first martyr. Tremendous sums have been raised by the IEB for this purpose without cutting into the budget for its regular work. The school will doubtless constitute a fine contribution to the Christian life of Imerina, though its evangelistic significance is not likely to be great.

All of these developments indicate a greatly strengthened program of operations through the years since 1920. Evidently the imposition of foreign supervision proved completely compatible with a stronger indigenous development. This is not to suggest that the source of the great advance was to be found chiefly in the influence of foreigners, for this was a period when foreign views were at a discount and foreign missionaries sometimes felt they had to ask Malagasy to express their views for them in IEB assemblies. The source of the advance lies more in the general economic improvement and the growing self-support in the churches, combined with the increasing power of nationalism.

The relation of self-support to the IEB advance disproves the all too common assumption that churches should make self-support their first goal and self-propagation their second. In earlier years, there had been occasional complaints from foreign missions that the

[73] M. Rabetafika in LMS, *Ten Years Review of Mission Work in Madagascar, 1921–1930*, pp. 202–205; Peyrot, *op. cit.*, p. 56. *Ny Fiangonana Isan Enim Bolan' Imerina*, Faha 174, pp. 28–32; Faha 175, pp. 28–32; Faha 176, pp. 26–27; Faha 179, p. 4; Faha 170, p. 11.

Imerina churches continued to expect subsidies for their pastors and internal activities while they gave funds freely to evangelism through the IEB.[74] The missions might better have rejoiced in the fact that Imerina churches were doing something to help others rather than concentrating all of their efforts on taking care of themselves. When a drive for self-support got under way in the 1920's, churches rapidly took over the full cost of their own operation and at the same time increased their contributions to their missionary work.[75] Such was the advantage of having a missionary program in church life from the beginning, rather than delaying it until after self-support was achieved.

But a more important reason for advance than the self-support program was the growth of national spirit which found expression in the IEB and enhanced the interest in its work. It was only natural that nationalism as well as evangelism should take a place in the life of this body. Before the French conquest the IEB had been the major national church organ for the country even though it was made up of Imerina churches only. True, as time went on it had devoted itself more and more exclusively to evangelism while effective ecclesiastical decision had been relegated more and more to the representative bodies related to the three principal Protestant missions of Imerina— LMS, Friends' Mission, and Paris Mission. Yet the IEB continued as a unifying force and a reminder of the time when there was only one Protestant church of Madagascar. Thus the IEB was a natural vehicle for the expression of the national sentiments of Imerina and it was closely watched by the French government for just this reason.

The nationalist tendency was accentuated in the years following 1920 by the presidency of a Tananarive pastor named Ravelojaona. As a young man he had been elected to the governing committee, in 1911, and in 1915 he became president, an office to which he was to be re-elected thirteen times before his death in 1956. In 1916 came an unfortunate incident which heightened the national sentiment in the organization. The French government discovered a conspiracy among some students and learned that these youths were planning to elect certain pastors, including Ravelojaona, as leaders of their proposed independent republic. The pastors were not guilty of the conspiracy but were jailed nonetheless. Ravelojaona was condemned

[74] E.g., Houghton *et al.*, *op. cit.*, pp. 29, 56; McMahon, *op. cit.*, p. 79.
[75] Chirgwin, *op. cit.*, p. 96.

to death before a special decision in France set him free. He resumed his leadership in the IEB and became accepted generally as the finest representative of Malagasy nationhood and the real center of all IEB activities. He was elected in 1939 as the Malagasy delegate to the Conseil Supérieur de la France d'Outre-mer.[76]

In those years many church leaders like him became strongly nationalist. They maintained that the IEB was the true Malagasy church and they objected to the domination of missions and missionaries. In some quarters the IEB was regarded as a revolution against missions. It is true that there were examples of anti-missionary sentiment in it, but any knowledge of the way in which it accepted missionary supervision of its work and missionary leadership of its assemblies should have been sufficient to discredit such a view. However, some missionaries had a feeling of suspicion toward the IEB, and when about 1950 discussions began to be held for the formation of a united church in the north, there was a clear rejection of the claim that the IEB should be the nucleus for it and the assertion instead that it was but the missionary arm of the church. At the same time there has been restlessness among Malagasy leaders about the missionary supervision which still exists over the IEB evangelists. Some of the most responsible officials of the church feel that the IEB should again have full responsibility for its districts as it had in the pre-1920 years. However, it should be recognized that wherever foreign missionaries now supervise IEB workers they do so as the responsible appointees of the Malagasy church, and their function may be taken over by the Malagasy nationals whenever the church appoints such as supervisors. In some places, nonetheless, circumstances are still such that Malagasy themselves insist that foreign supervision is desirable for the most effective advance in the Christian mission.

The Isan Enim Bolana: Prospects and Problems

As the churches in northern Madagascar move toward unity and the Malagasy themselves take over the complete responsibility for church life and work, the role of the Isan Enim Bolana as a center both of unity and of mission will need to be clarified. In the past it

[76] Daniel Ralibera, "Les Disciples du Seigneur," unpublished dissertation in Theological Faculty of Paris, p. 82.

has rendered important service to the churches in both respects, and if a united church should come into existence in the future, the IEB committee would presumably become its missionary board and the IEB assemblies would be its great convocations. If the relationship to the developing church life can be kept strong there is no reason why the future of the IEB should not be bright. With a growing budget, a full-time secretary, and an increasing number of workers, it stands now in what is probably the strongest position it has ever held. It still has the devoted loyalty of the Imerina Christians and is the chief heir of their long tradition.[77] Tradition is a weakness as well as a strength, however. It can and does prevent the development of new approaches to new conditions.

Effectiveness will depend most of all on whether the IEB can secure able workers and whether its workers can reach humbly and sympathetically to non-Merina. These two problems, it will be recalled, have always been the chief ones of the IEB. From the very beginning it has had difficulty procuring the quantity and quality of evangelists that it has needed. There have always been more calls for its services than it could meet with the men available. Although in recent years there has been serious shortage of funds for existing commitments, the more common problem over the years has been a lack of adequate personnel.[78] To leave the familiar culture and higher life of Imerina and go out to live in relatively backward, isolated, and unhealthy places has called for a greater degree of devotion and sacrifice than most of the church people possessed, though funds to help those who would go have been readily forthcoming. The result has been that the IEB has been chronically understaffed and all too commonly has included in its staff men who were barely able to finish their schooling. A historian surveying the scene a generation ago came to the conclusion that the men sent out simply were not equal to the task of founding a serious and well-established work among people of different customs and backgrounds. A more recent survey has repeated the conclusion that some churches give in to the temptation of offering to the IEB the men they do not want for

[77] For example, when the leaders of the Christian Endeavor in Tananarive felt their group should have some definite work and aim, they proposed the support of an IEB evangelist. *The Chronicle,* July, 1926, p. 151.

[78] In some years there has been more money contributed than could be used for the men available. See LMS, *Ten Years Review, 1870–1880,* p. 156; *JME,* 1902, part 2, p. 466; Houghton *et al., op. cit.,* pp. 55–56.

themselves.[79] The dangers of nepotism have also not been unknown in the selection of workers; those with relatives holding important positions have a better chance, among the weaker candidates, of being accepted.

Yet a recognition of the weakness of many of the workers should not obscure the devotion and deep commitment which has been characteristic of the group as a whole or the reliability and self-sacrificial zeal of a considerable number. In carrying on the work the majority have been required to undergo hardships and privation. Their salary on the average is about one-third the amount which is earned by pastors with similar training in city churches of Imerina, though not greatly different from the amount earned by evangelists employed by foreign missions. In past times it was common for IEB workers to supplement their salary by engaging in trade, like the other Merina who moved about the island. They have always received their rice from the local congregations and have sometimes expected the local people to cultivate their gardens for them. Formerly, through trade and the opening up of land some of them even became wealthy and established themselves as planters. But since the mid-1930's, when government salaries began to be pushed up rapidly, anyone who has been interested in making money has not been tempted to enter the service of the church and certainly not of the IEB. Those who have gone out have been men of devotion who were willing to make sacrifices for the work in which they believed.

Some have proved themselves fine workers. French missionaries still speak of Charles Ranaivo, who graduated from their seminary in the 1930's after a period of experience as a teacher and offered himself to the IEB. He worked in the Moramanga district, where the railway line from Tananarive to Tamatave drops down toward the coast, and in a few years quite transformed the area. He showed such ability that he was later called to further study in France and to teaching in the theological seminary until his untimely death. LMS missionaries speak with appreciation of many others of his kind. The LMS Survey of 1920 said that there were no better men on the island than the kind employed by the IEB.[80]

The other great problem for the IEB arises from the difficult rela-

[79] Mondain, *op. cit.*, p. 275; Peyrot, *op. cit.*, p. 57.
[80] Lewis *et al.*, *op. cit.*, p. 37.

tions existing between the various peoples of the island. Suspicion and hostility from other tribes have blighted the efforts of Merina missionaries from the beginning and they are not dead yet. With the spread of national feelings and the advance of Western civilization the problem may diminish. One does not see as many references now as formerly to circumscription of IEB work by the Hova community. A generation or two ago most observers pointed out this circumscription as the almost fatal weakness of all IEB efforts. It was noticed that in IEB territory where there were no Hova there were no churches. One Britisher in 1919 estimated that 90 per cent of the work of the IEB evangelists was concerned with the Hova settlers.[81] In a sense the Merina workers were more foreign than the foreigners in the Christian mission because, though they spoke the language and understood the customs better than Europeans, they often had a higher wall of hostility to pass. This was especially true in the early days when Hova rule was a reality or a recent memory, and became less so as the memory receded and nationalistic sentiment in opposition to European rule took its place. Even though the difficulty is diminishing, it has been sufficiently pervasive to warn us against using the Malagasy experience as a fair test of what home missions may be able to do in comparison with foreign missions. In some respects Madagascar can be better taken as an example of two kinds of foreignness in missions.

It certainly should not be thought that the ethnic problem made the IEB work completely useless. The strengthening of Merina churches, which would otherwise have been in a very backward condition, has in itself been an important achievement. Beyond this, evangelism to the non-Merina has been a constant concern. One gets very different views as to how effective the evangelism has been. Some say that the IEB has had only a very small part in the evangelization of the island while others maintain that it has been the major cause of the growth of the church in the north. Reports on some of the workers, such as one evangelist who has founded at least twenty-five new—and presumably therefore largely non-Merina— churches, would indicate that the evangelism has been of significant

---

[81] Griffith, *op. cit.*, p. 69. See also McMahon, *op. cit.*, pp. 78–79; Houghton *et al.*, *op. cit.*, p. 53; A. M. Chirgwin, *On the Road in Madagascar* (London, SCM Press, 1933), p. 73.

proportions and effectiveness even though it has admittedly not been a mighty movement sweeping the country such as might have been hoped for from a dedicated and mission-minded indigenous church. The fact that IEB speakers presenting their cause to the churches emphasize those occasions when there has been some response from the non-Merina reveals that the missionary purpose is recognized as central by all concerned. IEB workers are not expected to settle down as pastors of the existing churches but to itinerate in their area, giving supervision to the teachers and encouragement to the congregations for the purpose of a larger outreach. Recently some reorganization has been effected so that two of the stronger stations have taken over the full support of their own workers and two others have taken over half support, thus releasing the IEB evangelists to move on to less evangelized places. Here are clearly the marks of an effective agency in the mission of the church.[82]

Yet it must be admitted that Madagascar has had a more effective agency, one which has not been seriously handicapped by ethnic divisions, one which has been more fully indigenous than the traditional missionary society, and one which, like the Isan Enim Bolana, started out with other interests and then turned toward evangelism. This was the Soatanana revival movement.

The Revival in Soatanana

The great hills and empty spaces of Betsileo have bred a people known for their mystery and mysticism. Their religious life before the advent of Christianity was not infrequently swept by strange frenzies where people in the possession of spirits would do mad things, running along the ridges of houses or lying in stream beds, sometimes being killed in the process. The early experience of the Betsileo with Christianity did not make them eager to propagate the faith. They thought of it as a Hova imposition, and even when the Norwegian mission came into their land and a truly Betsileo church began to develop, they did not desire to win others[83] but left any missionary activity to the Hova churches of the LMS in their midst.

[82] Much of the material in the foregoing paragraphs on the latter history of the IEB is derived from discussions with church leaders in Madagascar.
[83] Burgess, *op. cit.*, p. 130.

It looked for long as if the Merina people alone would catch the missionary quality of Christianity.

But in an unknown village something happened to an unknown man which changed all this. Rainisoalambo was a sorcerer in the little village of Ambatoreny close by the Norwegion mission station of Soatanana, which in turn is not far from the city of Fianarantsoa. The sorcerer had been baptized by an English missionary but not till he was in middle life was his baptism followed by a conversion of the heart and he burned all his fetishes, gave up many of his evil ways of life, and began to attend church regularly. He had been completely illiterate but church attendance and a deepening faith led him to learn to read and to study the Bible. In 1892 all of his family fell ill and in his worry he heard a voice say, "Pray for them and I will heal them." He prayed and they were healed. After this he was sure of the gift of healing of which he had read in the Bible. He went to his old fellow sorcerer Rainitiary, who was sick, and called on him to renounce his sorcery and sin and to be cured by Christ. The cure was effected and the two men became a team going out to preach and heal. Rainitiary, an active man, was the perfect complement to the meditative Rainisoalambo. Their example of changed lives and their preaching of the foolishness of idols, the seriousness of sin, and the need for love and sanctity made a great impression.[84]

On June 9, 1895, there came together twelve of those who had been healed of their diseases and most deeply affected by the preaching. They took the name Mpianatry ny Tompo or Disciples of the Lord. Rainisoalambo gave the people a set of rules for their life. All were to be able to read and write for the sake of their Bible study. Their hairdress was to be modest and appropriate, for among the Betsileo hairdressing had great importance and extremely elaborate techniques involving the services of professional hairdressers who required a whole day to arrange one person's hair. The house and its surroundings were to be kept clean and each house was to have an outside kitchen so that the one room of the house would not be

[84] Élisee Escande, *Les Disciples du Seigneur* (*Un Mouvement d'évangélisation indigène à Madagascar*), Les Cahiers Missionnaires No. 8 (Paris, Société des Missions Évangéliques, 1926), pp. 19–22; E. Pechin in *JME*, 1904, part 1, p. 275.

blackened with smoke. More food was to be grown and fruit trees were to be planted. Extensive funerals and pagan ceremonies in connection with them were to be avoided. Every act was to be begun in the name of Jesus.[85] The times were those of disturbance and suffering with the French conquest, the Jesuit attack, the pagan rebellion, and various epidemics, and people were disturbed and open to something new. Many were attracted by what they heard of at Soatanana and soon there was a whole community there owning the land in common, cultivating it co-operatively, and building their houses together.[86]

The Revival Turns Outward

If Rainisoalambo had felt that his vocation was fulfilled in this revived community with its strict Christian life, Soatanana would never be mentioned in connection with the self-propagation of the church. It would be just another example of an awakening within the church accompanied in this case by an idealistic Christian community life. But a much greater future opened up before this group of simple villagers. Without any outside suggestion, simply from Bible study and meditation, Rainisoalambo developed the conviction that they should send out messengers (*iraka*) to preach the Gospel widely.[87] At a meeting of the community, October 20, 1898, he chose eight disciples who were to be trained for the apostolate. Their method of training, he said, was to be according to the parable of the sower. As the seed is put in carefully and grows bit by bit, so the truth of the Bible is to be put into the hearts a little at a time and allowed to grow, for men cannot receive all the truth at one time. Six basic truths were to be inculcated in this "missionary training program," each founded on Biblical passages: repentance, humility, perseverance, prayer, love for one another, and the unity of believers. The trainees participated fully in the life and work of the community during their period of training. Finally, on July 2, 1899, they were sent forth, though only five were judged ready to go at that time. They were to go for only two weeks and then return for further training. Later the periods of service were lengthened to

[85] Burton, *op. cit.*, p. 74; Ralibera, *op. cit.*, pp. 31–36.
[86] Peyrot, *op. cit.*, p. 59.
[87] Escande, *op. cit.*, pp. 84–85.

three months, six months, and even a year or two depending on the distance to be traveled.[88]

The path for the messengers was difficult. The government was suspicious of any gathering. It was hard even to get permission for the existence of the home community in Soatanana since it was not a regularly organized village. The administration told the community that if they met for prayer in their prayer center that would become an unauthorized church building, so the members had to go over to the church at the Soatanana mission station and there the missionary gave them regular instruction as well as hospitality.[89] When the messengers started their travels they were severely limited by official travel restrictions, such as the requirement of passports for passage from one province to another. Also, outdoor preaching was forbidden. Missionaries were sometimes opposed and forbade their preaching in the churches. Even when, as usually happened, they were allowed to use the churches, preaching that stirred up the people sometimes brought down an interdiction from the authorities. Rainisoalambo was himself thrown in jail shortly after the messengers started on their tours since he seemed like the leader of a suspicious popular movement. The intervention of a missionary secured his release. When he went to Antsirabe he was expelled by the government because of the great crowds he attracted. When five messengers tried to begin preaching in Tananarive in 1901 they were forced to spend fifteen days in jail and to leave the city because their presence produced crowds, which were forbidden by law. At the big meetings in Fianarantsoa confusion reigned as the cries for healing of the sick mingled with jeers of those opposed to the Disciples. The government ordered the expulsion of the messengers and the closing of the church if they should come there again.[90]

But these limited beginnings were opening the eyes of the Disciples and especially of their leader to the great task of evangelism to be carried out in Madagascar. Their movement was showing such strength and receiving such a response that they could dream of the possibility of evangelizing the whole country. About 1903 at one of the great gatherings of the Disciples which took place at Soatanana each year, Rainisoalambo said to his followers,

[88] Ralibera, *op. cit.*, pp. 39–42, 101.
[89] *JME*, 1924, part 1, p. 326.
[90] Escande, *op. cit.*, pp. 23–25, 27–28; Ralibera, *op. cit.*, pp. 45–50.

The missionaries have given up all to bring the Gospel to us, but consider how many areas they have not been able to enter. They are too few to evangelize all the parts of our land. There are also truths of the Gospel such as the healing by the laying on of hands and perfect sanctification which they have not taught us. After having meditated long on the Word of God I have arrived at the conviction that in the thought and plan of God it is by the Malagasy especially that Madagascar ought to be evangelized. I propose that we today send all those who will volunteer into all the provinces of Madagascar. Their task will be to work with the missionaries and churches where there are such and alone where there are none.[91]

From this time the work expanded very rapidly. The number of messengers increased so that by the spring of 1904 there were forty-one at work in addition to nine who had died in the course of their labors.[92] The rules by which their work was to be governed were derived from New Testament examples. They were to go two by two, a married couple often forming a team. They took no money and no possessions except a Bible and a hymnbook. They usually walked. They would stop in each village to announce the Gospel and to heal, staying in a place as long as the people would listen to them and could provide food and lodging. They were to receive no money personally, but the assembly of the Disciples might accept money for its work as a whole.[93] Since the Malagasy are renowned for their hospitality and are always ready to take in strangers and provide for them, it was possible to operate effectively in this simple way.

Rainisoalambo, who had been weakened by old age for some time, died shortly before the annual assembly in 1904, but the dedication of his followers did not diminish. Three thousand poured into Soatanana for the assembly that year from different parts of the country, and seventy-six pairs of messengers were sent out. A strong organization was given to the movement; a general synod and regional synods were established. There was to be an executive committee and certain members were chosen as "professors" to undertake the training of the messengers.[94]

[91] Escande, *op. cit.*, pp. 29–30.
[92] Burgess, *op. cit.*, p. 134.
[93] Escande, *op. cit.*, pp. 29–30.
[94] Ralibera, *op. cit.*, pp. 58–63.

Dispersion of the Messengers

All parts of Madagascar now began to be touched by the emissaries of Soatanana. The area immediately north of Betsileo, that is, the region around Ambositra and the Vakinankaratra which lay between Betsileo and Imerina, had been the first region beyond the homeland of the movement to be powerfully affected. A French missionary writing in 1908 reported that since 1900 Vakinankaratra had seen magnificent results of the work of God through the revival.[95] The missionary in Ambositra reported that in 1900, fifty people had asked for baptism following an evangelistic tour by the Disciples.[96] The churches of this region were deeply affected and a strong following for the Disciples developed among them. As the messengers returned there year after year their influence grew. Years later, in 1922, another French missionary in the area reported that after a visit from the messengers not only were churches crowded with two or three times their usual congregations but 1,500 people had consecrated themselves to God and 500 pagans had burned their amulets.[97] Villages where there had formerly been no churches, after frequent visits from the messengers, secured government permission to establish churches.[98]

Farther north Imerina with its powerful churches was strongly affected though here it was naturally more a revivalistic than an evangelistic movement. The villages round about Tananarive were especially influenced, and the great churches of the city became the source of the principal contributions to the headquarters at Soatanana. Along the railway line which leads from Tananarive to the northeast coast the messengers began churches among the settlements of woodcutters.[99] To the northwest the apostles entered Sakalava country and the province of Boina. By 1912 they had evidently penetrated the farthest north among the Antakaranana people and into Diego-Suarez.[100] Such a distant area required more time for the completion of tours than the few months which were usually allowed. A missionary long familiar with the movement tells of two men and

[95] H. Rusillon, in *JME*, 1908, part 2, p. 229.
[96] Ralibera, *op. cit.*, p. 49.
[97] M. Forget, in *JME*, 1922, part 2, p. 373.
[98] *Ibid.*, 1926, part 2, p. 666.
[99] Ralibera, *op. cit.*, p. 50; *JME*, 1922, part 2, pp. 370–371.
[100] Ralibera, *op. cit.*, p. 67; *JME*, 1922, part 2, pp. 370–371.

their wives who took three months for the journey up to Diego-Suarez in 1926 and stayed there two years before returning; one of them died on the trip. To the south from the early period of the Disciples work was done among the Bara and in the southwest of the island.

Perhaps the greatest achievement in evangelism was effected among the Betsimisaraka along the east coast. The leader of the French mission in 1958 estimated that half the churches in the east coast area of that mission were founded as the result of Soatanana work. The most striking reports of success in this region come from the period just after the First World War. Élisée Escande, who came to this area as a missionary in 1907, reports that in the southern part of the area, below Tamatave, there were fourteen churches in 1915. The Disciples of the Lord came in sometime before 1922 and by that year there were sixty-four churches. In 1924 there were 113 and the next year 124. In the important port city of Vatomandry where there was an old Hova church which the missionary had often tried to revive, the congregation was awakened to their missionary responsibility by a visit from two Disciples. Church members joined the messengers in helping to evangelize the villages of the locality, and when the foreign missionary returned in 1919 after some years abroad there were thirteen churches instead of one; two years later there were twenty-five. The same kind of thing happened in the northern part of the area.[101]

The number of men who went out is impossible to state but certainly many hundreds of messengers were sent from Soatanana over the years. It was a much larger operation than the Isan Enim Bolana has ever been and accomplished much more in the spread of the church. Soatanana, of course, could send out men much more easily than could the Isan Enim Bolana because each additional IEB worker represented an additional burden of financial support, while additional messengers cost nothing when they went out and their work often resulted in the winning of new followers who would send in contributions—more workers meaning more income rather than more expenditure. Sometimes a little money was sent from Soatanana to help those workers who had to stay out a very long time, such as the group who were two years in Diego-Suarez, and of course there

101 Escande, *op. cit.*, pp. 51–65.

were costs involved in training additional people even though the trainees worked in the rice fields of Soatanana. But on the whole, those who went forth received nothing from headquarters while they were on tour. They kept in touch only in the most casual way with their headquarters, sending an occasional letter as the spirit moved them. Sometimes a member of a team might leave his group and not be heard from further.[102] Those who had children were allowed to leave them at headquarters and eventually a boarding school was established there for their care.[103]

Their method of work was twofold. They would visit people in their homes, often making their approach to a village by visiting every home in it, and they would preach in the churches where there were any. The visiting was more important than the preaching, especially in reaching the non-Christians. In both visiting and preaching they repeated one theme over and over: sin, perdition, healing, the Cross, brotherly love. Wherever they went they said exactly the same things, often in a monotone, rather chanting their words as if repeating a lesson they had learned. The texts they liked to use were "Repent for the kingdom of heaven is near" and "A new commandment I give unto you, that you love one another." If they had stayed longer in each place, they would have needed to say more, but they stayed just long enough to state their message. Part of their appeal lay in their mystery; no one knew who they were, whence they came, or whither they went. There were exceptions to this methodology. In some cases a messenger confronted by a village suddenly converted to Christianity agreed to stay with the people until they secured a pastor from the church officials. But normally the messengers moved on and returned to Soatanana in time for the great annual gathering.[104]

Only in eyewitness reports can we begin to sense what was involved in the labors of these simple and uneducated missionaries, so different from those of the Western church tradition. A Frenchman describes vividly two teams he saw in 1940:

[102] Ralibera, *op. cit.*, p. 50.

[103] Burton, *op. cit.*, p. 74. Ralibera, *op. cit.*, p. 102, disputes the assertion of Rusillon, *Un Petit Continent Madagascar*, p. 392, that a center was established for the children; he maintains that they have been left with the families of Soatanana.

[104] Rusillon, in *JME*, 1908, part 2, pp. 227–228; Forget, *JME*, 1922, part 2, p. 373; Escande, *op. cit.*, pp. 62–64.

Three women formed one team, composed of an older woman with
experience, a vigorous manager, and a novice who was making her
first tour. They were moving in the region of Moramanga. The local
synods had asked for their visit and had assumed responsibility for
organizing their tour. The oldest one affected by the cold of the forest
had to break her trip in order to enter a hospital while her companions
continued their route toward the south. When we met her she was
desolate because of the weakness which obliged her to remain behind.
She was a frail old woman practically without baggage. She exercised
a profound spiritual influence upon her listeners. Submission and patience struggled visibly in her with the desire to be going ahead. The
second group were met in the low country forty kilometers from the
ocean at Ravinala. We were stretched out overcome by the heat of
midday. Suddenly through the glare of the open doorway there appeared on the main road a strange silhouette. A small man entered,
wearing a lamba with a pointed straw hat. He was followed by his
wife and a daughter of about twelve years who carried a light basket
on her head. We had before us a family of the "Mpianatry ny Tompo"
en route to the north where some churches were expecting their visit.
They had stopped to greet us in passage. The head of the local church
and the owners of the house formed with us an audience. Immediately
the man and the woman brought out their Bible which was wrapped
under their lamba. With an authority and a relevance which we ad-
mired among such simple people, they began to exhort us and to exhort themselves with a tone almost prophetic. Their visit finished, we
saw them going off towards the evening on the dusty road. They had
yet before them several months of journey in unknown territories. The
daughter followed courageously her mother and the man walked ahead.
With the wrapped Bible in his hand he could in some way feel as he
walked the validity of the promises made to those who follow Christ
without a place to put their heads.[105]

It is evident that this kind of witness can go only so far as to sow
the seeds of faith; it cannot build up a strong and instructed community of Christians. The Disciples of the Lord did not attempt to
do more than the initial work. They deliberately left to others the
whole constructive work which had to be done once they had stirred
up interest. Thus they depended on the church and on the foreign
missionaries for the fruitage of the seeds they planted. Often the
churches invited them into a region and thus provided the continuity

[105] Peyrot, *op. cit.*, pp. 60–61.

for their work. On a few occasions missionaries actually worked
with them using them as auxiliaries in the task of evangelism, sending
them into areas where their type of witness was needed, and following up their results with care.[106] On the whole the messengers were
not amenable to such close and limiting co-operation. Yet it was
where the church and the foreign missionaries and the messengers
strengthened one another's efforts that great results were achieved.

Divisions and Decline in Soatanana

The problem of relation to the church and foreign missions has
been the undoing of the Disciples of the Lord. It was natural that
there should be difficulty in this relationship. Soatanana represented
a highly emotional movement with charismatic leadership, so it did
not fit in well with any institutionalized body. Furthermore it was
strongly indigenous in its spirit and this made for a casualness of
operation, a looseness of financial arrangement, and an exaltation of
one-man authority which were often repugnant to the foreign missionaries. The local pastors often resented the suggestion that Christians needed the blessing of the revival, as if the blessing of the
church were not enough, and splits in the churches sometimes followed on the Disciples' work. An example of the difficulties that
were bound to arise appeared early in connection with the practice
of healing in the churches. Many churches were sharply divided
over this practice. In consequence, about 1902 those who went out
from Soatanana began to give up the healing sessions in churches,
confining them to private homes. Some said that from that time the
movement lost some of its power and its ability to attract people.[107]

It was only by grace that a break did not come early. The great
missionary scholar Maurice Leenhardt, visiting Madagascar in 1924,
said that the Disciples had naturally dreamed of becoming a separate
church of greater purity, uncompromised by the life of the ordinary
church members around them, and that it was only their constant
preaching of brotherly love which kept them bound to the church
in humility and discipline. As he put it, "They loved their ministry

[106] *JME*, 1923, part 2, p. 173; 1924, part 1, p. 327.

[107] Ralibera, *op. cit.*, pp. 120–126; E. Pechin in *JME*, 1904, part 1, p. 279.
This article by Pechin provides an excellent summary of the movement up to
1904.

more than themselves."[108] They accepted guidance and instruction from the missions and referred their converts to the church or the foreign mission of the area for the organization of Christian life.

Rainisoalambo's successors were faithful men who maintained the ties that had been established. At the death in 1918 of the then leader two successors appeared and a split developed in the movement. The two groups represented basically the Betsileo and the Merina influences that had been developing in the body of the Disciples. The Norwegian missionaries labored to bring about a reconciliation and in 1925 the division was healed with the recognition of one of the two contestants, named Augustine, as Ray aman-dreny, or "father and mother," as the head of the movement had come to be called.

The mission then suggested, and the Disciples agreed, that there be a definite constitution or "discipline." In that constitution the missionary at Soatanana was given a most important place. He was to head the organized life and the Ray aman-dreny was to be the leader of the spiritual life. There was to be an executive committee consisting of these two along with the pastor of the Soatanana church and certain elected members, and these under the missionary had responsibility for the activities of the organization. The committee had final power over the selection of the messengers. As in years past the selection was to be made by the Ray aman-dreny each year after the whole community had prayed for ten days and then three people had kept up a day-and-night vigil of prayer in the holy of holies, the Ray aman-dreny's room. But now when the selection had been made, presumably under the guidance of the Holy Spirit, it was to be submitted to the committee for final decision. The missionary was established as the treasurer in order to bring some accountability into the situation, where there had thus far been no records. Augustine had shown a tendency to send messengers chiefly to places from which there was hope of receiving funds rather than to those which needed evangelism. Large sums were coming in particularly from persons touched by the revival in the Tananarive churches and there was need to handle the funds properly.

Augustine died about 1930. His successor was a good man but short-lived. Then came Rajoelina, who was the Ray aman-dreny till 1960. He represented a new generation that did not go back to the early spirit of the revival and was much interested in money. A great church, a kind of cathedral of the revival, was built in the headquarters with funds collected from all over the island. There were several bad incidents involving the use of funds, and with them the influence of the movement declined in its homeland, though not in the more distant areas where the messengers traveled. A report of 1950 stated that many of the churches of the Norwegian mission, which covered all of Betsileo and most of the south, had become disinterested in the movement. The messengers who came to Soatanana for training were mostly from the north and those who did come from the Lutheran churches usually had no authorization from their missionaries.[109]

Nevertheless in 1949, 110 pairs of messengers were sent out. By this time most of them went at the call of churches which asked them to come for revival meetings and visitation programs. They walked only if the inviting church could not pay their fare by some other method of transport. Their course of training, which could last from two to eight years, was well established: revival history and doctrine taught by the Ray aman-dreny, Bible lessons taught by the pastor of the Soatanana mission station church, and reading and writing taught by the local school teacher.[110]

In 1955 the break came. The missionary in charge made certain demands which are said to have included the right to give all the training to the messengers. The Disciples refused and absented themselves thereafter from the mission church. In consequence they were declared to be out of the church. The Intermissionary Conference of 1958, which created the National Council of Churches for Madagascar, was appealed to to heal the rift and it made all the concessions possible to bring the Disciples back. It sent its apologies to the Disciples for mistakes that had been made in dealing with them. It offered them the right to have their own organization, to keep their own treasury, and to send out their own messengers as long as they were members of the church and would work with the church in the area where they were traveling. But it also said clearly that the Disciples could not be accepted as a separate church related directly to the new National Council of Churches. The representatives of the Conference who carried this message to Soatanana were accepted

[109] Ralibera, *op. cit.*, p. 86.
[110] *Ibid.*, pp. 94, 101.

hospitably by the Ray aman-dreny with ceremonial foot-washing and food. But the offer of reconciliation was summarily rejected. These were simple people who were set in their opinions, and the earlier desire for independence was now fully in control.

The Disciples have been losing vitality and influence rapidly since the final break took place. They can still command much loyalty inherited from the past, and the majority of the pastors in Imerina are still within the ranks of the movement, but the most responsible Malagasy leaders in the denominations which have been most favorably inclined toward them now feel that the churches have gone as far as they can in making concessions. The future of the movement can be viewed only with great uncertainty.[111]

Other Missionary Forces

Soatanana is in any case no longer the only home of revival, though it remains the original fountain of revival for Malagasy Christians. Partly because of its example prophets other than Rainisoalambo have appeared and other movements have burst forth. Near Antsirabe lives the old woman Ravelonjanahary, who drew thousands of people to her especially in the period following 1927 when she claimed to have died and been brought back to life. She showed great gifts as a healer and has been called to various churches where she has preached and has converted great numbers, both Christians and non-Christians. A man who was touched by her and also secured the blessing of Soatanana was Daniel Rajaofera, a great revivalist preacher from the time of his conversion by Ravelonjanahary in 1927 to near the time of his death in 1936. Another woman of great influence is Nenilava, whose headquarters are in the little town of Ivohipeno on the east coast south of Manakara. She is closely connected with the greatest of all these more recent revival movements, that of Farihimena.

Farihimena is a cluster of a few houses atop one of the barren and inaccessible hills in the region of Antsirabe. Here an impressionable and emotional young preacher named Daniel Rakotozandry began his first pastorate in 1946. His ministry was short for he died at the

[111] Much of the material in the foregoing paragraphs on the later history of the Soatanana movement is based on discussion with church leaders in Madagascar.

end of 1947, but he preached with great power and his fame spread far and wide so that people poured into his little chapel. After his death his movement, which emphasized weeping for sins, spread to many parts of Madagascar. Church services were commonly held up for hours or given up altogether because the congregations became so uproarious in their weeping. Pilgrims poured into Farihimena especially on the great anniversaries of the revival, and from their contributions a large stone church was built which dominates the valleys round about. The movement has kept close to the Lutheran church. Its organization and treasury are controlled in the same way as those of other local churches.

In 1955 one further revival began at Mandua, farther to the north. Its distinguishing feature was the vomiting of its adherents to get rid of evil spirits and sin. This movement, however, has broken with the churches and has failed to exercise a continuing influence.[112]

But it is a strange fact that none of these movements have shown as much missionary zeal as Soatanana. They have followed the example of the Disciples of the Lord in their healing and their preaching, in their messages of sin and deliverance, but they have given their attention more strictly to the Christians. True there have been non-Christians in not insignificant numbers who have been converted through hearing of their works and attendance at the meetings. But the evangelism has been more incidental and secondary in these movements whereas with Soatanana it was consciously undertaken and was kept as an important concern.[113] One does not hear of plans by their leaders for assuming responsibility for the evangelization of the non-Christians of the island such as Rainisoalambo enunciated about 1903, nor does one hear of new congregations in considerable numbers coming from their work as have been reported for Soatanana.

There have of course been other evangelistic forces besides the revivals. Various small societies have been formed from time to time

---

[112] Ralibera, *op. cit.*, pp. 68–94; Arnold, *op. cit.*, p. 13. *Ny Fifohazam-Panahy eto Madagascar* ("The Spiritual Revival in Madagascar"), by Rajosefa Danielson, published by Imprimerie Volahamitsy in Tananarive, is a fanciful and exaggerated report on the revivals by an enthusiast, important for showing the way such people view these movements.

[113] Cf. the treatment of the revivals in Burton, *op. cit.*, pp. 71–73, in which this difference seems to be evident.

for missionary purposes. A medical missionary society was formed by young doctors in 1890 but it was short-lived.[114] The Anglican church on the island began a missionary society of its own in 1913.[115] The churches connected with the Evangelical Lutheran Church around Fort Dauphin have in recent years organized a mission of their own as a result of Bible classes where the missionary vocation was brought home to them. To the work of this missionary committee the American church is glad to make block grants to be used by the national church as it may see fit.

The Protestant churches of Madagascar as a group have also launched evangelistic programs. In 1928, 1939, 1945, and 1954 they organized co-operatively what they called "Tafika Masina," or Holy Wars. During a given month or two every local church held prayer meetings followed by visits to all the homes of its town or village. At the same time meetings of witness and exhortation took place and nearly every church saw an increase in its membership, some gaining as many as two hundred new members in one of these campaigns.[116]

Most important of all, the process of spontaneous expansion through Merina migration continues. Though many non-Merina are still suspicious of the religion of these people who formerly dominated them and still regard Christianity as taboo for themselves, there are others who are affected by what they see of the religious life of the Merina as they settle in empty parts of the island. The women of other groups see the Merina women taking Sunday as a day of rest and hear them singing the Christian hymns as they go about their household duties. The men see that once a week the Merina men gather to read from the Bible and pray. And so an interest in Christianity develops. A survey made by a French missionary in 1944 in the region north of Tamatave showed 289 new churches which had appeared in the previous thirty years; the commonest cause for their appearance had been the impression made by immigrants. The wandering preachers of the Disciples of the Lord were often the catalysts in this kind of situation, bringing the natives to the decision to form a church. This is a great change from the early days of Hova domination, when the IEB workers reported that

[114] LMS, *Ten Years Review, 1880–1890,* p. 83.
[115] McMahon, *op. cit.,* p. 80.
[116] Hardyman, *op. cit.,* p. 144; Peyrot, *op. cit.,* pp. 57–58; G. E. Burton in *World Dominion,* 1947, pp. 285–289.

the greatest obstacle to their work was the drunken and licentious life of the Hova immigrants.[117]

Conclusion

Thus in many a way the church in Madagascar has brought the Gospel of God to the people round about it. Looking over the whole story we can clearly discern three main efforts that have dominated the organized mission of the Malagasy: first, the officially related missions of the older days of Hova rule; second, the long efforts of the Isan Enim Bolana, which span the early period and the most recent, showing greater strength as they go on; and third, the more recent and widespread but now declining efforts of the Soatanana revival.

From all of these the missionary movement of the Western churches has much to learn. The first and last of them have been quite foreign to the ways of the Western churches. The first was in fact subject to constant restraining efforts from the European missionaries, who believed more in the freedom of Christian life than did their newly won converts. And time seems to have borne out the reservations of the missionaries about this kind of evangelism. It is often suggested today that a new church must be given full freedom to carry on the Christian mission in its own way rather than copying the ways of the West. In principle this is true, but at the same time the experience with the official evangelists and evangelistic officials of Madagascar seems to indicate that the Western missionaries also must be true to their own understanding of the faith and try to influence the new church to carry on its mission in accordance with that understanding. Neither party to the endeavor can resign its responsibility before God for the appropriate presentation of the Gospel.

The second major effort, that of the Isan Enim Bolana, has been the least successful of the three. In this very fact lies a suggestion that missionary methods which are simply copied from Western experience are not likely to have the same power as those which spring from a more indigenous way of life. The foreign missionaries are surely right in inspiring and forwarding a body like the Isan Enim Bolana in its missionary endeavors. But at the same time

[117] *The Chronicle*, 1880, pp. 28–34.

they should be alert to those expressions of the mission which spring up in quite unexpected ways and do not fit into their familiar forms of activity. Even more notice should be taken of and encouragement be given to these types of missionary endeavor.

The Soatanana movement has been just such an irregular and indigenous type of mission. It has certainly manifested all of the problems and pressures that it might be expected to generate. Yet the fact that it has proved the most effective of the organized indigenous missions abundantly justifies the wrestling with those problems. It has also shown the importance of co-operation with the foreign worker for procuring the best results, and its future without that co-operation looks dim.

In fact, all three of the movements show the value of the assistance of missionaries from the older churches. The first effort, that of the early Hova, found in the foreign missionaries a needed restraint on its possible excesses and in the teaching of the missionaries a provision of gospel content where otherwise there would have been only oppressive form. The second effort, that of the Isan Enim Bolana, found in the foreigners a needed supervision and guidance that kept its scattered workers more aware of their mission and more effective in their evangelism. And the third effort, that of Soatanana, relied heavily on foreign missionaries as well as on national pastors to give to its new converts the continuity and the instruction without which all its sacrificial labors would have been only ephemeral in their effect. The content, supervision, and continuity provided in these three cases have been immensely important contributions from abroad. They emphasize the importance of maintaining an active missionary assistance from the older churches. Proposals for handing over the mission entirely to the younger churches fail to take account of the serious losses that would be involved.

But in all these examples it must be borne in mind that the foreign missionaries have made their contribution to a mission of the Malagasy church. More important than the usefulness of the foreign mission is the national mission with which the foreigners could work. It is to this central effort that the foreign missions is auxiliary and it is the responsibility of the foreign workers to pay all possible attention to the development of that national misison. As they are able to strengthen it by their various contributions, they accomplish their most important work.

It is no easy thing to develop the national mission, just as it is no easy thing to maintain a foreign mission. Both the national churches and the foreign churches are always all too ready to settle down in their own life and forget their missionary responsibility. Therefore the awareness of a missionary call must always be regarded as a precious gift in any church. It is something to be appreciated and provided with every chance to grow rather than being thwarted or opposed. The national church must appreciate and try to develop the sense of mission in the foreign churches, and the foreign workers must do the same for the development of the sense of mission in the national church. Each must examine its own policies in light of their possible effect on the awareness of missionary responsibility in the other. When each appreciates the preciousness of that awareness in the other and each offers and calls forth the fullest co-operation with the other in the common calling, the mission will have its greatest effectiveness. It is in this way that the church has grown in Madagascar.

APPENDIX

Authorization and Instructions Given to the Evangelists Sent Out by the Queen in 1869

I, Ranavalomanjaka, Queen of Madagascar, accept the men chosen by the Assembly of (name of church) of Antananarivo to go forth to preach the Word of God, according to the commandment of Jesus Christ written in Mark 16:15 in these terms: "Go ye into all the world and preach the Gospel to every creature." This is why I, Ranavalomanjaka, Queen of Madagascar, and the congregation of the palace and the congregation of the (name of church) have all given money in order to form a Malagasy Society to help you who go out to teach and to preach the Gospel of Jesus Christ.

In consequence, I, Ranavalomanjaka, Queen of Madagascar, give these instructions to you who are about to depart:

1. You are about to depart, but if instead of teaching exactly the word of God and extending the Kingdom of Jesus Christ according to the Holy Scriptures you do any other thing and especially if you teach that which is not in conformity with the Word of God, remember what Jesus Christ has said: "It would be better for him if a millstone were hung round his neck and he were cast into the sea than that he should cause one of these little ones to sin." (Luke 17:2) Walk

uprightly then and be worthy of this mission which you receive so that there may not be applied to you the words of Jesus Christ: "Cast the worthless servant into the outer darkness; there men will weep and gnash their teeth." (Matthew 25:30)

2. And I too declare to you that if instead of accomplishing this useful instruction in conformity with the above order you should exploit my people for increasing your own well-being and your fortune, especially if you do evil and violate the laws of my kingdom I will treat you as a criminal and a condemned one: for my kingdom is not a kingdom which I turn over to those who are uncaring, but is a kingdom which I establish on God.

3. "Finally be zealous and persevere as good soldiers of Christ Jesus." (II Timothy 2:3) "Tend the flock of God that is your charge not by constraint, but willingly, not for shameful gain, but eagerly." (I Peter 5:2) May God help you to accomplish perfectly the good work of Jesus Christ for which your congregation has chosen you. May Jehovah aid and protect you. May Jehovah cause his face to shine upon you and be gracious unto you. May Jehovah lift up his countenance upon you and give you his presence. To you and to all the people who will be taught by you the grace of the Lord Jesus Christ and the love of God the Father and the fellowship of the Holy Spirit. Amen.

[Here followed the seal of the Queen with this attestation:]

These are truly the instructions given by Ranavalomanjaka, Queen of Madagascar, to the persons who will go to teach.

Signed

Rainilaiarivony
Prime Minister

Antananarivo
18th of November, 1869

(Taken from De la Vaissière, *Histoire de Madagascar*, Vol. II, pp. 44–46.)

BIBLIOGRAPHY

Becker, Robert. *Dao, l'Antankarana: Vie d'un Évangéliste Malgache.* Paris: 1932.

Birkeli, Fridtjov. *Politik og Misjon.* Oslo: Egede-Instituttet, 1952.

Boudou, Adrien, *Les Jésuites à Madagascar au XIXe Siècle.* Paris: Gabriel Beauchesne, 1950.

Burgess, Andrew. *Zanahary in South Madagascar.* Minneapolis: 1932.

Burton, George E. *The Waiting Isle: Madagascar and Its Church.* London: Livingstone Press, 1953.

Chapus, M. G. S. *L'Église du Palais*, Tananarive: 1937.
Chirgwin, A. M. "The Growth of the Church in Madagascar," *International Review of Missions*, January, 1933.
———. *Report After a Secretarial Visit to Madagascar*. London: London Missionary Society, 1931.
———. *On the Road in Madagascar*. London: SCM Press, 1933.
Danielson, Rajosefa. *Ny Fifohazam-Panahy eto Madagascar*. Tananarive: Imprimerie Volahamitsy.
Escande, Élisée. Les Disciples du Seigneur (Un Mouvement d'évangélisation indigène à Madagascar). Les Cahiers Missionnaires No. 8. Paris: Société des Missions Évangéliques, 1926.
Friends' Foreign Mission Association. *Review of the Work of the F.F.M.A. in Madagascar from 1867–1880*. Antananarivo: 1880.
Gale, W. K. *Church Planting in Madagascar*. World Dominion Press, London, 1937.
Goodall, Norman. *History of the London Missionary Society, 1895–1945*. London: Oxford University Press, 1954.
Griffith, Robert. *Madagascar, A Century of Adventure*. London: London Missionary Society, 1919.
Halvorson, Mrs. P. C. *Lo-ha-ra-no*. Minneapolis: Augsburg Publishing House, 1948.
Hardyman, J. T. *Madagascar on the Move*. London: Livingstone Press, 1950.
Houghton, W. S., *et al. Report of Deputation to Madagascar, July–October, 1913, including joint report of London Missionary Society, Friends' Foreign Mission Association and Paris Missionary Society*. London: 1913.
Jackson, A. C. "Evangelistic Work in Madagascar," *International Review of Missions*, April, 1939.
Journal des Missions Évangéliques, 1895–1955.
Lewis, H. E., Griffith, Robert, and Hawkins, F. H. *London Missionary Society Madagascar Mission Report of the Deputation, 1920*. London: 1921.
London Missionary Society. *The Chronicle*, 1862–1958.
———. *Report for the Year*, 1869–1930.
———. *Ten Years Review of Mission Work in Madagascar*, 1861–1870; 1870–1880; 1880–1890; 1901–1910; 1911–1920; 1921–1930.
Matthews, T. T. *Thirty Years in Madagascar*. London: Religious Tract Society, 1904.
McMahon, E. O. *Christian Missions in Madagascar*. London: SPG, 1919.
Mondain, G. *Un siècle de mission protestante à Madagascar*. Paris: Société des Missions Évangéliques, 1920.

Mullens, Joseph. *Twelve Months in Madagascar*. London: 1875.
Nakkestad, Gabriel. *Fra Vekkelsene på Madagaskar*. Oslo: Egede Inst., 1955.
Ny Fiangonana Isan Enim Bolan' Imerina (semiannual reports of the IEB).
Peyrot, Alfred. "Action Missionnaire de l'Église Malgache," *Journal des Missions Évangéliques*, March–April, 1946, pp. 51–63.
Rahamefy, Henri. "L'Église du Palais à Madagascar," *Le Monde non-Chrétien*, No. 32 (October–December, 1959), pp. 381–422.
Ralibera, Daniel. "Les Disciples du Seigneur." Unpublished Ph.D. dissertation in Theological Faculty of Paris.
Rusillon, H. *Un Petit Continent Madagascar*. Paris: Société des Missions Évangéliques, 1933.
Sibree, James. *Fifty Years in Madagascar*. London: Allen and Unwin, 1924.
———. *Madagascar Before the Conquest*. London: Allen and Unwin, 1896.
———. *Madagascar and Its People*. London: Religious Tract Society, 1870.
———. *The Madagascar Mission*. London: 1907.
Syrdal, Rolf A. *Mission in Madagascar and the Beginnings of the Malagasy Lutheran Church*. Minneapolis: 1957.
Thunes, A. *Vaekelsen paa Madagaskar*. 1926.
Vaissière, de la, Père. *Histoire de Madagascar, ses Habitants et ses Missionnaires*. Paris: Libraire Victor Lecoffre, 1889.

CHAPTER VI

*The Christian Mission Since 1938:
Methods and Techniques*

CALVIN H. REBER, JR.
United Theological Seminary
Dayton, Ohio

His study of the history of Christian expansion has caused Kenneth Scott Latourette to see a close connection between missionary methods and Christian vitality. The periods in which Christian outreach was dynamic were those marked also by the discovery of new ways of proclamation. On the other hand, times of missionary recession were those when methods used were merely continued from an earlier period. Thus, of the period following 1914 Dr. Latourette wrote:

> This continuation of pre-1914 agencies and methods into the post-1914 age may be a symptom of recession. The seeming failure to produce new means to meet what is in so many respects a radically different world may indicate an ominous lack of resiliency.[1]

This penetrating observation imposes a special duty upon one making a study of missionary methods since 1938. It makes it insufficient to merely catalog the ways in which the mission of the Church is functioning. One must seek to determine the most significant ways, their relevance for our time, and their indication of vitality within the Church. This task may be entirely too large for the present paper, the period involved may be too short to determine a trend, and we may be too close to evaluate the era. Yet Dr. Latourette's

[1] K. S. Latourette, *The Unquenchable Light* (New York, Harper & Brothers, 1941), p. 167. Cf. also his *The Christian World Mission in Our Day* (New York, Harper & Brothers, 1954), p. 133.

observation cannot be ignored, and the question it poses offers the best hope of unifying a survey which could be very discursive.

Methods in 1938

To have a viewpoint from which to see what has happened since 1938, it is necessary to understand missionary methods at that time. Again Dr. Latourette is most helpful. For the Madras Conference he set forth the distinctive features of missionary methods in the preceding period. These marks were as follows:

1. First of all is the extensive geographic spread of Christianity and the wide range of cultures and religions with which missionaries have had to do. . . .
2. A second feature is the large number of kinds of Christianity which have been propagated. . . .
3. Almost in the same breath with this must be mentioned, as a third characteristic, the extensive cooperation which has arisen among Protestant missionary forces. . . .
4. A fourth feature, and one not so commonly noticed, is the partial, often complete, divorce of missions from the political policy of the lands from which missionaries have gone and to which they have come. . . .
5. . . . as never before missionaries have protested against the exploitation by their fellow-countrymen of the peoples among whom they live. . . .
6. Still another . . . striking peculiarity of nineteenth- and twentieth-century Protestant missions is the broad, popular base of the financial support of the enterprise. . . .
7. Probably never before has money given by older churches been used so lavishly in helping to bring into existence and nourish younger churches.
8. One of the most distinctive features of this present age of Protestant missions is the large part played by women. . . .
9. An outstanding peculiarity of nineteenth- and twentieth-century Protestant missions is the place occupied by schools, hospitals and various undertakings such as famine relief, agricultural improvement and cooperative societies. . . .
10. Still another unique feature of modern Protestant missions has been the high standards for admission to baptism. . . .
11. Interwoven with this last characteristic are two other phenom-

ena: the reduced frequency of mass conversions as compared with earlier centuries and

12. The small percentage of professed Christians in most of the lands to which Protestant missionaries have gone. . . .

13. In contrast with the diminutive size of the Protestant Christian communities . . . is one more feature. . . . That is a certain kind of mass conversion (or better, "mass modification") on a scale unprecedented in the history of any religion. . . . Millions have accepted ethical and social ideals which historically have been associated with Christianity.[2]

So comprehensive is this list that it is hard to add to it any further characterization. Some slightly different emphases were made in the discussion at Madras, but these can be seen better as we observe the changes. Dr. Latourette's list sketches well the methodological accents of missions at that time.

A Changed Situation

At Madras there was awareness of the need for changes in missionary policies. The recommendations of Section VI in particular point to needful improvement in method.[3] However, before the stimulus of Madras could be tested adequately, war came again to the world. The Christian mission faced a more urgent situation in every regard. By the shutting of normal channels of communication, younger churches[4] had to grow up quickly or perish. Because of the burdens and destruction of war, older churches had fewer resources to aid other areas. In the postwar period revolutionary forces such as nationalism, rising antagonism between West and non-West, increase of economic pressures, resurgence of the non-Christian religions, and racial conflict created a radically different situation from that foreseen at Madras. The total shaking of the foundations deepened within the Christian Church a concern for the truths of the Christian faith along with a desire to have Christian activity rooted

[2] K. S. Latourette, "Distinctive Features of the Protestant Missionary Methods of the Nineteenth and Twentieth Centuries," *Evangelism*, Vol. III in *Madras Series* (New York, International Missionary Council, 1939), pp. 16–29.

[3] *Ibid.*, pp. 396–407.

[4] The terms "younger" and "older" are used in this paper, with clear recognition of their unsatisfactory nature, only because there seem to be no substitutes as brief and as widely understood.

in theology. It was inevitable that some changes in method should
come. The only questions which could be asked were whether they
would be soon enough and adequate for the changed situation. The
insights of the world missionary conferences had to get out to the
actual administration in boards and fields and to the supporting constituencies of the world mission.

Partnership

The most powerful policy change demanded was suggested in the
call for partnership. The word and the broader phrase, "partnership
in obedience," came from the Whitby Conference in 1947. Neither
word nor phrase is to be regarded merely as a catch phrase to stir a
conference. They mark rather the recognition of a new relationship
in service. There had been awareness that the existence of younger
churches would eventually necessitate different policies from those
which prevailed earlier. The nature of these policies was less certain.
Some spoke constantly of the need for the missionary to work himself
out of a job, and of the mission's being the scaffolding which would
not be needed when the Church was complete. If this were so, then
as soon as a church was established the missionary should go on to a
new area, as Paul did, or return home. He might stay on in the field
as a kind of symbol of ecumenicity but his usefulness was only sym-
bolical, while the real burden lay upon the indigenous church to
govern itself, support itself, and propagate itself.

The events accompanying and following the Second World War
showed grave weakness in these assumptions. First, there was the
urgency of the situation. "Each year's delay may mean the closing
of doors which may not be opened again till this generation has
passed away," said Whitby.[5] In the face of urgency like that, missionaries sent to witness to God's act in Christ cannot be content to
be symbols. Nor can a church obligated to proclaim the good news
to all the world wait indefinitely until a local church grows strong
enough to reach the whole of its own land. Second, the resurgence of
the non-Christian religions in the East and the advance of secularism
in the West made clear that evangelization has dimensions other than
geographic. The fact that the Church was everywhere in the world

---

[5] C. W. Ranson (ed.), *Renewal and Advance* (London, Edinburgh House,
1948), p. 174.

could no longer hide the fact that the world was not being won at any encouraging rate. Third, there were voices, like that of Stephen Neill, which reminded that idealizing the younger church could be as dangerous as idealizing the so-called Christian West.[6] Although no one could deny the amazing growth of the younger churches at a time when their mere existence was a miracle of God, it was both unrealistic and unfair to them to assume that they could carry alone the burden of evangelization of their lands. When less than 1 per cent of an area is Christian, the smallness of the minority requires help even to avoid the peril of defensiveness before effective evangelization can take place. Fourth, the end of missions seemed also to suggest an end of mission, and this did not make sense in a world so obviously far from being Christian. The words about "the uttermost parts of the earth" may be more than geographical, but they cannot be less than that. Knowledge of a world in need and a Gospel for it prevents any constriction. It was imperative, for these reasons, that ways of continued world-wide witnessing be found.

None of these pressing considerations, however, could be allowed to undermine the integrity of the growing younger churches. The fact that they were weak could not be allowed to doom them to constant domination by stronger churches. The fact that they could not carry alone the full burden of evangelizing their lands could not be allowed to take from them the primacy of this duty. Their being indigenous itself gave them possibilities of witness which are ever closed to the outsider. Moreover, the urgency of the situation demanded that every resource for evangelization be used, and the possible closing of an area to missions made it equally imperative that the Church be strengthened to stand alone in the event that outside connections were broken. In addition, the years of war had so tested the younger churches in this very situation that there could be no possible return to dependence. The teen-ager who has learned to support himself and make his own decisions cannot go back to being bottle-fed or to being instructed in every detail of behavior.

The need of the younger churches for room to grow and the need of the older churches for room to witness could produce irreconcilable conflicts unless some principles were found by which both needs

[6] Stephen Neill, *The Unfinished Task* (London, Edinburgh House, 1957), pp. 111–145. See also his "Missions Enters a New Phase," *Union Seminary Quarterly Review*, May, 1954, pp. 3 ff.

were unified under a common purpose. This unifying principle is "partnership in obedience." For now both needs are subjected to a higher loyalty, in which they contribute their strengths and weaknesses to the common cause of a common Lord.

It has become increasingly apparent since this principle was enunciated that stating it does not solve all the problems involved. Being human as we are, no one of us ever recognizes his need of advice so quickly as his need of money. Similarly, in our common humanity, the giver is certain to consider his advice of far more value than his financial assistance. So it was inevitable that younger churches should evaluate financial help most highly while older churches should regard their counsel as the greater contribution.

Quite apart from such comparative values, the personnel relations posed other problems. It is comparatively easy for all to understand the lack of wisdom and even offensiveness of sending younger churches persons to do tasks native leadership can perform as well. It is more difficult to attain agreement as to what local and imported leadership, respectively, can do. The outside expert is more likely to see most clearly his expertness, while the insider is more likely to see his outsideness. There is also the possibility that no outsider can be an expert on a particular inside situation.

Moreover, if the younger church is most ingrown, it is most in need of the stirring outsider to quicken it to its responsibility. Yet where that need is greatest, there will be the greatest tendency to resent the disturber. When the younger church is weak, it has the greatest need for help, which too easily becomes a crutch or a means of rule.

As a result of such complexities, there has been neither a surplus of satisfaction over the practice of partnership nor an avoidance of efforts to do better. The real difficulty lies in the fact that these relationships cannot be handled by mere structure or words. They demand a larger measure of commitment to the common purpose of effective proclamation and a greater sensitivity to the feelings of each other. They require awareness of the tendency to substitute one's own plans for the purposes of God and a willingness to hear God's voice in the words of a brother.[7]

Particular devices that aim to increase a sense of partnership must be examined by these criteria. The accent on "exchange of person-

[7] Cf. Max Warren, *Partnership* (London, SCM Bookclub, 1956), *passim.*

nel" seems positive in seeking to achieve true sharing of personnel. The substitution of the term "fraternal worker" for "missionary" is a mixed blessing to be judged largely by what this substitution really says to the younger church. The Western board method of solving problems by executive decisions, memoranda, and committees far removed from persons and issues involved must be seriously questioned. The substitution of the deputations for day-by-day missionary contact, and the efforts to keep missionaries from interfering with a board and younger church partnership can be actually destructive of the real partnership sought. New structures of partnership cannot replace the partnership of toil together in the heat of the day.

Mission

The second major accent in contemporary missionary methods is the emphasis on more dynamic outreach. This is best symbolized by the changed spelling of the key word of the undertaking from "missions" to "mission." The new spelling calls for a new emphasis on *totality* concerning both the Church and the world. It means a turning from the period in which missions were a concern of a minority in the West for some faraway people to an awareness that the whole Church has a mission to people everywhere. It also calls for *unity* in which there is less thinking about separate attractive projects in many places and more total thrust of the whole Church of Jesus Christ. It includes a renewed stress on *mobility*. "Missions" have come to represent more or less static arrangements like mission stations in a time when the fluidity of the world requires much more adaptability to change. "Mission" also demands a more *deliberate encounter* with the world to which it is sent than that which prevailed when institutional missions sometimes forgot their real reason for being.

It would be possible, of course, for this change in spelling to be nothing more than a promotional device to encourage an apparently needful new approach. There appears to be considerable evidence, however, that the verbal change represents actual changes already achieved.

Changes have taken place in this direction in the relationships of local sending churches. During the nineteenth and twentieth centuries, Protestant missions have been the primary concern of a part

of the Church. In Europe the separate structures of the missionary
societies gave evidence of that. In America most mission boards were
denominationally organized, but the whole Church has never fully
accepted missionary responsibility. Now, however, the gradual transformation of women's missionary societies into women's societies,
and the inclusion of missionary education within the children and
youth programs instead of providing separate organizations show a
new trend. It may be pointed out that, at the same time, independent
boards in America are increasing their proportion of the missionaries
sent. It may also be debated whether the mild missionary flavor of a
whole church is not likely to appear quite insipid compared with the
more pungent taste of the convinced minority. The existence of the
trend itself is less debatable.

This same movement to mission shows itself more fully on the
national and world level in the inclusion of the former Foreign Missions Conference of North America within the National Council of
Churches as the Division of Foreign Missions. The movement toward
merger of the International Missionary Council with the World
Council of Churches is similar. So also the joint meeting of the
Division of Home Missions with the Division of Foreign Missions of
the National Council of Churches in recent years testifies to the recognition of the unity of the mission. Apart from these larger structures there has been the growth of interdenominational co-operation
in numbers of specific projects—co-operation that has transcended
comity to bring into being united missions. These things have not
happened solely for pragmatic reasons. Rather there has been increasing awareness that those who are not reconciled cannot carry
the message of reconciliation, and that the structures by which we
work must reflect and encourage reconciliation.

Another particular method in the new spirit of mission has been
the reconstitution of the missionary force on a more international
and interracial basis. This reconstruction itself has been effected in
differing ways.[8] Some of them, of course, precede 1938. For example,
before that time there were union colleges, seminaries, and churches
in which two or more foreign nationalities worked together and
with the leadership of the national church. The significant differ-

[8] For a more detailed statement of these developments, see J. W. Decker,
"Internationalizing Missionary Action," an unpublished mimeo document made
available to professors of missions by the International Missionary Council.

ence is that since the last war this has been more widely accepted as a determined method of work. The variety of internationalization may be shown by citing some of the particular projects.

Among churches there has been the strengthening of international participation in Japan through special provisions such as Interboard, and in Indonesia through separate assignment of missionaries unrelated to societies formerly occupying the area.

Internationalization has also taken place through confessional alliances. It has been advanced among Lutheran missions as the result of war-orphaned missions. In Europe a similar confessional bond of several national churches has been established in the European Baptist Society.

Additional internationalization of institutions includes Vellore Christian College, Ludhiana Medical College, and the International Christian University of Japan.

In the United Mission to Nepal we have a situation in which international participation marked the project from its inception. Support in funds and personnel for this mission is reported from America, Canada, Britain, Norway, Sweden, Switzerland, Australia, and India. Greater participation is being sought from India and other Asian nations.

The larger participation of Asian nations as senders of missionary personnel is being stimulated by the East Asia Christian Conference, and it is becoming common for Asians to serve in other Asian lands and even in Africa.

In West Pakistan a concentrated evangelistic approach to a new area used a team drawn from several denominations with national workers matched with Western missionaries. Workers from the nearest churches were enlisted to take responsibility for continuing nurture and evangelism after the departure of the team.[9]

The importance of this total development for showing the worldwide nature of Christianity and the need for all people to share in sending participation cannot be overestimated. It must not be suggested, however, that all the problems are already solved. Two of them have a way of recurring. One is the problem of salary. When persons from a wide difference of home economies participate to-

[9] *Minutes of the Assembly of the International Missionary Council Meeting at Ghana,* December 28, 1957, to January 8, 1958 (New York, International Missionary Council, 1958), p. 60.

gether in a missionary situation, discrepancy of salary may put heavy burdens on fellowship. Like payment for like work may be equally unfair. Another problem is the relationship of personnel and financial support. Some areas may be able to provide one form of support rather than another, but experience shows that there are dangers whenever only one form is provided. The importance of internationalization, however, is so widely acknowledged that one can be sure that workable, even if not final, solutions will be found.

Accent on mission has also given rise to a large use of laymen in the world mission. At first this trend was nothing more than the extension of specialization. Builders, pilots, and office staff were added to the doctors and teachers without theological training. These people were regarded, however, as slightly less missionaries than the ordained personnel. Essentially the church and the mission were made central and contribution to its program or its institutions was the missionary criterion.

Since the last war two things have altered the relationship of laymen to the mission. The new situation produced thousands of laymen going overseas as representatives of governmental agencies and private companies. These people were bound to have some kind of influence. If they were Christians, here was a new evangelizing possibility. As Islam propagated itself largely through its laymen, Christianity too might utilize this resource. The other thing that happened was the theological recovery of the mission of the laity. To take Eugene Smith's strong comparison, there has been growing awareness that the pastor's being an assistant layman may be more important than the layman's being an assistant pastor.[10] The mission of the Church is to minister to those outside its life and not merely to maintain its own structure. In that ministry the layman is crucial because he has a contact with the world impossible for the professional religious leader.

This double thrust has affected the mission of the Church in a number of influential ways. Lay training centers have grown up in various areas of the world Church, and lay activity going out from the Church is due to increase. This will require a new education of the laity in the nature of the Christian mission. It will not be possible

[10] Eugene L. Smith, "The Role of the Laity in the Christian World Mission," *Occasional Bulletin* of the Missionary Research Library, February 20, 1960, p. 6.

to regard the world mission as the exclusive preserve of the professional.

So far the major concern of the world mission has been with laymen going overseas. The meetings of the International Missionary Council have spoken with increasing clarity to the possibilities of this ministry. The Ghana meeting pointed out that this service should be regarded as multi-directional and not merely aimed by older to younger churches. It also encouraged special training by member councils of the IMC and suggested that local churches, in the presence of the congregation, give letters of commendation to help persons going abroad to relate themselves to churches in the area of their service.[11] Meanwhile the Western churches are increasing their efforts through churches abroad to minister to their nationals.[12]

There is a quickening of general concern for laymen as witnessing Christians in the older churches, and it appears that a similar increase may soon appear among the younger churches. This will require more extensive help to laymen as persons who stand most directly at the point of mission—where the Church really meets the world. The total rediscovery of the layman may prove to be the most significant development within the church and mission in our time.[13]

Along with the new understanding of the function of laymen, the mobile conception of mission has stirred concern also for a new kind of professional ministry. Until Madras the ministry as such did not receive great consideration. Churches were created and ministries were trained according to the traditions of the missionaries, and some of this training was very good. Nevertheless, Madras reported, "Almost all the younger churches are dissatisfied with the present system of training for the ministry and with its results."[14]

The recognized need had three facets. The ministry needed more adequate training to fulfill its task without negative comparison with other professions. The preparation needed to be more fully related to the actual life of the church and less imitative of foreign seminary curricula. Ways were also needed to use a more adequately trained

[11] Ghana Assembly *Minutes*, p. 61.
[12] Cf. S. Alan Watson, "American Churches Overseas," *Christian Century*, Vol. LXXXIV (July 17, 1957), pp. 864–866.
[13] Cf. Norman Goodall, "New Frontiers of the Church's World Mission," in E. J. Jurji (ed.), *The Ecumenical Era in Church and Society* (New York, The Macmillan Company, 1957), pp. 118–120.
[14] *Madras Series*, Vol. IV, *The Life of the Church*, p. 188.

ministry in a church with a weak economic base. Since Madras the careful study of theological education in the younger churches and the launching of the Theological Education Fund promise to meet these needs in at least some measure. Whether this will mean simply a more adequate ministry in accord with present patterns or the rise of a new pattern of ministry this writer is not competent to say. Although the direction of the new developments is not yet apparent, they may prove to be most important in the new thrust of mission.

Community

The third major emphasis in missionary methods since 1938 has come from a new concern for community. Here again the mission is being influenced jointly by movements without and within itself. The currents of "togetherness," group dynamics, and the basic loneliness of mass man in an impersonal society have had their effect. At the same time the longings these manifestations reveal have stirred the Church to examine its message in regard to them. So there has come a realization of the necessity of community both in apprehending and in proclaiming the Gospel.

This emphasis has strengthened concern for the centrality of the Church even beyond that shown at Madras. There has been increasing awareness that neither the isolated winning of converts nor the permeation of society is an adequate way to work. People must be nourished by the community of love, and the permeation must be effected by a fellowship of witness.

This sense of the Church as community has caused both an emphasis on the renewal of the life of the local churches and an interest in new experiments.[15] At this time two novel types of development seem most promising. In the lands of the older churches there have arisen efforts like the East Harlem Protestant Parish to minister to people totally from a real church center of deep devotional commitment. In the lands of the younger churches community development projects in rural areas often have similarly made the church a center and fellowship redemption. In quite a different direction, the growth of indigenous communal movements seeks to recapture the genius

15 Cf. Norman Goodall (ed.), *Missions under the Cross* (New York, International Missionary Council, 1953), p. 216.

and spirit of the early church which held all things in common. One well-known example is the Jesus Family group of China.

The recognition of the importance of community has been shown also in a re-emphasis on the winning of previously existent communities to Christianity. Mass movements to Christianity are not new, and even as missionary strategy they have persisted through the time when the primary accent was on individual commitment. However, such works as Donald McGavran's *Bridges of God* suggest that the effort to capture natural communities for Christ may be revived.

The concern for community has also produced a growing number of retreat centers. All over the world there has been interest in providing places where people can live together under God for shorter or longer periods of time. In group prayer, study, work, and silence individuals have been helped to deeper levels of living and to an awareness of Christian community which overcomes modern loneliness.

The institutions of the Church such as schools and hospitals have been re-examined in the light of this new concern.[16] These missionary institutions are expected to be effective Christian communities of healing and learning. Moreover, they are expected to have a relationship with the Church as the central Christian community which nourishes them and guides their purpose.

The area generally considered as women's work has also felt the concern for community. In the earlier days of missions there was a primary and necessary concern for the protection of women and children and for helping them seek their full status as persons. Now that these individual rights have been largely secured, the point of greater urgency is the Christian family. Consequently more attention is being directed to achieving the kind of families in which not only women and children but all members find Christian meaning in life together.

The accent on the Christian community has affected also the compassionate ministries of the Church. The existence of chronic distress since the war and the necessity of governmental action provided external stimuli for the mission to rethink its serving activities.

[16] Cf. R. Pierce Beaver and W. F. Mills, *Toward a More Effective Ministry Through Missionary Institutions* (Division of Foreign Missions, National Council of Churches, New York, U.S.A., 1953), *passim*.

Within the Church, developing unity required that oneness be manifest in its ministry to the world. At the same time, there was equal need for reconciliation between those who stressed the primacy of evangelism and those who saw the urgency of Christian helpfulness.

The renewed understanding of the *diakonia* provided a firm principle for such revitalization and unity. Loving service was not to be considered an auxiliary activity but a manifestation of the very nature of the Church. The real test of it was not so much its quantity as the degree to which this activity revealed the love of God. To the advocate of the primacy of evangelism this conception provided the understanding that the cup of cold water given in the name of Christ is evangelism. To the advocate of simple helpfulness it provided the insight that Christian service should have a distinctive quality because it is the activity of a redeemed community showing forth the love of God.

Thus in a variety of ways new understanding of the unique nature of the Christian community is shaping the current activities of mission. As the younger churches find increased status within the world Church, unless they are disrupted by Western fragmentation, the accent on community appears likely to increase. Many of these churches are closer to cultures which long sensed the solidarity of the group. As the West leaves its excessive glorification of the individual, Christianity may show the way to new forms of community which respect and enhance individual personality.

Use of New Resources

The fourth major development in the methods of mission since 1938 lies in the use of modern technical resources. There is nothing new, of course, in the acceptance of new devices. The whole history of Christian expansion is marked by this. It does seem, however, that in our time technical advances have made available striking possibilities which are shaping the operation of the world mission.

It may be possible to consider all the advance in the realm of literacy and literature as simply the widespread extension of methods previously used. It may be possible also to regard the use of radio as merely the extension of evangelistic preaching. When, however, the nature of the audio-visual and mass communications devices is considered, a new dimension in all these areas becomes apparent.

For although radio makes possible the extension of the human voice, it also creates a different situation. It is not possible, for instance, for the audience to be seen by the preacher. Thus he cannot see the effect of his message or get an immediate response. His audience itself may come and go with an ease not usual in an assembled congregation. Offsetting these disadvantages is the size of the audience. It becomes necessary to increase the holding appeal of the presentation and to provide some way for the speaker to establish continued communication with the audience. As a result, new forms beyond preaching have been sought, and correspondence courses have been tied to radio presentation to provide two-way communication.

The importance of developments here is indicated both by the number of receivers available and by the number of missionary stations coming into existence. S. Franklin Mack, a leader in this field, sets the total number of receivers, exclusive of those in the United States and Canada, as 143,330,500 with an additional 28,918,500 wired speakers. In 1947 there were only two missionary broadcasting stations. By 1959 there were twenty-one such stations on the air and at least ten others being planned.[17]

Protestantism has also entered bravely into the field of audiovisual presentation, and an impressive number of production centers has arisen.[18] It is not equally clear that Protestant Christianity has faced fully the consequences of this new approach. From its beginning Protestantism has resorted almost entirely to the spoken word in the presentation of the Gospel. It was suspicious of any visual device because it might encourage idolatry through images. Moreover, Protestantism was suspicious of any externalization of feeling and any tendency to decrease the personal and intelligent comprehension of the Christian message. This created some rigidity in the proclamation of the Gospel even in cultures where there was a far greater preference for immediate and concrete experience.[19]

Modern audio-visual devices move the presentation of the Gospel out into less verbal and intellectual ways. At the same time, these new ways cannot be entirely equated with the preliterate emphasis

[17] F. W. Price, "Missionary Broadcasting and Audio Visual Work," *Occasional Bulletin* of the Missionary Research Library, September 25, 1959, pp. 1, 2.
[18] *Ibid.*, pp. 6, 7.
[19] Cf. H. R. Weber, *The Communication of the Gospel to Illiterates* (IMC Research Pamphlet), *passim*.

on the concrete because they come out of a highly literate and so-phisticated scientific tradition. The long, agonizing process of adap-tation seems as inevitable here as in other aspects of the Christian mission. The danger is that the deceptive similarity will blind its advocates to the differences; and the urgent theological task may be neglected which must be done if the new resources are to be used well.

Protestantism is more at home in the developing use of another contemporary resource. This is the use of research. As a result of the modern emphasis on accurate facts, there has probably never been a time so marked by an effort to base missionary policy on prior research. It is interesting to note that the Madras and earlier conferences had a category of co-opted members, while the postwar conferences at Willingen and Ghana have a new species of partici-pants called "consultants." This designation appears no idle tribute to persons not delegates but seems a recognition of the necessity of persons who represent nothing but the importance of knowledge in making decisions. The Willingen Conference was also marked by widespread consultation in preparation. Since the Evanston Assembly of the World Council of Churches, the creation of the Division of Studies has increased significant activity in this area. Although the Division was a part of the World Council, it was regarded by the In-ternational Missionary Council as its agent in ecumenical study. In addition to the service of the whole Division to missions, one of the four departments is specifically concerned with missionary studies. In this department studies have been made or are proceeding on the Christian enterprise in China, the life and growth of the younger churches, theological education, and African marriage and family life.[20] At the Ghana Assembly the department was requested also to undertake a study on the theology of missions.[21] A series of smaller studies is resulting in the very useful IMC Research Pam-phlets.

These specifically missionary studies are only a part of the increas-ing resources available from the Division of Studies. The department concerned with evangelism has produced regional studies on evan-gelism as well as a careful study of the theological basis for evange-lism. A joint study by the departments of evangelism and missionary

---

[20] *The Bulletin of the Division of Studies*, Vol. I, No. 1, p. 2.
[21] Ghana Assembly *Minutes*, p. 46.

studies is being made on "The Word of God and the Living Faiths of Men." The Department on Church and Society is engaged in a study, urgent for the world mission, on "The Church and Rapid Social Change."[22]

In addition to these world-wide efforts, there has been a corresponding growth of regional study conferences and study centers. They appear to be largely concerned with the relationship of Christianity to the non-Christian faiths of the region involved, but the increasing vitality and number of these approaches forbid any designation of particular topics or sites.

Lest the effect of these studies be overestimated, two observations may be added. There is still only limited evidence that administrative offices of boards of missions are taking the studies seriously enough either to accept full involvement or to implement the results disclosed. There is also not a great measure of participation by the professors of missions in the seminaries in the United States. Although good explanations exist for the latter fact, it seems desirable that some proper way of involvement be found to prevent the professors of missions from being regarded as little more than agents of missionary propaganda or as outside critics of the enterprise. For quite apart from the significant data and understanding provided by all this study, these efforts strengthen the entire Christian witness by their concern for truth and their encounter with the realities of the world. The development of a hard-headed approach is demanded by the opposition facing missions both from non-Christians in the East and from partial Christians in the West.

One point at which this more hard-headed approach has already shown itself is in the selection and training of missionaries. Since the need for postwar replacements has leveled off, boards have been able to raise their standards and require better training before appointment. They have used psychological studies to assist determination of fitness and have assisted in the special preparation demanded for the task assigned. The boards which formerly co-operated in providing six weeks of joint orientation have now developed an ecumenical center with a one-year orientation program. The disciplines of anthropology and linguistics are becoming an important

---

[22] The continuing report of these studies is to be found in the twice-annual publication of the *Bulletin of the Division of Studies.*

part of missionary training to foster better understanding of the culture and language of those they serve.

Conclusion

The time has come to return to the questions with which we began and to strike some kind of balance. We have seen something of the present thrust of missionary methods. It has not been possible to even name every individual technique in use. One mark of the mission today is the fact of considerable individual experimentation carried on without publicity. Perhaps enough has been said to suggest major trends and how these are demonstrated.

Yet we must ask whether the new methods we have described give evidence of a new vitality in the Christian world mission. Although a number of changes have been indicated, their significance is more difficult to evaluate. Many of them had their beginning before 1938. Others may be only superficial, or adaptations of older methods. For example, it is difficult to see any great manifestation of vitality in the use of such modern devices as the airplane or Biblical recordings. These appear to be rather simple adaptations of devices used by all agencies in our day and call for no new insight into the nature of the Gospel. At Ghana it was said again that "few new forms of mission have as yet arisen."[23]

One must ask, however, how radically and how rapidly new forms must arise to merit consideration. It does seem that the present witness of the world Church is quite different both in its over-all direction and in its specific aspects from that described by Dr. Latourette at Madras. True, we are only just now seeing action arising from ideas, and the actions may still be only as big as a man's hand. But these ideas of partnership, mission, and community are fraught with consequence, and action is following idea with encouraging speed. Whether or not we are in a new era of missionary advance, there is at least considerable evidence that new forms are being produced to cope with a changing world.

---

[23] Ghana Assembly *Minutes*, p. 58.

CHAPTER VII

Faith Missions Since 1938

HAROLD LINDSELL

Fuller Theological Seminary

Pasadena, California

In a very real sense the year 1938 marks the end of one age and the beginning of another. While it may be argued forcefully that one particular date does not lend itself with finality to this conclusion, nevertheless sufficient evidences point to 1938 as such a decisive year. This is true politically and economically as well as in terms of the Christian missionary enterprise.

Politically, 1938 witnessed the beginning of World War II, which commenced formally on September 1, 1939, with the invasion of Poland by Germany, but which was occasioned by events transpiring in 1938. On September 30, 1938, the Munich Peace Pact was signed by the great European powers. Czechoslovakia was occupied by the Germans with the consent of these powers in an effort to "preserve the peace of Europe." On October 5 Eduard Beneš resigned as President of Czechoslovakia. By the end of November the partition of this state was completed. Édouard Daladier of France and Neville Chamberlain of England assented to the terms and conditions of this defeat. Anthony Eden had resigned from the British cabinet months before the Munich Pact in protest against British capitulation to German and Italian pressures and aggression.

This same year was marked by other political events of significance. The Spanish Civil War was still in progress. The New Reform Government of the Republic of China was set up. Japan in its expansionist war against China occupied the major cities of Canton and Hankow. The first session of the "Red Parliament" convened in Russia with members elected to the supreme Soviet under the new constitution. Joseph Stalin was one of the delegates. At the close of the year France and Germany signed a "good neighbor relations" pact and the Italian Parliament was dissolved, to be replaced by a totalitarian government under the control of Mussolini.

Economically the United States was still in the grip of the depression. The New Deal of Franklin Roosevelt had mitigated the suffering attending the economic dislocations of the early thirties (by mortgaging the future with borrowed money) but had wrought no lasting solutions for the underlying problems. With the advent of World War II the whole economic situation in the United States underwent a profound change, and a new age began in American life. Europe had suffered economic disaster earlier than the United States after World War I. By 1938 new patterns of totalitarianism had risen to bring solutions to European economic woes. However, the rise of dictatorships by no means solved these problems; rather the attention of the people was directed toward nationalist and imperialist ambitions which led directly to World War II.

In Protestant missions too the year 1938 marked a milestone. The International Missionary Council met at Tambaram, Madras, India—the last such meeting before the advent of war. Indeed, the dark clouds of the approaching war hung heavily over the meeting. Inasmuch as the Council convened at the end of 1938 (December 12 to 29) it did so against the background of portentous political changes which so clearly marked the imminence of war. When the war was over and such meetings were resumed the whole world picture had changed unbelievably. Truly a new age had commenced.

In 1911, just prior to World War I, there were over 19,000 Protestant missionaries scattered around the globe.[1] Most of them came from Europe. By 1925 the number had increased to over 28,000. Then the effects of the postwar depression struck forcibly. The missionary situation worsened. The number of foreign missionaries decreased. By 1938 some recovery had been effected but the total number of foreign missionaries was still between four and five hundred fewer than in 1925. Of the total number of missionaries in 1938 a shade over 40 per cent came from North America.[2] In the period since 1938 a reversal has taken place; indeed, the disparity

---

[1] Joseph I. Parker (ed.), *Interpretative Statistical Survey of the World Mission of the Christian Church* (New York, 1938), p. 17.
[2] *Ibid.*, p. 43.

has widened so that today more than 60 per cent of the Protestant foreign missionary force comes from North America and the financial undergirding of the enterprise has been assumed in even greater proportion by it.

Since 1938, then, there has been a definite and decisive shift of the major home base for missions from Europe (and particularly the British Isles) to North America (particularly the United States of America). During this same period the total world situation has been altered: mankind has been brought face to face with new problems, even as the old ones have increased in intensity and aggravation. In the political arena the expansion of the Russian Communist bloc has affected the balance of power profoundly. The resurgence of nationalism among the smaller nations of the world has produced staggering problems. All over the world minority groups are calling for self-government and freedom from the white man's historic domination. This is true in Africa, Asia, Indonesia, and elsewhere. One of the peculiarities of the phenomenon lies in the reverse process by which minority groups who used to be free have been swallowed up by Communism. Thus Poland, Czechoslovakia, Hungary, East Germany, Estonia, Latvia, Finland, etc., have lost their independence.

Scientific advances have further complicated the world situation. The development of nuclear weapons has brought fear to men, and the threatened use of such weapons portends the destruction of vast numbers of mankind. The other side of the story has to do with constructive advances which have reduced distances and improved communications in a way hitherto undreamed of. Jet-propelled airplanes have brought almost every place on the globe within man's reach in a day or two. Improvements in communication make the global transmittal of news a matter of minutes. Medical achievements have lengthened the span of life, and preventive medicine has cut infant mortality to a new low. In turn, these and an increasing birth rate have led to a world-wide population explosion the ominous side of which has alarmed sociologists, economists, politicians, and missionary leaders.

In missionary endeavor this new age has been characterized by a pronounced hostility to missions, serious curtailment of missionary activities, and an intensified antagonism toward the white race in particular. The closing of China to missions has cut off at least 20 per cent of the world's population from foreign missionary outreach.

Restrictions placed upon foreign missionaries in various other countries have either reduced or kept at the same level the number of
missionaries. Antagonism toward the white race has hastened the
transfer of mission properties and leadership to national churches
led by national leaders in what might be called the fulfillment of the
indigenous ideal.

The period since 1938 has also brought a new age of ecumenicity
amid shifting economic, social, and political conditions. This has not
been a movement with a single focus and objective, however. Centripetal and centrifugal forces have pointed up the sharp cleavages
which exist among a divided Protestantism. The World Council of
Churches (officially launched in 1938), the majority representative
of the Protestant world, has been the most dynamic force with centripetal tendencies. While it has not effectively reached the grass
roots, its voice and power have been manifested in unmistakable
terms in the last decade. In the United States, at least, strong passive
and positive Protestant opposition to the World Council has arisen.
This resistance movement has found expression in agencies like the
National Association of Evangelicals, the Interdenominational Foreign Mission Association, and the American and International Councils of Christian Churches. In addition to these ecumenical bodies
one can find strong Protestant denominations like the Southern Baptist Convention (with a constituency in excess of nine million people) which have never aligned themselves with any ecumenical body.

Against this brief historical backdrop, the position, ministry, and
significance of faith missionary agencies will be traced from 1938
to the present. That these agencies have been affected by all of the
forces in motion during this time admits of no doubt. The consequences flowing from these forces may be measured in part and
certain conclusions drawn. Later history will, of course, modify any
conclusions arrived at by those who are a part of the period for
which the evaluations are made. What appraisal, then, can be made
of faith missions in the last quarter-century of cataclysmic change?

Finances

Faith missions have been so named because of their approach to
the problem of personnel and financial support. All of them are

theoretically nondenominational or interdenominational in that they welcome workers and support from diverse sources. In practice this theory is not carried out consistently. Thus a particular board may refuse to accept a confirmed Pentecostalist who believes that speaking in tongues is a necessary evidence of a conversion experience. Some boards with a Calvinistic emphasis refuse to accept stanch Arminians who believe that a man may fall from grace subsequent to his conversion experience. Often the decision is made on the basis of the individual and an appraisal of his willingness to maintain the doctrinal harmony of a station when he is likely to be in disagreement with other workers about certain doctrinal beliefs. But faith boards do not normally inquire into the doctrinal persuasions of those who support the work financially.

Faith missions have not altered their general nonsectarian approach in the past quarter of a century. However, misunderstandings have arisen from time to time about finances. The label "faith mission" has been thought by some to imply a better brand of Christian faith or at least one which connotes greater faith and trust in God. Faith mission leaders have been among the first to deny this charge, insisting that they have followed what they believe to be the leading of God for them without reference to the financial policies of any other groups or denominations.

The financial policies of faith missionary endeavor are usually twofold. First and foremost is the concept of sharing according to the income received. Thus the missionaries receive no guaranteed income or allowance. Each one is expected to look to God for the supply of his needs and not to the mission board.[3] In almost every instance particular amounts are designated as the allowance for an individual, or a married couple, with an additional amount for each child depending upon his age. Allowances do not exceed the stipulated amount although they may fall below it. Normally the allowance figures are qualified by the phrase "as the Lord provides."

The second facet of the financial arrangements of faith boards is the method by which money is raised. It varies slightly from board to board but ordinarily falls into one of two types. The first ap-

---

[3] An illustration of this general practice may be found in *The Principles and Practice of the Sudan Interior Mission* (Holland, Mich., 1958), p. 24. See also *Introducing the IFMA* (Brooklyn, N.Y., n.d.), pp. 1, 2.

proach is used by the China Inland Mission (now known as Overseas Missionary Fellowship), one of the oldest of the faith mission boards, whose example has been followed by many other agencies.[4] The China Inland Mission operates on what might be termed a "pure faith" basis.[5] Its members do not make their financial needs known nor do they solicit funds directly or indirectly. They pray in faith, expecting God to supply their financial and other needs. The second type of faith board is one which has modified one phase of the policy of the China Inland Mission. It does not solicit funds either but provides full public information about its financial needs. Most of the faith boards probably fall under the latter category. Boards of both types usually agree that the monies which come in represent God's appraisal of their real needs and mark the limit of the agency's responsibility to its missionaries. In the first instance when the mission board has discharged its obligation by prayer, and in the second instance when the agency has discharged its obligation by the presentation of its needs and prayer, the results are left in the hands of God. There has been no substantial change in the financial policies of faith boards in the past two decades.

Theology

Faith missions have always been identified as part of the fundamentalist wing of the Christian Church. At this point the mentality of fundamentalism is not being considered, only its theology. Faith agencies have been, and still are, highly conservative in their theological convictions. Anyone may read the doctrinal platform of almost all the faith mission boards without discovering major differences either in the convictions enunciated or in the items included. Indeed, there is not a faith mission board which does not have an explicit doctrinal platform to which cordial assent must be given by all of the personnel. Such theological statements are spelled out in some detail.

The doctrinal platforms generally include the following items: (1) the verbal or plenary inspiration of the Bible as the only infallible rule of faith and practice; (2) the Godhead—a trinity of the Father, Son, and Holy Spirit; (3) the person of Jesus Christ who is

---

[4] The China Inland Mission dates from 1865. The Woman's Union Missionary Society of America began in 1860.

[5] *Handbook of the China Inland Mission* (1959), pp. 10, 11.

true God, virgin born, sinless, resurrected from the dead in the same body, ascended into heaven and coming again; (4) the condition of man as lost and undone apart from regeneration through the New Birth; (5) the substitutionary or vicarious atonement of Jesus Christ whose blood propitiated God; (6) justification by faith alone; (7) the eternal life of the redeemed and eternal punishment of the lost; (8) the Church a spiritual body comprising the saved of all ages.[6]

Faith mission board theology has become more rather than less important during the last quarter of a century. The advent of Liberalism before World War I and the growth of Neo-orthodoxy after the decline of liberalism have caused faith missions to stress their theological orthodoxy as a bulwark against apostasy and as a touchstone by which the Christian public could measure their doctrinal integrity. This has become true even for incidental details not spelled out in doctrinal platforms. One might go so far as to say that there are two sets of standards for some boards: those which have been put down in writing and those which exist *de facto* rather than *de jure* but which have assumed the status of unwritten law. One illustration will suffice. Few, if any, faith boards have anything in their official statements about speaking in tongues. But a confirmed Pentecostalist would rarely, if ever, be accepted by the average faith board.

The intensified concern with basic theological tenets has been due, in part, to the deep-seated suspicion that the major denominations have departed from the historic faith of orthodoxy.[7] There is room for this suspicion once an agency has adopted any statement a departure from which is regarded as heresy. Faith boards do not look with disfavor on the historic creeds of the great denominations. Rather they argue that large numbers of key leaders within the denominations no longer accept these creeds or at best give lip service to what they do not really believe. Nor can it be denied that the major denominations allow wide latitude with respect to theological commitments, and little or no effort is made to disfellowship those who are not in accord with the historic statements of faith. This theological diversity has increased the suspicions of the faith boards,

[6] *IFMA News*, February, 1960, p. 2.
[7] See, for example, the brochure *Congress on World Missions* published by the IFMA. "Many who had that vision in 1910 have been overcome with apostasy and liberalism."

who contend that the large denominations have departed from their own standards.

Undoubtedly faith boards will continue to be suspicious of the large denominations and will continue to ignore them and their organizations. This does not imply that faith boards regard all of the members of these denominations as apostate or unconverted. In fact, a substantial proportion of faith mission support derives from fundamentalist believers who are dissatisfied with their own denomination and missionary program. They will not leave the denomination of their upbringing but they will not support the program of the denomination, choosing instead to channel missionary money to conservative agencies.

While acknowledging that there are many true believers in the great denominations, faith missions regard the denominations either with suspicion or look upon them as apostate for still another reason. Consciously or unconsciously they believe in and practice the concept of a pure church. By "pure" church they mean a church which has in its fellowship only those who have had a genuine conversion experience. The measuring rod of this experience is adherence to a creedal statement. The failure, therefore, to embrace such a statement of faith cordially is looked upon as *prima facie* evidence of unbelief or of an unregenerate state. For the churches not to root out such tares is to disobey the Biblical command to excommunicate those who are not converted. Faith boards apply their standards rigorously to their own personnel, and any significant deviation is just ground for dismissal from a particular board. It would be most difficult to find a single person in any of the faith boards who is not at least externally in accord with the doctrinal platform of his own board. There may be secret nonconformists among them, that is true, but once their presence becomes known their fate can be prophesied beyond a doubt. It may even be that rigid conformity has occasionally resulted in the dismissal of missionaries whose differences with their boards were more semantic than theological.

No evidence is available in the last quarter of a century to show that there has been any major shift in the theological base on which faith missions operate, or in their zeal to perpetuate their convictions, or in their feelings that fellowship with the great denominations represents compromise of vital convictions. Rightly or wrongly, this is the way they feel. Each theological tenet is immeasurably important, for the loss of a single distinctive precept is looked upon as the ruination of all. The continuing characteristic of faith boards is the unbending tenacity with which they cling to their own theological convictions. Nowhere is this attitude expressed more forcefully than in the statement

> In these days, when many are being "tossed to and fro and carried about with every wind of doctrine," the China Inland Mission Overseas Missionary Fellowship still remains unshaken in its adherence to the faith which was once for all delivered unto the saints. The directors and councils reaffirm their agreement with the strictly conservative and evangelical interpretation of the great doctrines of the Christian faith.[8]

Constituency

Behind every missionary agency there is a constituency comprising those who support the endeavor financially, who back it up by prayer, and from whose fellowship the board enlists its new recruits for overseas service. It is difficult to determine who the people are who support faith missions, how many of them there are, and how strong their influence is. But some tentative answers must be sought when considering faith missions for the past quarter-century.

Historically faith boards are of recent vintage. The majority of them have been in existence for fifty or sixty years. Many are not more than thirty years old. Contrasted with this pattern, the large denominations have operated for a much longer period of time. The Congregationalists, Methodists, Presbyterians, Episcopalians, and Baptists have mission boards well over a hundred years old. Their respective constituencies have been easily identified, for the distinctive denominational names have marked them off clearly. Each denomination has published annual statistics indicating how many church members each group had and how much money the people gave for local support, general benevolences, and foreign missions. But no such statistics exist by which faith agencies may be evaluated.

In order to appraise the constituency of the faith missions certain religious movements on the American scene must be understood. They are three in number. The first is the development of independ-

8 *Handbook of the China Inland Mission*, p. 5.

ent churches, the second the rise of the Bible school movement, and the third the development of antidenominational missionary spirit within denominational churches and among individuals.

The rise of the independent or Bible churches has been associated with changing theological viewpoints.[9] The movement has been characterized by a sturdy independence and a strong sense of individualism, without which it would never have succeeded. Theologically the major reason for the rise of independent churches was Modernism. Modernism had both negative and positive thrusts, but it was the negative one which aided most in the development of these churches. Modernism's denial of key theological doctrines led to schisms, withdrawals, and pioneer church planting. Among the doctrines Modernism denied were the plenary inspiration of the Bible, the virgin birth, the vicarious atonement, the physical resurrection of Christ from the dead, and in some instances the deity of Christ. These denials struck at what had always been regarded as the heart of the Christian faith.

The vigorous battle waged by optimistic liberals produced internal friction and strife within the denominations. Ministers unable to co-operate with colleagues who were theologically loose faced three possible choices. One was to remain silent but to preach faithfully their own conservative message in their local churches. The second was to seek to disfellowship those who no longer believed the church's doctrinal standards. When this proved, in general, to be unsuccessful these men became silent, withdrew, or were themselves ejected from the old-line denominations. The third choice was to leave the denomination immediately, and some did this.

Among those churches affiliated with congregational-type denominations three kinds of response were elicited as the battle progressed. First, large groups of churches defected, forming new church organizations. The General Association of Regular Baptist Churches is an example of this type of response. It included those churches which withdrew as a body from the Northern Baptist Convention (now the American Baptist Convention). The second response was to withdraw the local church from the national fellowship without joining any other organization. Thus the church became an independent entity in isolation. The third response was to remain within

---

[9] E.g., see *What Is the I.F.C.A.?* (Independent Fundamental Churches of America), a pamphlet on this subject.

the framework of the denomination but refuse to co-operate with its program or to support it financially.

Another effect of the advance of Modernism was the reaction it produced among the laity. Those with unbending theological convictions often withdrew from their churches in protest against what they believed to be apostasy. They either formed new churches, which led to the erection of new structures and the calling of independent ministers, or united with existing independent churches. Some remained within their own churches but ceased to be financially co-operative.

The rise of independent churches in America could not have continued without training centers for ministerial candidates. Thus the Bible institute movement and the development of Bible churches are interrelated. They supplement and complement each other; the one could hardly have existed without the other.

The Bible institute movement began with Dwight L. Moody, who founded what was to become the Moody Bible Institute but was originally a training school for lay workers. When its original perspective changed it became a post high school professional institution whose graduates served as missionaries or ministers. The number of Bible institutes increased rapidly so that ultimately there was hardly a major city without one. Their impact has been profound. Just as Modernism in the old-line denominations created a constituency for faith missions, so these Bible institutes became the training ground for their candidates and a major source for the supply of ministers. Graduates of the institutes often began store-front churches or opened up new works in unchurched areas or in areas where they competed with the established churches but offered a highly conservative theology with particular emphasis on personal separation from the world and from theological apostasy.

The Bible institute graduates also strengthened the faith missions in still another way. Some discovered that their training was inadequate when they preferred to work within the old-line denominations. They secured sufficient further training which enabled them to enter the ministries of the older denominations. Coming as they did out of conservative Bible institutes, they carried their theological views with them into the denominational churches. They tended to regard their denominations with suspicion, particularly with respect to missionary work. Consequently they sometimes supported faith

mission work and encouraged their people to do so either directly
or indirectly. Furthermore their young people were encouraged in
their suspicions of the denominations. Those who sought to become missionaries did not hesitate to find an outlet for their service
through the faith mission organizations rather than through their
own denominations. Or the young people obtained Bible institute
training, which was regarded as insufficient by the denominations.
Refusing to take further educational work they were forced to channel their enthusiasm through faith mission agencies. It was not un-
natural for a local congregation to support, through a faith mission
board, one of its own young people who had grown up in the
fellowship and who commanded the affections of the congregation.

The third movement which explains the developing constituency of faith mission agencies was one which led to the erosion
of missionary loyalty in local denominational churches and among
individuals within those churches. The development of an antidenominational missionary spirit was occasioned by theological considerations. Once again Modernism is a key to the problem. Churches
and individuals often concluded that they could not have confidence
in their own denominational missionary program. This attitude was
aided and abetted by some of the graduates of Bible institutes who
infiltrated some of the denominations. But it was also hastened by
those who had no connections whatever with Bible institutes. Dismayed by the encroachment of Liberal theology on the mission
fields, individuals and churches reacted in the only manner possible
so long as they retained their connections with their denominations.
Churches withheld their financial support of the denominational
program and gave instead to the work of nondenominational agencies; or the people diverted their individual giving to outside agencies.

Two examples of the above development will suffice. The Park
Street Church (Congregational) of Boston, Massachusetts, currently
has the largest foreign missionary budget of any Protestant church
in the United States. But its monies have been channeled largely
through faith missionary agencies. Its minister is not a Bible institute
graduate but a strong theological conservative. The Congregational
Christian denomination was widely penetrated by liberal theology
and its missionary outreach was influenced by that penetration. Con-
servative-minded missionary candidates either sidestepped the agency
or were refused by it and sought service elsewhere. This local church

wanted its monies spent for the propagation of a conservative theology. It turned to agencies created for precisely that purpose. And they were faith boards. The church has continued its connection with the Congregational Christian denomination (the merger between the Evangelical and Reformed Church and the Congregational Christian Churches may alter this connection) although its missionary offerings have gone to agencies other than those of the denomination.[10]

A second illustration is that of the Lake Avenue Congregational Church in Pasadena, California. Its former minister, who served the church more than thirty-five years, was a graduate of a Bible institute. Further study led to admission into the ministry of the Congregational Christian communion. Conservative theological convictions made it undesirable for the church to support a denominational missionary program which was infiltrated by Liberal theology. The net result was the same as that at Park Street Church. The bulk of its missionary giving went for the support of those who found service under the banner of faith missionary agencies.[11]

Faith missions, we may conclude, have a constituency which is made up of three groups of people. The first group includes independent churches removed from the orbit of the old-line denominations whether these churches now have nominal ties with other churches and denominations or not. The second group includes those churches within the old-line denominations whose allegiance to the missionary program of their respective groups has been diluted to the point of either nominal support or none at all. The third group is less definable, but nonetheless existent, and comprises individuals whose missionary loyalties bind them to faith mission boards either by direct financial support or through indirect support sent via their local churches in the form of specific designations in which the churches are simply agents for the transfer of funds earmarked for an individual or a faith mission board.

How many supporters faith missions have cannot be determined by any certain yardstick. But using a rough standard it is possible to guess approximately the number of people who make up the true constituency of the faith agencies. Assuming an annual income of

[10] Weekly church calendars of the Park Street Church, Boston, Massachusetts.
[11] Weekly church calendars of the Lake Avenue Congregational Church, Pasadena, California.

approximately twenty millions of dollars for faith missions and assuming that the $2.54 average annual per capita gift for missions reported by the Department of Stewardship of the National Council of Churches may be applied, one can conclude that the constituency of the faith boards is approximately eight million people.[12] This figure, of course, excludes agencies in the conservative tradition which are not normally included in the category of faith missions. The Southern Baptist Convention (1959 report), with more than nine million people, a foreign missionary force of almost thirteen hundred, and a missionary budget in excess of fifteen million dollars; the Christian and Missionary Alliance denomination, with more than seven hundred missionaries and a three-million-dollar-a-year budget for missions; and the Conservative Baptist Association of America would be among those agencies not included. Nor would denominational and nondenominational Pentecostal missionary endeavors be included.

Growth

The period from 1938 to 1960 has been one of extraordinary growth and financial enlargement for faith missions. This forward movement is all the more significant when reviewed in the light of the progress of denominational agencies. Just as the nineteenth century has been referred to as "The Great Century" for Protestant missions by Kenneth Scott Latourette, so may the past twenty-five years be referred to as the period of "Great Advance" for faith missions. Even more impressive than the advance itself is the fact that it has taken place in a time characterized by dislocation, the greatest of all world wars, the closing of missionary doors, the rise of a formidable nationalism, and the forward movement of world Communism. The reasons for this advance, reasons which appear illusory but which may be offered with some degree of risk, are of supreme interest to the missionary historian.

The statistics for personnel are not readily available for all of the faith missionary agencies for the year 1938. Indeed, a number of these boards were not in existence at that time or were so small as to be of no particular significance. Another reason for the difficulty

[12] *Statistics of Giving,* Joint Department of Stewardship and Benevolence, National Council of the Churches of Christ in the U.S.A. (New York, 1959).

in arriving at correct statistics is that some of the major North American agencies were at that time British societies with incidental North American connections. The movement of the missionary base from Europe to the United States altered this picture. Societies which were formerly British have become essentially American agencies both in the number of personnel and in financial support. A few exceptions may be noted, such as the China Inland Mission, which still employs more missionaries from sources outside North America, as do the Sudan United Mission and the Regions Beyond Missionary Union. Yet about 75 per cent of the faith missionaries now come from North America. The remainder are recruited from all of the other countries in the missionary sending world, most of them from English-speaking countries.

In gauging the growth of the faith missionary enterprise it is not possible to make the analysis by the use of total figures. It is easier to look for comparisons within individual agencies and to note the progress or decline of each.

Looking at the faith mission picture negatively, we note that the China Inland Mission is one of the few examples of decline.[13] In 1938 it had 1,387 missionaries in its employ. This figure comes from missions sources. The *Interpretative Statistical Survey of the World Mission of the Christian Church* (hereafter referred to as *ISS*) listed 1,326. The latest available figures showed a total of 699, of which 253 were North American, 348 were from other sources, and 98 were attached to the permanent home staff. This means that from 1938 to 1960 there was a shrinkage of approximately 700 missionaries. The explanation is quite simple. This mission commenced in 1865 to work exclusively in China. Its ministry was concentrated in inland China. When China turned to Communism, all foreign missionary endeavor was eliminated. Since its work was limited to China the board's activities came to a halt. After the doors to China were closed the CIM was reorganized. Some of its personnel retired from missionary work completely; some were redeployed into new fields.

---

[13] The figures which follow for the various faith boards have been collated from the following sources: Parker, *op. cit.; Occasional Bulletin* of the Missionary Research Library (New York), Vol. IX, No. 10; *Statistical Report* of the Interdenominational Foreign Mission Association of North America (New York, 1959); *Missionary Statistical Report* of the Evangelical Foreign Missions Association (Washington, 1959); and letters received from the various agencies in response to a request for information.

The board changed its name to the China Inland Mission Overseas Missionary Fellowship. It retained the old China Inland Mission name for purposes of identification, and with the hope that China would be reopened to missionary activity at a later date. It added Overseas Missionary Fellowship to its title to designate more properly the new thrust of its work. Considering the sudden and drastic end of its China ministry it is remarkable that the CIM survived, and the fact that it now employs almost 700 workers is a tribute to its recuperative powers. But this is the only example of a faith board which has suffered any serious shrinkage of forces, and the decline can be explained logically by circumstances beyond control.

On the positive side the picture is very bright. The Africa Inland Mission in 1938 was listed in *ISS* as a British agency. Its foreign staff numbered 143, but board correspondence supplied a higher figure of 220. Today the North American personnel alone number 422, personnel from other sources 64, and the permanent home staff 16. The growth factor for this agency is about 130 per cent since 1938. The annual income for the mission in 1938 was $163,000 in round figures. The IFMA 1959 report showed an income of approximately $1,200,000. The growth factor was over 700 per cent.

The Sudan Interior Mission, like the Africa Inland Mission, is listed in *ISS* as a British agency. The figure given there for personnel is 211. Board correspondence supplied a figure of 310. Undoubtedly the board figure included American as well as British personnel. The growth of this agency has been extremely rapid. The latest statistics showed a total strength of 1,285 divided as follows: 1,023 from North America, 201 from other sources, and 61 assigned to the permanent home staff. Using the 310 figure for 1938, the growth factor for the mission since 1938 is just over 400 per cent. The financial figures also indicate the progress made by this board. In 1938 the income was just short of $300,000. In the 1959 report of the IFMA the figure was about $2,875,000. The growth factor is over 950 per cent.

The Evangelical Alliance Mission (formerly known as the Scandinavian Alliance Mission) grew tremendously in the 1938–1960 period. The *ISS* reported a foreign staff of 95 for 1938; the correspondence with the board revealed the number as 163. The 1959 IFMA report listed 744 North American missionaries, 29 from other sources, and 16 on the permanent home staff. Latest correspondence supplied a total figure of 803. Using the 163 figure for 1938 and the 803 figure for the present, the personnel growth factor is approximately 500 per cent. In 1938 the income for the board was $143,-000. In the IFMA 1959 report it was approximately $2,600,000. This means that the financial growth factor was over 1,800 per cent.

The Wycliffe Bible Translators is one of the most interesting examples of the forward thrust of faith missions since 1938. This agency began work in 1933. It was incorporated in 1942. In 1938 there were 25 workers connected with the unincorporated association. The 1959 IFMA report revealed 762 North American workers, 70 from other sources, and a permanent home staff of 5. The personnel growth rate of this agency between 1938 and 1960 is 3,200 per cent. The income in 1938 was negligible and the informal organization without adequate bookkeeping records. Thus there are no certain financial figures available for 1938. But the income according to the 1959 report of the IFMA was close to $1,700,000. The financial growth factor cannot be computed without the 1938 figure but one can conclude that it is phenomenal.

Up to this point the statistics show that the rate of growth for the agencies cited was extraordinary. However, one cannot assume that the same rate of growth prevailed among all of the boards operating on a faith basis. But these other boards registered impressive, if not equally dramatic, gains in the same period. While it is not possible to trace the experience of all faith boards, a few further illustrations will suffice.

The Orinoco River Mission had 21 persons on its staff in 1938. The 1959 IFMA report showed 55 foreign staff members and one on the permanent home staff. The growth factor is over 250 per cent. The 1938 income for eight months was $10,000. The IFMA report for 1959 showed $135,000. The growth rate is around 900 per cent. The Bolivian Indian Mission showed 53 workers in the *ISS* 1938 report. The 1959 IFMA report showed a total of 74. The growth rate is less than 50 per cent. Income rose from $18,000 in 1938 to $173,000 in the IFMA report. The growth rate is approximately 950 per cent.

The Belgian Gospel Mission had 12 staff members in 1938, 33 in 1959. Income rose from $33,000 in 1938 (of which $26,000 came from America) to $155,000 in the 1959 report (of which $61,000 came from America). The rate of growth is appreciable. The Central

American Mission rose in number of workers from 64 to 181 in the same period. The 1959 report of IFMA showed an annual income of $532,000. The figure for 1938 is not available. The Regions Beyond Missionary Union grew from 71 members in 1938 to 163 in 1959. The South American Indian Mission personnel figure rose from 47 to 99; income rose from $29,000 to $290,000. Personnel of the World-wide Evangelization Crusade rose from 117 in 1938 to 390 in 1959. The Oriental Missionary Society went from 36 to 130 in the same period. Almost without exception the story is the same: substantial growth of the faith missionary agencies from 1938 to 1960.

One of the features of faith mission development has been the inauguration of new agencies since 1938. Among them may be listed New Tribes Mission (388 members); Far East Broadcasting Company (15); European Evangelistic Crusade, Inc. (109 in 1956); Brazil Gospel Fellowship Mission (25 in 1956); Far Eastern Gospel Crusade (147); Greater Europe Mission (66); Missionary Aviation Fellowship (55); and Soldiers and Gospel Mission of South America (40). In a later discussion when we evaluate the new methods developed and used by faith missions for the past quarter of a century reference will be made again to some of these agencies which have been brought into being to meet changing circumstances in response to the challenge of a new age.

There is one method by which it is possible to test the thesis that the period from 1938 to 1960 has been one of unprecedented growth for faith missions. That method is to analyze the growth factor for denominational missions during the same period. From the results of such a survey it may be possible to come to some conclusions about the growth of missions in general and of faith missions in particular.

Again it would be well to look at the negative side first. From this approach it becomes obvious that a number of the old-line denominations suffered considerable shrinkage in missionary personnel while the faith boards were experiencing enormous growth. The United Presbyterian Church in the U.S.A., a combination of the Presbyterian Church U.S.A. and the United Presbyterian Church, employed approximately 1,300 missionaries (not including home missionaries) in 1958. The figure for the combined churches in 1938 was approximately 1,700—a shrinkage of about 400 people. The Congregational Christian Churches (American Board of Commissioners for Foreign Missions) supported about 500 missionaries in 1938. By 1958 this figure had sunk to about 350. The American Baptist Convention employed 632 missionaries in 1938, but its force was reduced to 407 in 1958.

On the positive side, many of the denominational boards enjoyed some increase in personnel but it was a modest one in most instances. The Presbyterian Church U.S. enjoyed a 25 per cent increase, from 402 to 504. The Protestant Episcopal Church (Episcopalian) increased less than 10 per cent, from 376 to 395. The Evangelical and Reformed Church went from 116 to 143, an increase of less than 30 per cent. The Methodist Church's missionary force increased from 1,346 to 1,453, or less than 10 per cent. The Southern Baptist Convention registered a substantial increase, its roster of foreign missionaries rising from 405 to 1,293, or more than 300 per cent. The Seventh Day Adventists also registered a substantial increase, the number rising from 1,240 to 2,000, or about 70 per cent.

Some of the Lutheran bodies registered gains. The Evangelical Lutherans went from 141 to 315, a gain of more than 120 per cent. The United Lutheran Church went from 163 to 294, a gain of more than 80 per cent. The United Church Missionary Society grew from 173 to 242, an increase of about 40 per cent. The Assemblies of God jumped from 230 to 676, a sharp increase of almost 300 per cent.

When eleven of the key denominations connected with the Division of Foreign Missions of the National Council of the Churches of Christ in America are lumped together, they employed about 7,400 of the approximately 11,000 missionaries listed in the statistical figures for 1958 printed in the Missionary Research Library report. These same agencies employed about 6,800 missionaries in 1938, which means there was an increase of 600 in personnel. But the Seventh Day Adventists accounted for 760 of those listed in the 1958 figure of 7,400, or more than the total increase. Thus if the Adventists are left out there was a decrease rather than an increase.

One other facet of the statistical problem has to do with the combined figures for all of the faith boards when contrasted with the figures for denominational agencies. The Missionary Research Library report of 1958 listed about 11,000 missionaries for the denominations connected with the Department of Foreign Missions. It listed about 6,000 for the faith boards affiliated with the IFMA (this figure, however, is not correct because some of the statistics included, while others excluded, missionaries coming from sources outside of North America; e.g., the Sudan Interior Mission statistics excluded missionaries from other sources whereas the Africa Inland Mission statistics included missionaries from all sources). Accepting the 6,000 figure as realistic (since the 1959 report of IFMA puts total personnel at 8,000, of which at least 6,000 are from North American sources), we must add the number of missionaries from nondenominational independent boards—in round figures approximately 1,000. To this must be added those faith agencies related to the EFMA (missionary arm of the National Association of Evangelicals). Of the more than 5,100 staff members reported in the EFMA report of 1959, approximately 1,200 were attached to faith mission boards. This means that one can reasonably assume that a total of 8,200 staff members for North American faith boards is consistent with the statistical information. Therefore approximately one-third of the North American missionary personnel (8,200 out of about 25,000) derived from faith sources.

It has become plain, then, that the faith missions have experienced a dramatic increase in numbers while the denominations (with the exception of some like the Southern Baptist Convention, the Assemblies of God, and the Seventh Day Adventists) have remained static or have experienced either a slight increase or a decrease. What is the explanation for the phenomenon and what general conclusions may be drawn?

One cannot assume too quickly that the great denominations have ceased to be missionary-minded. Nor can one suppose that the failure to grow is solely the result of the inroads of Liberalism. These are possibilities and to some extent both of them have exerted an influence. But there are two other factors which may have a real bearing on the issues. The first is the factor of maturity. In the growth of organizations there seem to be limits beyond which pronounced growth is halted. Organizations, like individuals, mature and in maturing tend to become static. The faith boards are younger and more likely to be influenced by the normal laws of growth. The denominational boards may have reached their apex and will either maintain the level to which they have grown or perhaps decline slightly. This, of course, leaves out the possibility of some genuine missionary reawakening, which could conceivably change the course once again.

The second factor is the deployment of personnel. Some of the old-line denominations have increased their incomes considerably without increasing their foreign staffs. In some instances this has been part of a strategy to subsidize the national churches and to support national rather than foreign personnel.[14] Faith boards rarely use North American money for the support of national personnel, whereas denominational boards do so increasingly. Hence one cannot assume that the difference in personnel per se is the sole basis on which to determine whether a missionary program has gone forward. It is possible that a new stage in the strategy of missions whereby North American money supports national workers may do more in the long run than the sending of foreign workers without the use of North American money for the support of foreign personnel. Time alone will tell.

With these qualifications in mind the affirmative reasons for the growth of faith missions may be adduced. It is impossible to evaluate the proportionate worth of each reason for growth, nor should it be supposed that the order in which each is considered is an index of priority. One can confidently affirm, however, that all of them together offer an explanation for the great advance of faith missions in the past quarter of a century.

The theology of the faith mission boards is one explanation for their unprecedented growth. But this reason cannot be isolated from the normal processes of growth and the maturing of faith organizations. Since the theology of faith missions has not changed substantially across the years one may well ask why they have experienced their great growth in the past quarter of a century and not earlier. Since faith missions commenced one hundred years ago and many of the boards which at present have the largest number of missionaries have been in existence for sixty years, why did they grow so slowly in the years before 1938? Possibly the cause was not theology alone, for had it been, the agencies should have grown more substantially in earlier years. But there may have been a time lag looking

---

[14] A case in point is the United Presbyterian Church, U.S.A., which resulted from the union of the United Presbyterian Church and the Presbyterian Church U.S.A. In 1938 the two agencies expended $3,141,000. They supported 1,698 missionaries. In the 1958 report the income for foreign missions was in excess of $10,600,000. There were only 1,293 missionaries in the combined agencies. At the same time the Sudan Interior Mission was supporting almost 1,300 missionaries with less than $3,000,000.

to the moment when the theologically conservative forces had regrouped and were strong enough to spearhead a new and dynamic forward movement in missions.

There is one historical circumstance which should not be overlooked. The period between 1925 and 1935 has been called "The American Religious Depression" by Robert Handy. He states that "one sensitive indicator of a religion's vitality is its missionary program." This missionary enthusiasm and conviction waned between 1925 and 1935. In 1920, some 2,700 students presented themselves for overseas service. In 1928 the number had dwindled to 252.[15] The decline may not be attributed to the economic depression alone since the trend was clearly apparent before the debacle of 1929. Postwar spiritual apathy was undoubtedly one of the factors to be considered, but the tremendous growth of faith missions since the Second World War makes this thesis questionable. This leaves as one of the causes changing theological convictions, for Liberalism has never been noted for its missionary zeal. The inroads of scientism, behaviorism, and humanism may well have been the consequence of an uncertain theological note which carried no impelling conviction of the Gospel imperative for those without Christ.

What is there about the theology of faith boards which encourages missions? Undoubtedly it is the conviction that (1) all men are lost and will be eternally separated from God apart from salvation in Jesus Christ; (2) all men have a probationary period in this life without the possibility of a second chance; (3) there is no universal salvation in any guise; (4) if the heathen are to be saved they must hear of Jesus Christ, who alone can bring eternal life; (5) the time is short and those who never hear will soon perish in sin; (6) Jesus Christ is coming soon and obedience requires that the world be evangelized (not Christianized) before his Second Advent. This theology provides a tremendous thrust for missions, but it is still related to historical patterns and circumstances. Thus, before 1938, the growth of faith boards would not have occurred without the theological presuppositions, but the presuppositions were still subject to the laws of growth.

There is at least one notable exception to this generalization. This is the Wycliffe Bible Translators, begun in 1933. By 1959 it had over

[15] Robert T. Handy, "The American Religious Depression," *Church History*, Vol. 29 (March, 1960), pp. 4–6.

800 workers and an income close to $1,700,000. It had a short infancy, becoming an adult with extraordinary speed. This progress may be accounted for in several ways. First, the organization commenced at a time when there was great growth for faith missions in general. It came into the kingdom at the proper time and in a favorable climate. Secondly, it had for its rationale a compelling thesis which attracted to it dedicated hearts and enthusiastic financial support. Having concern for those tribes with no portion of the Word of God, it became exclusively a pioneering agency for translating the Word of God into the languages of these unreached people. Moreover, World War II brought many soldiers into intimate contact with isolated tribes all over the globe. It gave them a foretaste of what missionary work would be like. Psychological barriers were broken down. Hundreds of these young men and women turned their guns into pruning hooks and ploughshares with the advent of peace. They sensed the spiritual needs of the nations and hastened to meet them. But they had seen the fruits of foreign missions and were sold on the results. Neither the old-line denominations nor the faith boards were prepared for a gigantic forward movement designed to bring the Word of God to these hundreds of unreached tribes. Hence the creation of an agency which had this specific objective resulted in an amazing forward movement. Had the existing agencies, denominational and faith, caught the vision of Wycliffe it is safe to predict that similar results would have obtained.

The decline of Liberalism, as we have seen, must be adjudged a reason for the expansion of faith missions. Subsequent to World War I Liberalism looked for the advent of a millennium. The Locarno and Paris Peace pacts promised that there would be war no more; it had been abolished as an instrument of national policy forever. But the European and American depressions, followed by the rise of dictatorships in Europe, changed all this. The advent of Hitler and Mussolini and the consequent darkness produced by a second world war debunked the optimism of Liberalism. In the process, Neo-orthodoxy lifted its head and conservative theology was strengthened. Everywhere the movement was away from Liberalism toward a more conservative theology. There was a more mature approach to Biblical criticism and a return to a theology based on the Bible itself. During this period, then, faith missions drew to themselves a constituency. Many of the laity who had forsaken their denominations for Bible churches and other independent associations never returned. They strengthened the arms of faith missions and remained committed to the program. But this too must be understood within the context of the Bible institute movement.

The Bible institutes of America have been the seedbed out of which the faith boards have obtained personnel. They have also been the source from which thousands of pastors have come to minister to independent churches all over the land. Even as late as ten years ago large numbers of churches affiliated with the American Baptist Convention were pastored by men whose training had been secured in Bible institutes. In the past quarter of a century the Bible institute movement reached maturity.[16] This was true in two senses. First, Bible institute graduates were widely spread over America and the independent churches were firmly established and financially able. Second, the institutes reached their optimum growth at the same time. Moreover, during this same period a new maturity developed within the movement. Concerned with academic standards as never before, they entered a period of self-examination which produced two changes. They created an accrediting agency designed to establish standards, provide academic respectability, and fill in the gap created by the refusal of liberal arts college accrediting associations to admit Bible colleges into accredited membership. And, with a few notable exceptions like the Moody Bible Institute, they extended the normal three-year course to four years and added a nucleus of liberal arts courses in order to offer a bachelor of arts program with a Bible major. Often the names of the institutions were changed to reflect this new approach. The Providence Bible Institute became the Providence-Barrington Bible College; the Bible Institute of Los Angeles named one branch of its multiform organization Biola Bible College. Later it added its own theological seminary (Talbot Seminary). The Azusa Bible Institute ultimately became Azusa College, going so far as to drop the word "Bible" from its name. This, then, was the era in which the Bible institute movement matured. And its maturity, growth, and stability occurred during the same period that faith missions matured. There is an interlocking aspect to this phenomenon which cannot be overlooked. Each aided the other.

Another explanation for the growth of the faith boards turns on

[16] There is a need for a standard work on the history of the Bible institute and college movement.

the use of new media by which the Gospel can be made known to men. New ideas were developed and used by existing agencies or by the newly created ones. It so happened that denominational boards were already deeply committed to a program involving a thrust which the faith agencies rejected in principle; this involvement kept the denominations from employing new media too quickly for spreading the Gospel. The two are interrelated.

Faith boards have been traditionally cold to the social aspects of the Gospel. Thus they have always been less interested in agriculture, medicine for healing without direct and aggressive evangelism, certain forms of education, etc. Instead they have stressed the evangelistic side of the Gospel, endeavoring to reach individuals who needed to be saved from eternal death.[17] Any reading of faith mission literature will disclose that personal salvation has been the primary emphasis. The stories speak of individuals who have come to a place of personal commitment to Jesus Christ or who through secondary means of medicine and the like have been reached with the saving message of the Gospel. A reading of denominational materials will reveal a different accent.[18] Further evidence may be seen in the promotional materials of denominational and faith agencies. Faith boards reach the hearts of their constituency by their appeal for the salvation of individual souls; denominational promotion stresses the program, the humanitarian, the less personal. When new media developed which made possible more direct access to individuals with the Gospel it was the faith agencies that responded to the challenge, or individuals who began new faith ventures for that purpose. Both responses were characteristic, as the evidences show.

Translation work is one of the evangelistic methods in question. In the nineteenth century it was essential to bring the Word of God to people in their own languages. This was done for the Chinese, Koreans, Japanese, Burmese, etc. But once the major language groups had been given the Bible in their national tongues the denominational mission boards were satisfied to limit their service to these groups.

---

[17] A survey of the largest faith mission, the Sudan Interior Mission, reveals that 70 per cent of the staff are in the evangelistic category; 12 per cent are in teaching situations; 18 per cent include physicians, dentists, and nurses; and there are a few pharmacists, laboratory technicians, and airplane pilots.

[18] A survey of any issue of the *Sudan Witness, The Millions,* or *Inland Africa* over against *Overseas News, Missions, World Outlook, Presbyterian Life,* or *Outreach* will lead to this conclusion.

In fact, most of them had more than they could do in the lands and for the peoples to whom they were committed. As the faith boards developed they followed a similar pattern of translating the Bible into the language of the particular peoples they were seeking to touch. Not until the Wycliffe Translators came into being was a really new thrust developed. Realizing that there were still millions of people without the Word of God in their own tongues this pioneer agency reached out to the unreached. Neither the major denominational mission boards nor the faith boards caught this vision. A new faith agency was required to fill the gap. The rapid growth of the Wycliffe Bible Translators is evidence of the need and of the willingness of Christian people to back such a program. It is also interesting to observe that an international leader in the American Bible Society today (Eugene Nida) sprang out of this context. Furthermore, Wycliffe has produced a substantial number of linguistic experts who are making a tremendous contribution in this field of endeavor.[19] But of still greater significance is the contribution which Wycliffe has made to denominational and faith missions by the creation of schools of linguistics for prospective missionaries. At these summer institutes they teach linguistics, phonetics, phonemics, etc. Two major values have accrued. First, missionaries going to a field where the Bible has been translated are helped in learning the language of their people much faster and better. Second, those who are going to unreached tribes to do translation work are given the basic principles by which they can learn unwritten languages, create alphabets, translate the Scriptures, and teach the people to read in their own newly written languages.[20]

A second medium which has been exploited in depth by faith missions is radio. Again denominational boards have been slow to use this modern method of communication. Perhaps the best known of all the agencies using the radio for communicating the Gospel is the World Radio Missionary Fellowship, which has flourished under the leadership of Clarence W. Jones. This board operates the Voice of the Andes, HCJB, in Quito, Ecuador, and publishes its own periodical, *The Call of the Andes*. The agency was organized in 1931. By

---

[19] Nida, Pike, Cowan, Pittman, and Townsend are only a few of the men who have made such a contribution.

[20] The Wycliffe Bible Translators and the Summer Institute of Linguistics of the University of Oklahoma are two separate legal entities. They interlock in the sense that ultimate control is vested in the same people.

1938 its income was slightly over $20,000. Two married couples and their children comprised the staff. By 1959 there were 140 staff members, of whom 120 came from North America, 4 came from other sources, and 16 were on the permanent home staff. The income had increased to almost $700,000.

The Far East Broadcasting Company, Inc., was organized in 1945. It mushroomed quickly. Transmitters are maintained in Manila and time is purchased for broadcasting from transmitters in Taiwan. It reaches all of the Far East with its coverage. Trans World Radio, known as the Voice of Tangier, was incorporated in 1952, under the name International Evangelism, Inc. It operated out of Tangier until December of 1959. At that time the Moroccan government halted all nongovernmental broadcasting and nationalized radio communications. Fortuitous circumstances enabled the mission agency to relocate in Monte Carlo, Monaco, and to begin the installation of a 100,000-watt transmitter. This brought Russia, one of the chief targets of the board, 1,000 miles closer. By May of 1960 the station was expected to commence broadcasting, at which time it was to cover Europe using all of the major languages, with African and Asian languages to be added later.[21]

Some of the faith mission boards have added radio to their existing programs. The Sudan Interior Mission operates ELWA in West Africa. The Latin America Mission has a radio station in its Central American area. From all of this it may be concluded that faith missionary agencies have gone into radio work on a large scale covering vast portions of the world through this medium. The denominations have not risen to the challenge of this method as the faith boards have.

Another area in which faith missions have reached out is aviation. Actually the largest work is being performed by a new faith agency called the Missionary Aviation Fellowship, which exists as a service organization to missionaries of denominational and faith boards.[22] The 1959 IFMA report listed this agency as having 40 North Americans in the field and 6 on the permanent home staff. The income was in excess of $200,000. The board was organized in 1944 and incorpo-

---

[21] *Voice of Tangier* (newsletter issued periodically; not all dated); *It Happened in Monaco* (pamphlet).
[22] *What Is the Missionary Aviation Fellowship?* (pamphlet); *Missionary Aviation*, October–Novembmer, 1959.

rated in 1945 so it is rather young. The Missionary Aviation Fellowship is the only North American agency whose exclusive ministry
is limited to supplying transportation as a service agency. But other
faith mission boards have used the airplane in connection with their
activities. Two stand out. One is the Sudan Interior Mission (five
pilots) and the other the Wycliffe Bible Translators (through another corporation known as Jungle Aviation and Radio Service—
JAARS). Both have effectively joined aviation to missionary endeavor as an instrument for the furtherance of their work. The use
of the airplane as a tool for evangelism has not been exploited by
denominational missions. It was left for the faith boards to develop
and work out.

Still another new missionary method has been promoted by Joy
Ridderhof, the founder of Gospel Recordings, Inc. This organization dates from 1939. A woman missionary who had been invalided
home permanently provided the leadership. Seeking in some way to
serve God despite her physical difficulties she conceived of using
recordings to reach people with the Gospel. She realized that multi-
tudes of people were unable to read or had no written language. But
they could and would listen to records which would provide a stop-
gap evangelistic medium until their languages were reduced to writing or until they learned to read. In the 20 years since the idea was
first employed Gospel Recordings has sent out almost 2,500,000 records to 150 countries in 2,003 languages.[23] This has involved the
enormous labor of visiting each tribe to find someone who was lin-
guistically equipped to make a tape recording in the language of
that group of people. The tapes were processed, plates made, and
platters pressed. Gospel Recordings has been a service agency providing records for faith and denominational missionaries. No other
faith board or denominational agency has entered into this type of
ministry in any competitive sense. Once again faith missions indicated
their genius for the use of new methods and their willingness to venture upon untried pathways because of their urgent desire to get the
message of the Gospel to those who have never heard it.

One additional medium remains to be mentioned and that is the
publication of literature in a world which has become increasingly
literate. Here again faith missions have entered the field and have

[23] *Annual Report for 1959*, Gospel Recordings Incorporated (Los Angeles,
1960).

secured a commanding lead over denominational agencies. The motivations for literature distribution was the knowledge that the printed page in a more literate world had already shown itself to be a worthy medium of communication. Communism has used it everywhere successfully. Cults such as Jehovah's Witnesses, Unity, and others have used the printed page to increase their numbers dramatically.

The publication attainments may be broken down into several categories. First there is the setting up of overseas printing presses, from which have come thousands and thousands of books, booklets, pamphlets, magazines, and papers. Examples include large printing establishments like the Niger Press in Nigeria, the Africa Inland Mission press in Kijabe, the Christian Witness Press in Hong Kong, the printing ministry of the Evangelical Alliance Mission in Japan, and scores of small but effective presses from Beirut to Manila.

Faith missions have also entered the tabloid paper business. Literally hundreds of thousands of copies of inexpensive tabloid papers and magazines are sold every month. The Sudan Interior Mission produces *The African Challenge*. Others, like *The Caribbean Challenge*, *Dengta*, and *Kiran*, are coming forth from the presses at an increasing rate. The fact that faith missions employ this medium, in view of their intense concern for individual salvation, indicates their conviction that it is an effective means to an evangelistic end. On the other hand, it connotes an imperceptible, but nevertheless certain, inroad into their governing philosophy that everything must be evangelistically centered. Since these magazines and tabloids enter more fully into the totality of life and do not limit themselves to spiritual matters alone, the implication is that circumstances are forcing faith missions to become involved in the life of their people in its totality.

One might mention, in incidental fashion, still another medium, which is small now but may very well develop. This is the use of Bible correspondence courses, begun under faith mission auspices through the genius of the Hillis family. The "Light of Life" Bible course has been used widely and with excellent results. At least one denominational group has exploited this area. The Brethren have developed the Emmaus courses, which have also enjoyed a good response.

One more accomplishment of faith missions (and in combination with denominational representatives) also pertains to literature. In 1953 Evangelical Literature Overseas was incorporated. Its vision was not to become a missionary sending organization but to be a service fellowship assisting evangelical agencies, both faith and denominational, in providing literature to a literate world which is being subjected to mountains of words from Communist sources. The vision looked toward the goal of fellowship and co-operation with those working in given language areas. The stated objectives were "to coordinate the total literature program, embracing writing, translation, production, distribution and training of personnel."[24] On the board of directors are men from key faith boards as well as Kenneth Taylor, the director of the Moody Press, and H. Wilbert Norton, president of Trinity Seminary and Trinity College of the Evangelical Free Church. On its international council are Eugene Nida of the American Bible Society and Raymond Buker, professor of missions at the Conservative Baptist Theological Seminary in Denver. A representative from EFMA, Clyde Taylor, is also listed. The usual faith missions representatives comprise the remainder of the international council. ELO has a conservative statement of faith which is prominently displayed. ELO is the "recognized literature arm of EFMA . . . and IFMA . . . but has also worked with many other missions and literature organizations."[25] Eight annual conferences have been held and much has been accomplished by this agency. It does not publish or distribute literature but it does give technical assistance and help for those who do. It provides a library of available manuscripts on pertinent subjects and supplies funds to assist in publication. Thus ELO is representative of the vision and drive of faith missions to employ every possible means to get the Gospel to those who so desperately need it.

The past quarter of a century, then, has been a period of extraordinary growth for faith missions. The reasons for this growth have been delineated. They are external reasons which do not take into account the mysterious providence of God. Providence has been at work and always is at work. No one can deny this. However, any effort to evaluate this factor is impossible. We can suppose the continued interest of God in the fulfillment of the Great Commission, which faith mission boards take very seriously. And we can conclude

[24] *Capturing Men with Books,* Evangelical Literature Overseas (Wheaton, Ill., n.d.), p. 3.
[25] *Helping Place the Printed Page in Hungry Hands,* Evangelical Literature Overseas (Wheaton, Ill., n.d.). Pamphlet.

that the role faith missions have played in the plan of God in the last twenty-five years is somehow related to God's will that every nation and tribe and kindred and people hear the good news of salvation in Jesus Christ. But God is working, and has been working, through other than faith agencies. We shall therefore review the relationships of faith missions to the ecumenical movements of the present day. By this is meant the relationships which exist among faith agencies themselves, and the general relationship of all the faith agencies to the denominations of our day.

Faith Missions and the Church

Faith mission boards have been traditionally independent in that each is a separate legal entity responsible only to a self-perpetuating board of trustees. They have gone their own ways for many years and have had few or no intimate contacts with other mission boards or denominations. Nor have they given much thought to their relationship to the whole Church of Jesus Christ. This state of splendid isolation has been modified somewhat in recent decades in the relationships among faith boards and in some instances to organizations which have included other groups besides the faith mission boards themselves. At the moment our interest is in the relationships between agencies of like form and not with relationships in the larger ecumenical framework of the National and World Councils of Churches.

There are a number of nondenominational, independent faith missionary agencies unrelated to any ecumenical group. Some are not interested in any relationship; others have not been accepted by the larger fellowships. The total number of unaffiliated agencies may be somewhere in the neighborhood of forty and they employ fewer than a thousand missionaries. The largest and undoubtedly the best-known agency in this category is the New Tribes Mission, which accounts for more than one-third of the missionaries and one-quarter of the amount of money raised by them all. One agency is deliberately excluded from our account at this point for it will be considered later in another connection. This is the Wycliffe Bible Translators, formerly affiliated with the IFMA but now withdrawn from that association.

The ecumenical fellowship of faith boards is to be found within three associations. The first, the largest, and the most important is the Interdenominational Foreign Mission Association (IFMA). Most of the large faith boards are members of IFMA and they employ more missionaries than any other group or total of groups. The second ecumenical fellowship is the Evangelical Foreign Missions Association (EFMA), which is an agency of the National Association of Evangelicals. EFMA includes in its membership conservative denominational boards as well as conservative faith missionary agencies. Theologically both groups are identical except for two major distinctions. The IFMA has no "tongues" or "pentecostal" groups in its fellowship and generally looks with disfavor upon this emphasis. The EFMA and the National Association of Evangelicals include within their fellowship Christians of this persuasion. The second distinction is that the EFMA includes conservative denominations within its orbit whereas the IFMA has no denomination, large or small, in its fellowship. The EFMA thus is a hybrid of denominations and independent organizations linked together in a loose way for fellowship and for the accomplishment of tasks which can be done better in a co-operative rather than in an independent framework.

The third ecumenical organization is the Associated Mission Agencies of the International Council of Christian Churches. This agency represents the extreme right wing of American Fundamentalism. About 85 per cent of the missionary personnel connected with this group are employed by the two missionary boards belonging to the General Association of Regular Baptist Churches. More than 80 per cent of the monies collected are received by the same two agencies. The AMICCC does not associate with any of the other two ecumenical groups and is inordinately critical in its attitudes. This critical spirit is reserved particularly for the NAE and its agencies which it considers competitive and accuses of compromise. The same hostility is not outwardly as apparent toward the IFMA as toward the NAE and the EFMA.

The IFMA was organized in 1917 as a "fellowship of missions without denominational affiliation. . . ."[26] It brought together a number of mission boards whose theological commitments were generally similar and who were willing to commit themselves to a creedal test for fellowship. The IFMA doctrinal statement is ap-

[26] *IFMA News*, January, 1960, p. 2.

proximately the same as that of the average faith board. In the membership of the IFMA are 41 boards with more than 7,000 missionaries. These figures take into account the withdrawal of the Wycliffe Bible Translators.

In one sense the IFMA is more than an association of people of like mind. It has become, in effect, an accrediting agency for faith mission boards. Statements from IFMA publications make this quite clear. "Membership is an indication that societies have met the stringent regulations of the Association and are worthy of the prayers and support of God's people."[27] By implication it may be assumed that those who do not meet the stringent regulations are not worthy of the support of God's people. Undoubtedly the accrediting aspect of IFMA's ministry has resulted from unfortunate experience. Not all agencies denominated "faith missions" have been worthy of anyone's support. Since it is possible for any individual to incorporate and for anyone to start a faith board, unethical promoters with ulterior motives have mulcted a gullible Christian public by appealing for funds which have been used for personal gain. It should be noted that there is less danger of the misuse of funds in denominational missions because their programs proceed from a defined constituency to which the missionary agency is responsible. But even here there have been defalcations, such as the Southern Baptist Convention experienced some years ago.

A recent internal difficulty in the IFMA reveals evidences of tension normal to the operation of any agency. It involved the operational policies of the Wycliffe Bible Translators in its relationship to the IFMA. Apparently the prolonged discussions of the problems did not result in their satisfactory resolution because the Wycliffe Bible Translators resigned from IFMA and its resignation was accepted. This was done by mutual consent. Wycliffe submitted an extract from its own mission minutes to the IFMA: "Whereas, it has been increasingly apparent that some of our God-given methods are the cause of misunderstanding with some of the Board of the IFMA we of the Board of the Wycliffe Bible Translators, Inc. hereby tender resignation of our organization from the IFMA to become effective February 1, 1960. This action is taken after considerable heartsearching and prayer. Carried."[28]

[27] *Ibid.*
[28] *Ibid.*, February, 1960, p. 4.

Under date of January 7, 1960, the IFMA replied to the memorandum as follows: "The IFMA Official Board acknowledges the resignation of Wycliffe Bible Translators effective February 1, 1960, and regrets the circumstances involving differences of policy and practice which necessitated this action. We would express appreciation for Wycliffe Bible Translators' Christian fellowship and services to Member Missions through the years and assure them of our prayers."[29]

Since all of the facts are not available it is impossible to render a true historical judgment of this late development in the IFMA. The specific problem which brought about the resignation of Wycliffe seems to have been too close collaboration with Roman Catholics in Wycliffe's work in various parts of the world. This included providing occasional plane transportation for Roman priests and nuns. It also involved Wycliffe's procurement of jungle aircraft with the consent of certain South American governments (Roman Catholic) and the use of aircraft in the service of government officials (the organization is known as the Jungle Aviation and Radio Service —JAARS—and is separately incorporated).[30] Evidently these actions by the Wycliffe Bible Translators were regarded as contrary either to the letter or to the spirit of the "stringent regulations of the Association." There are no available statements outlining the "stringent regulations" which govern IFMA-affiliated mission boards. Whether they are written or unwritten, they seem to have the effect of law. The Wycliffe Bible Translators had to submit to the IFMA's request to change policies long in effect or to resign. The resignation can only be interpreted as a refusal to change policies. Faced with abandoning those policies or resigning from IFMA it chose the latter course of action. One cannot say with finality whether the IFMA would have disfellowshipped the Wycliffe Bible Translators had the latter insisted upon maintaining its own principles without resigning voluntarily from the IFMA. One must suppose that the organization would have been ejected. Evidently the differences of opinion were not resolved, but the separation was effected without scandal or un-Christian charges and countercharges.

The Wycliffe Bible Translators has been asked whether its with-

29 *Ibid.*
30 *Work Paper as a Basis for Discussion*, Wycliffe Bible Translators, October, 1959, *passim*,

drawal will cause it to align itself with the EFMA arm of the National Association of Evangelicals. That door is wide open. At the moment it appears as though the second largest faith mission in North America will remain independent of all ecumenical commitments. The withdrawal of Wycliffe reduces the number of missionaries affiliated with IFMA by more than 10 per cent but IFMA remains the largest single agency for ecumenically related faith boards.[31]

The second substantial ecumenical agency for faith missions is the EFMA. As previously stated, this group includes both theologically conservative denominations which have never joined the National Council of Churches and faith boards. Among the denominations are the Assemblies of God, the Nazarene Church, the Evangelical Free Church, the Christian and Missionary Alliance, and the International Church of the Foursquare Gospel. Among the nondenominational missionary agencies are Worldwide Evangelization Crusade, Orient Crusades, Inter-Varsity Christian Fellowship, the Oriental Missionary Society, Youth for Christ International, and the International Child Evangelism Fellowship.

The EFMA doctrinal platform (that of NAE, the parent organization) is approximately the same as that of the IFMA. EFMA is more of a service organization and less of an accrediting agency. Its constituency is theologically conservative but there is room for vast differences within that limitation. The literature of the EFMA does not suggest that it is governed by the same kind of stringent regulations common to IFMA. Indeed, even a superficial examination of the agencies in EFMA will reveal an absence of homogeneity obvious in the IFMA.

The EFMA seems to have made a splendid contribution to the advancement of missionary work through its Washington office, which keeps track of political developments and acts as a lobby with legislators for the benefit and protection of its missions' overseas work. Its Washington passport activities have been genuinely helpful. The fact that the EFMA and its parent organization, the NAE, have been able to maintain an ecumenical agency comprised of groups so diverse is a tribute to its skillful leadership and indicates that it is possible for those of different viewpoints to work together.

[31] As per letters exchanged between EFMA and the Wycliffe Bible Translators.

This accomplishment is especially noteworthy since divisiveness has been a latent characteristic of independence.

In an age of ecumenicity centripetal forces breaking down the barriers which have separated Christians for years are operating among the faith missionary agencies. This may not be said, however, when faith missions are considered within the context of the whole Christian Church. Therefore one must analyze the opposing forces governing the relations of faith missions to the major denominations of the day.

The major ecumenical agency in the United States is the National Council of the Churches of Christ. Its international counterpart is the World Council of Churches. The former agency represents most of the old-line denominations except the Southern Baptist Convention. It claims a constituency in excess of thirty million people. The National Council brought into a co-operative relationship the old Federal Council of the Churches of Christ along with the Foreign Missions Conference, the Home Missions Council, the International Council for Religious Education, and others. The National Council has been quite successful in its operations and has within its fold the greatest number of people in any American Protestant ecumenical agency. But it has not succeeded in uniting *all* Protestantism and is unlikely to be successful in this in the discernible future.

The problem of the National Council of Churches is not one which answers the question whether unity is good or bad per se. Few individuals or groups remain in splendid isolation. The Southern Baptist Convention is one that does, although even here isolation appears to be breaking down. The burning issue is quite another question. All are agreed on the essential unity of the Church. Everywhere organizations have been formed to express that unity. But the form it should take, the foundations on which it should be built, and the safeguards by which its theological integrity can be maintained are the real problems. This leads to an examination of the three major ecumenical agencies which are outside the National and World Councils of Churches.

The most determined single enemy of the National and World Councils of Churches is the American Council of Christian Churches and its International Council of Christian Churches. The ACCC represents extreme right-wing Protestantism and has for its major spokesman Carl McIntire, editor of the *Christian Beacon*. The American Council is a militant organization whose chief thesis is that the National and World Councils of Churches are apostate. Since the ACCC practices first- and second-degree separation, its people believe that they must separate from "the apostasy" and that they must not have fellowship with those who are themselves orthodox but who have not separated from this apostasy. Therefore they attack the National Council of Churches as apostate, but they also attack the National Association of Evangelicals as an organization of compromise. Although the American Council is numerically small, its voice is influential. The General Association of Regular Baptist Churches is the largest denomination in the fellowship. The American Council claims to be a true council of churches like the National Council of Churches and distinguishes itself from the NAE, which makes room for individuals as well as for denominations. On the roster of its co-operating missionary agencies, however, the American Council does list faith missionary organizations and to this extent it impinges upon the present discussion of faith missionary boards in an ecumenical atmosphere. The faith boards connected with the American Council are anti-denominational and militantly opposed to the National Council of Churches and its Division of Foreign Missions.

The second agency is the NAE, of which the missionary arm is the EFMA. The NAE was formed to counter the influence of the National Council. Within its fellowship are some individuals and individual churches who are related to the National Council of Churches through their own denominations. Since they are not in accord with the general denominational program respecting the National Council, these have registered their dissent by identification with the NAE. The agency also has in its fellowship smaller denominations not otherwise related to an ecumenical agency. In the EFMA are mission boards, both faith and denominational. Individuals in these faith boards are separately related to the NAE, which has room in its fellowship for such membership. The NAE and EFMA differ from the American Council in two respects. First, they provide fellowship for those who are committed to a conservative doctrinal platform and who are not otherwise adequately represented by an ecumenical group. Automatically this implies a judgment upon the National Council of Churches: that it is not exclusively in the conservative theological tradition. This attitude is in accord with the facts for it is well known that Neo-orthodoxy and Liberalism are represented in the National Council. The desire to provide ecumenical fellowship caused the NAE to embrace the tongues and pentecostal groups, as well as individuals and individual churches, all of whom are excluded by the American Council.

The second difference between the NAE and the ACCC lies in attitude and outlook. The NAE has sought to preserve a positive testimony whereas the ACCC has been an agency of negation. Moreover, the NAE has never adopted a position of second-degree separation, by which it would have to refuse fellowship to those with membership in the so-called apostate denominations. The existence of the NAE presupposes that the National and World Councils do not properly represent the NAE constituency, otherwise there would be no reason for its existence. While dissent underlies its framework, the method of operation is more positive and constructive than that of the ACCC. From time to time the ACCC has accused the NAE of collaboration with the National Council. At all times it has accused it of compromise. In the early days an effort was made to bring the NAE and the ACCC into one fellowship. This effort failed so that today there appears to be no hope whatever of the organizations' merging.

Underlying the protest of the NAE against the National Council are doctrinal considerations, and objections to Liberalism and leftish economic pronouncements. There is nothing in the present situation which would lead anyone to imagine that the NAE will disband or become an integral part of the National Council. Even if the latter option were in the offing, it would leave certain of the NAE groups stranded, for the National Council of Churches with its monolithic denominational structure has no place for individuals, independent churches, or faith mission boards. There has been no organized effort for the NCC and the NAE to engage in conversations to discuss their differences. Each pursues its separate existence as though the other were virtually nonexistent. Any ecumenical program which overlooks the necessity of working out the differences between these two forces is hardly ecumenical.

The third conservative ecumenical agency is the IFMA. It has a limited constituency—faith mission boards. It does not include in its fellowship denominations, churches, or individuals. Behind it lie all of these, but membership is limited to faith missionary boards which meet its doctrinal standards and its stringent operating regulations. The IFMA stands apart from the ACCC and the NAE. For it to move in either direction would be difficult. The reason is obvious. Many IFMA missionaries are supported by people and churches militantly opposed to the NAE. Others are supported by churches and people who are in the NAE and who favor it. If the IFMA moved in either direction some of its support would be lost. In this kind of situation the IFMA has little room to maneuver.

There are two sides to the coin of ecumenicity for the IFMA. It cannot join the NAE or the ACCC. But there is no room for it in the NCC either. If there were, the IFMA would not move into its orbit. The NCC has never made any particular overtures to engage in conversations with the IFMA. It is extremely doubtful that the IFMA would agree to such conversations if they were suggested. Nor has the IFMA made any overtures to the NCC. Nor will it. There was a time when faith missionary leaders did have fellowship with, and speak under, the auspices of denominational agencies. Thus in 1902 the Student Volunteer Movement (uniquely associated with the name of Dwight L. Moody and the Northfield Conference grounds) held its Toronto World-Wide Evangelization conference. Along with men like John R. Mott and J. Ross Stevenson were Dr. and Mrs. F. Howard Taylor of the China Inland Mission.[32] In 1910 the World Missionary Conference convened in Edinburgh, Scotland. It was essentially an ecumenical gathering. Representatives were invited from all missionary "Societies having agents in the foreign field and expending on foreign missions not less than £2000 annually, and . . . such Societies . . . [are] entitled to an additional delegate for every additional £4000 of foreign mission expenditures. It is a notable fact that both America and the Continent, as well as Great Britain, sent the full quota of delegates to which the Societies were entitled under this rule."[33] Faith missionary endeavor was represented by the China Inland Mission, Ceylon and India General Mission, Egypt General Mission, North Africa Mission, Regions Beyond Missionary Union, South Africa General Mission, Africa Inland Mission, Scandinavian Alliance Mission of North America, and the

[32] *World-wide Evangelization,* Student Volunteer Movement for Foreign Missions (New York, 1902), *passim.*
[33] *The History and Records of the Conference,* World Missionary Conference, 1910 (New York, Fleming H. Revell Company, n.d.), Vol. 9, p. 7.

Women's Union Missionary Society. Today there is nothing like this. No key missionary leader from a denomination connected with the National Council's Division of Foreign Missions has appeared, or will appear, on the annual programs of the IFMA. Nor have key leaders of the IFMA been invited, or appeared, on programs sponsored by the Division of Foreign Missions.

The IFMA distrusts the Division of Foreign Missions and the NCC. This distrust is basically twofold. First, the IFMA is convinced that Liberalism and Neo-orthodoxy have crept into the NCC so that the theological foundation of the enterprise is not truly orthodox. The IFMA does not pass any final judgment that *all* missionary activity and *all* missionaries connected with the NCC are unorthodox but it certainly believes that *some* of them are. Second, the distrust is based upon the belief that the churches of the NCC reflect their true theological coloring by their emphasis on the social aspects of the Gospel rather than on the message of individual salvation through the merits of Christ.

The great denominations have done little to allay the distrust of the faith boards and the faith boards have sought no interchange by which they might alter the theological perspective of the denominations. While the faith boards have not gone out of their way to be negative in their approach to denominational missions which have been infiltrated by those holding nonconservative theological convictions, they still have made it plain that they are standing for the historic Christian faith in a way which distinguishes them from those who do not. The *IFMA News* commends its members to "God's people" as worthy of their support because of "a oneness of heart and mind in the things of the Lord and a common adherence to the historic Christian faith as expressed in the following doctrinal statement."[34] The constant repetition of doctrinal soundness and the frequent printing of the doctrinal statements of IFMA agencies reveal the importance of the distinction which they make between sound and unsound theology. Recent missionary literature published by denominational mission boards fails to reveal any similar approach by them. The exceptions to this generalization occur in the literature of the smaller and particularly conservative denominations not connected with the Division of Foreign Missions.

One of the clearest evidences of the gulf separating faith from

[34] *IFMA News*, Vol. 11, No. 2, p. 2.

denominational missions at the theological level was the recent call to the Congress of World Missions. This call was issued under the sponsorship of the IFMA. The Congress convened December 4–11, 1960. The preliminary publicity revealed an attitude of separation from the other agencies who are engaged in overseas missionary work.[35] It was a Congress in a limited sense. The missionary arm of the American Council of Christian Churches was not involved. The EFMA arm of the NAE was not included. The Division of Foreign Missions of the National Council has no connection with it. Yet it denominates itself a Congress "designed to awaken evangelicals in North America." Perhaps who has been left out is as significant as who has been included.

The brochure specifically mentions the famous Edinburgh Missionary Conference in 1910. By implication the IFMA suggests that the mantle of this conference has fallen upon its own shoulders. The slogan of that conference, "The world for Christ in our generation," has become the slogan of the IFMA. "Many who had that vision in 1910 have been overcome with apostasy and liberalism."[36] It is difficult to determine from this statement whether Liberalism means apostasy or whether there is a distinction between a Liberal church and an apostate church. This much is clear: The use of the word "apostate" (which means desertion of the professed principles of the faith) must mean two things. First, it is a pronouncement that apostasy has taken place and that the facts in the case warrant such a conclusion. Second, it requires those who are non-apostate to separate from those who are.

Moreover, an examination of the preliminary list of speakers indicates that the conference will be almost exclusively one of independents. Even those denominations which by no means could be identified as Liberal or apostate are not included. One further exception should be noted. Dr. Vincent Brushwyler of the Conservative Baptist Foreign Mission Society appears on the speakers' list. All of this is indicative of the depth of the chasm which separates North American missionary forces in this generation. In an ecumenical age the divisions continue, and they mark off, not only those who are theologically conservative from those who may not be, but also those who are theologically conservative from those who are equally

---

[35] *Congress on World Missions* (pamphlet published by IFMA).
[36] *Ibid.*

conservative. It is too early to sing "all one body we" even for those of the same theological persuasion, and the divisions beyond this are so profound as to make comment unnecessary.

It is regrettable that fifty years after Edinburgh there cannot be a world congress for missions which transcends some of the unimportant differences dividing those of similar missionary aims. It is also unfortunate that few efforts or none are being made to engage in conversation about the important and unimportant issues which separate. It is even more unfortunate that conversations among those with whom faith missions are in theological disagreement are regarded by many as a departure from orthodoxy. All of this shows how deep are the divisions which exist and how tortuous the road of reconciliation.

Perhaps the faith missions may be able to enlarge their vision and provide a creative and dynamic leadership for a new age of missionary advance. This could be accomplished by the following steps. First, the IFMA could bring into a united fellowship all of the faith boards. Then they could join in a larger fellowship with those denominations which are committed to a conservative theology. Then they could reach out to embrace at least those within the great denominations who are also in the conservative tradition and who have a zeal for the fulfillment of the Great Commission. If this much could be accomplished, the rapid and impressive growth of faith missions in the past quarter of a century would not have been in vain. It is too much to hope for or expect that there will be any suitable rapproachment between the Division of Foreign Missions and the faith boards now or in the foreseeable future unless vast changes occur and concessions are made by both sides—concessions which are unlikely.

Until the horizon is lighted by more stars than now appear it seems reasonable to expect that there will continue to be five strands which go to make up the missionary endeavors of Protestant Christianity in America—the IFMA, the EFMA, the Division of Foreign Missions, the independents, and those associated with the American Council of Christian Churches. And among the stars which do shine, that of the faith missions has shone brightly for a quarter-century of unprecedented advance with nothing to suggest that it will not continue to do so and with every indication that, while there may be a slowing down of its growth, it will continue to move forward impressively in the decades ahead.

CHAPTER VIII

Kenneth Scott Latourette: Historian and Friend

E. THEODORE BACHMANN
Pacific Lutheran Theological Seminary
Berkeley, California

1. *The Making of a Historian*

In the case of Kenneth Scott Latourette, the making of a historian covers the first twenty-five years of his life, 1884–1909. From his birth in Oregon to his doctorate at Yale, there extends a line of development which points with promise to a future not of his own choosing. The salient features of these years may be sketched here in hopes that they will prove helpful in understanding the man to whom many are indebted as historian and friend.

In a region of Oregon rich in folklore and pioneer history, Kenneth spent his boyhood. Of Huguenot descent and himself a third-generation Oregonian, he was born on August 9, 1884, in Oregon City—remembered as the seat of territorial government under the noted Hudson's Bay agent John McLoughlin.[1] His grandfather, L. D. C. Latourette, a native of Lodi in western New York and the son of devout Baptist parents, had sought his fortune in the Far West. Arriving in Oregon in 1848, he taught school briefly, joined the gold rush to California, and then returned in 1851, settling on a farm near Oregon City.[2] Kenneth's father, De Witt Clinton Latou-

---

[1] *Who's Who in America, 1950–1951. Current Biography, Who's News and Why* (New York: H. W. Wilson Company, 1953), p. 342. C. H. Mattoon, *Baptist Annals of Oregon* (McMinnville, The Pacific Baptist Press, 2 vols., 1906, 1913), Vol. I, p. 68.

[2] Mattoon, *op. cit.*, p. 68. The Latourette ancestry is Huguenot, the first generation in America having come from France in the late seventeenth century and settled in Staten Island, New York. Letter, K. S. Latourette to E. T. Bachmann, June 17, 1960.

rette, took up law and banking, while his uncle, W. H. Latourette, upheld the family's Baptist heritage by entering the ministry.[3]

The Latourettes were "mainstays" of the First Baptist Church in Oregon City, today the oldest surviving congregation of its communion west of the Rocky Mountains.[4] By marriage the family was also related to that of Ezra Fisher, pioneer missionary of the American Baptist Home Mission Society, whose career had led him from work in Indiana, Illinois, and Iowa out to Oregon as early as 1845.[5] Latourette's grandfather, L. D. C., had married Eliza, daughter of Ezra Fisher.

Enjoying the advantages of an exemplary Christian home, young Latourette received a public school education and was graduated from Oregon City High School in 1900. He and his older brother, Howard Fenton, who later studied law, were youthful participants in the affairs of the First Baptist Church, where their father served as deacon and also superintendent of the Sunday School.[6] Later, the father's service to the larger work of the denomination included membership in the board of directors of Berkeley Baptist Divinity School in California.[7] His mother, née Rhoda Ellen Scott, taught

---

[3] Mattoon, *op. cit.*, p. 68.

[4] "A Brief Historical Sketch," by K. S. Latourette, *100th Anniversary, 1847 . . . 1947*, First Baptist Church, Oregon City, Ore. (privately printed), pp. 3 ff. Kenneth L. Holmes (ed.), *Linfield's Hundred Years: A Centennial History of Linfield College, McMinnville, Oregon* (Portland, Binfords & Mort, 1956). Introduction by K. S. Latourette, p. vii.

[5] *Correspondence of the Reverend Ezra Fisher* [1800–1874], *Pioneer Missionary of the American Baptist Home Mission Society in Indiana, Illinois, Iowa and Oregon.* Edited by Sarah Fisher Henderson, Nellie Edith Latourette, Kenneth Scott Latourette. (Printed originally in the *Oregon Historical Quarterly*, Vol. 20.) Pp. 12–13. On the Fisher side of the house, K. S. Latourette is related to George Park Fisher, noted professor of church history at Yale prior to Williston Walker. He is also related to the family of President William Howard Taft and to the late Senator Robert Taft. K. S. Latourette to E. T. Bachmann, June 17, 1960.

[6] Mattoon, *op. cit.*, p. 68. *100th Anniversary, 1847 . . . 1947*, p. 3.

[7] Sandford Fleming, President Emeritus, Berkeley Baptist Divinity School, interview accorded E. T. Bachmann, June 5, 1960. D. C. Latourette's service on the BBDS Board began after that school's reorganization in 1910. His brother, W. H. Latourette, "was for years secretary of the California State Baptist Convention and was later financial agent of McMinnville [Linfield] College." *100th Anniversary, 1847 . . . 1947*, p. 8. K. S. Latourette has pointed out that he is the only one in his own generation, on either side of the house, who entered the ministry, and that on his mother's side "there is a strong strain of independent thinking." K. S. Latourette to E. T. Bachmann, June 16, 1960.

Sunday School at First Church for a generation, and as he himself has said "was the mainstay of the missionary interests."[8]

In 1900, First Church was a key congregation in the Willamette Association, reflecting the ordered work of many laymen as well as of the competent preacher. Young Latourette had the good fortune of growing up in a church of which it could be said:

> Its internal harmony and vigor, its extraordinary Sabbath schools, its home and foreign mission work, its thorough organization in every department of Christian work in accordance with the most effective modern methods, all gave cause for praise.[9]

From solid environment in home and community, Kenneth went on to college. In not far distant McMinnville he spent three years at Linfield College, graduating as valedictorian in 1904, and receiving his Bachelor of Science in chemistry. Linfield was a Baptist institution that traced its beginnings to the vision and pioneering of Ezra Fisher and a handful of associates. "It was symbolic," writes Latourette in retrospect, "that the school which they started in the Pacific Northwest (in 1856) was first held in the meeting house" of First Church, Oregon City.[10] Attendance at Linfield strengthened Kenneth in the family heritage, for his uncle, the Rev. W. H. Latourette, was the traveling agent for the college.[11] As to his studies, the sciences fascinated him, and geology has remained a lifelong hobby. Yet his interest in history dated from boyhood and appeared to him congenital.[12] Over and above scientific and historical interests, his expectation was to follow his father in the profession of law and banking. To that end his membership on Linfield's championship debating team lent promise.[13]

Meanwhile, his continued cultivation of the Christian faith had

---

[8] *100th Anniversary, 1847 . . . 1947*, p. 4. The Scott family, originally from North Carolina and Virginia, had come from Kentucky by way of Illinois and settled in Oregon in 1852. Rhoda Ellen Scott's brother, Kenneth's maternal uncle, Harvey Scott, became the long-time editor of the Portland *Morning Oregonian*. Her sister, Kenneth's maternal aunt, Abigail Scott Duniway, became famed in her day as an advocate of women's rights. K. S. Latourette to E. T. Bachmann, June 17, 1960.

[9] Mattoon, *op. cit.*, Vol. II, p. 21.

[10] *Linfield's Hundred Years*, p. vii.

[11] Mattoon, *op. cit.*, Vol. I, p. 68.

[12] Letter, K. S. Latourette to E. T. Bachmann, April 27, 1960.

[13] *Linfield's Hundred Years*, photo facing p. 7.

opened wider vistas and challenged his personal commitment to missionary service. It is said that when the student YMCA was organized on the Linfield campus in 1887, a revolution in outlook followed. Where religious activities had formerly been centered in the denomination, they now rose above denominational horizons and aroused interest in a movement that was spanning the nation and linking many nations.[14] In his junior and senior years, Kenneth was president of the Linfield YMCA. Besides, the Student Volunteer Movement for Foreign Missions had come on the campus with vigor, proclaiming its watchcry, "The evangelization of the world in this generation." He himself responded and signed the forthright declaration "It is my purpose, if God permit, to become a foreign missionary."[15] Yet the decision was not easy and, as he put it, came only after a good deal of anguish of soul and from a compelling sense of duty.[16] The treasured ties with home and community were loosened and, as a young man of twenty, he headed east, across the continent, to round out his education before going overseas as a teacher.

Latourette entered Yale as a senior, being drawn to a college and university that was outstanding not only as a seat of learning and culture but also as a center of missionary fervor.[17] He became "a Yale enthusiast from his first year there."[18] Majoring in history, he received his A.B. with the class of 1906 and was elected to Phi Beta Kappa. Awarded a graduate fellowship, he stayed on, earning his M.A. in 1907 and his Ph.D. in 1909. For his missionary teaching task, he wanted to prepare himself as fully as possible; and for his prospective position on the faculty of the then new (1901) and struggling Yale-in-China the doctorate seemed highly desirable. To be sure, he had canvassed the possibilities of a doctorate in geology

[14] *Ibid.*, p. 157.

[15] *Addresses and Papers of John R. Mott*, Vol. I, *The Student Volunteer Movement* (New York, Association Press, 1946), Vol. 39 (1892), p. 89. (Hereafter cited as *Addresses and Papers.*)

[16] K. S. Latourette to E. T. Bachmann, April 27, 1960.

[17] K. S. Latourette, *A History of the Expansion of Christianity*, Vol. IV, *The Great Century, A.D. 1800–1914, Europe and the United States of America* (New York, Harper & Brothers, 1941), p. 101, and regarding Yale's missionary bands in the westward expansion across the United States, pp. 210–211. Roland H. Bainton, *Yale and the Ministry. How a Puritan School Molded Generations of Americans* (New York, Harper & Brothers, 1957), pp. 131–135.

[18] K. S. Latourette to E. T. Bachmann, April 27, 1960. *Yale College, A History of the Class of 1906* (New Haven, Yale University Press, 2 vols., 1911), Vol. II, p. 415.

or economics, but settled for one in history, a field in which for him it was possible to fulfill the requirements more quickly, while also satisfying "a deep-seated and long-standing major interest."[19]

His academic fare in the historical field included a variety of eras and global areas. His one course in Church history was the survey offered by Williston Walker.[20] Here he met a scholar trained in the historical discipline at Leipzig, oriented to the European heritage, and devoted to "the cult of historical objectivity." Walker saw the meaning of Church history as implicit in "the bond of unity which runs through all the variety of forms, of organization, or types of worship, and of theological statement in the Christian Church, [and] which is to be found in Christian experience."[21] If this interpretation paid homage to piety, Walker balanced it with his respects to rationality, declaring that the story of the Church "is essentially that of divinely guided process, and one moving forward to a larger realization of the Kingdom of God."[22] We shall see later how these perspectives found reflection in Latourette's thinking.[23]

Conventional as much of his historical study was, his field of specialization was unconventional. He took all the courses in the Far East which were offered at that time at Yale. This brought him into close company with Frederick Wells Williams, who in 1900 had become assistant professor of modern Oriental history. Williams, a one-time literary editor of *The National Baptist*, was the son of missionary parents who had served in China. Himself a graduate of Yale, in 1879, Williams had done further study at the universities of Göttingen, Berlin, and Paris and had then assisted his father[24] in bringing out a revised edition of *The Middle Kingdom* (2 vols., 1882–1883), long a standard history of China.[25] Professor Williams had already written a couple of books of his own on the Far East prior to 1904. In his teaching, as Latourette recalls, "he covered Central Asia, India, and the Far East, and did much to stimulate interest

[19] K. S. Latourette to E. T. Bachmann, April 27, 1960.
[20] *Ibid.*
[21] Bainton, *op. cit.*, p. 234.
[22] *Ibid.*, p. 235.
[23] See following two footnotes below.
[24] Samuel Wells Williams. (See *Life and Letters of Samuel Wells Williams*, 2 vols., ed. by F. Wells Williams.) *Dictionary of American Biography* (hereafter *DAB*), Vol. 20, p. 260.
[25] The biographical sketch of F. Wells Williams is by K. S. Latourette. *DAB*, Vol. 20, p. 260.

in fields generally neglected in the curriculum of American colleges
and universities. It was to China, however, that he devoted the major
part of his attention."²⁶

With Williams as his mentor, Latourette wrote his doctoral dissertation on "The History of Early Relations Between the United
States and China, 1784–1844." Two things about this work were
typical of future developments—the one personal, the other more
general. In personal terms, his thesis revealed a young man who had
disciplined himself to the demands of historical research and scholarly
objectivity, so that subsequently, when his thesis was published and
the reviewers got at it, one experienced "China hand" commented,
"The author has accomplished his task with a precision which is
quite exceptional."²⁷ In general terms, Latourette later observed that
the Far Eastern scholarship of the United States

> . . . has tended to devote itself to diplomatic and commercial relations,
> to economic problems, to contact between the Far Orient and the
> Occident, and to current changes in the culture of the Far East. The
> most distinguished European Savants, who have majored in the Far
> East, on the other hand, have devoted themselves almost exclusively to
> the older history and culture of this region. They have not understood
> the current situation. Nor have they cared to do so.²⁸

In his formative years as a scholar, young Latourette had thus
come into a field which was calling for men to communicate and
interpret its story to the Western world. Son of the farthest North
American frontier, he had begun to link its young story to that of
the venerable Far East. For in his thesis he confidently pointed out
"that the Oregon country was preserved to the United States because of the importance it was felt to have in the Canton commerce."²⁹

With the place of his birth set in a world-wide context, his life

²⁶ *Ibid.*
²⁷ Marshall Broomhall, Editorial Secretary, China Inland Mission, London,
in *International Review of Missions* (hereafter *IRM*), Vol. 7 (1918), p. 255.
²⁸ K. S. Latourette, *Biographical Memoir of Berthold Laufer, 1874–1934*
(Washington, National Academy of Sciences, 1936), p. 55.
²⁹ *The History of the Early Relations between the United States and China,
1784–1844* (New Haven, Yale University Press, 1917), p. 57. See also *American
Historical Review*, Vol. 23 (1918), pp. 408–409. In passing, it may be noted that
1909, the year of Latourette's doctorate, was also the fiftieth anniversary of
Oregon's statehood.

was poised to enter upon a vast and global adventure. There was existential logic in this like the logic of a well-reasoned debate; as such it was characteristic of the argument used by John R. Mott and other promoters of the Student Volunteer Movement. All of life was seen within a great encompassing divine purpose. And Yale was a place where the student commitment to foreign as well as home missions had a continuous history back to 1818. The Student Foreign Missionary Society, active since 1854,[30] had in 1901 undertaken the major support of the exciting project to share a bit of Yale-in-China. Professor Williams was closely associated with this venture and worked tirelessly for its success.[31] Also in 1901, a Yale band of five students spent the year traveling and working among young people's societies, visiting 70 cities, addressing 884 meetings, and holding 364 missionary conferences at which some 2,000 local young people's societies were represented; influencing many of them to organize missionary committees, to buy books on missions, to undertake mission study, to adopt systematic giving, and to promote intercessory prayer for missions.[32] By 1909, Yale was leading all other collegiate mission groups by its then annual giving of some $10,000 to missionary objects.[33]

It was this spirit at Yale that stimulated the enthusiastic young Latourette. True, there was smugness and self-satisfaction in some quarters, which draped itself over portions of Yale's faculty and student body,[34] but this seemed to prod the committed Christians to greater effort. Latourette, for example, took his turn at teaching student Bible classes and thus helped to ready himself for the coming task in China.

As he came to the close of his studies, these seemed to blend with his other experiences into a purposeful composite. Today, as he recalls, no one teacher seemed to stand out above the others as an influence in his life.[35] Yet it may be that ideals of Christian service, which he and others felt strongly,[36] gave substance to an otherwise

[30] Bainton, *op. cit.*, pp. 131 ff.
[31] *DAB*, Vol. 20, p. 261.
[32] *Addresses and Papers*, Vol. I, p. 81.
[33] *Ibid.*, p. 125.
[34] For a critique of Yale during these years, see G. F. Gundelfinger, *Ten Years at Yale, 1905–1915* (New York: Shakespeare Press, 1915), *passim*.
[35] K. S. Latourette to E. T. Bachmann, April 27, 1960.
[36] *Yale College. A History of the Class of 1906*, Vol. II, p. 417.

trite slogan, "For God, for Country, and for Yale." From the ivy-clad academy, however, his way led out literally into the world.

2. The School of Experience

True to its aim, the Student Volunteer Movement for Foreign Missions was in the early years of our century a dynamic, spirit-filled recruiting fellowship. Mott could characterize it as an offering of living young men and women that seemed to personify the event of Pentecost.[37] Many who took part in it, moreover, saw the Christian faith as the vital bond between the world of thought and the community of nations. Before heading for China, Latourette was engaged by the Movement to spend the academic year 1909–1910 as one of its traveling secretaries. His journeys that year took him to many colleges and universities, mainly in the eastern part of the United States.[38]

The high point of the year was the sixth International Convention of the SVM. Held at Rochester, New York, December 29, 1909, to January 2, 1910, it sought to capture the imagination of the hundreds of assembled students with a clear picture of the challenge confronting them and their student generation. With characteristic breadth and incisiveness, the report under Mott's chairmanship reviewed the preceding quadriennium as well as the nature and aim of the Movement as a whole. To all came the reminder that the primary function of the Movement is that of recruiting, and that this takes place in close co-operation with the mission boards of the denominations and in association with the YMCA and YWCA movements and other student religious societies as well.[39] With gratitude it could be shown that in the 23 years of SVM, 1886–1909, 4,346 volunteers had gone forth. On the list of the receiving countries, China led with 1,253. India was next, with 840; then Africa, 466; Japan, 374; South America, 266; Korea, 200; and so on, to lands in all parts of the earth.[40] To be sure, not all who volunteered could or actually did go overseas. But even this had its salutary effect by emphasizing increasingly "that the work of Christ at home and abroad is our work." Besides,

[37] *Addresses and Papers*, Vol. I, p. 12.
[38] *Yale College. A History of the Class of 1906*, Vol. II, p. 417.
[39] *Addresses and Papers*, Vol. I, p. 121.
[40] *Ibid.*, pp. 122–123.

"many of the students who are becoming clergymen regard their parishes not alone or chiefly as a field to be cultivated, but primarily as a force to be wielded on behalf of the whole world." The same was true of those becoming teachers or professional and business leaders, and of many others. Whatever their work, their vocation was to be Christians amid the main currents of modern life.[41]

Undergirding such results was the growing cultivation of Bible study, mission study, and intercessory prayer on the part of students across the land. And during his year as traveling secretary young Latourette was deeply involved in stimulating these elemental parts of the SVM. Nor could he miss the pointed significance of certain indirect results: notably, that the SVM was having a strong influence "on the religious life of the institutions of higher learning throughout the United States and Canada." The Rochester report reminded the members that, as a result of SVM activities, "more students have forgotten or lost themselves in the great cause of Christ than at any time in the history of colleges. Thus the Movement has dealt a powerful blow to some of the gravest perils of modern student life in North America—the perils of selfishness, of narrowness, of materialism and worldly ideals, of extravagance and luxury, of softness and love of ease."[42]

Soon bound for China as he was, Latourette was probably warmed by the repeated recognition that the SVM, through the World Student Christian Federation (1895), stood in a living relationship with students around the globe. Attention was called to "the most remarkable series of student missionary conferences ever held—those of Nashville (1906), Liverpool (1896, 1908), Halle (1897, 1901, 1905, 1909), and Cape Town (1906),"[43] besides the international conferences of the WSCF in Tokyo in 1907 and in Oxford in 1909. "Recent years," it was said, "as no preceding period, have seen a coming together of the students of the world in recognition of their common responsibility for the world's evangelization."[44]

Indeed, if anything could sum up the mind and will of the SVM in those years, it is the watchword, "The evangelization of the world in this generation." For it laid emphasis on the urgency of the task,

[41] *Ibid.*, pp. 124–125.
[42] *Ibid.*, p. 128.
[43] Ruth Rouse, *The World's Student Christian Federation: A History of the First Thirty Years* (London, SCM Press, 1938), *passim.*
[44] *Addresses and Papers*, Vol. I, p. 130.

the thoroughness of preparation for it, and the personal commitment to it. The times were seen as crucial in many parts of the world, and the opportunities for the Gospel as immeasurably great.[45]

A half-year after the Rochester conference Latourette set out for China. Sailing from New York on July 5, 1910, he spent part of the summer in England and on the Continent. Unfortunately, he missed the World Missionary Conference at Edinburgh, which had taken place June 14–23 and was to prove of such decisive significance for the ecumenical movement in our time.[46] He continued his journey via Russia, taking the Trans-Siberian Railway. Arriving in China from the west, he made his way to Changsha, the provincial capital of Hunan province, and found a hearty reception among his colleagues. After a half-year of intensive language study, plus a teaching assignment of five hours a week in history and Bible, he regarded his task humbly but hopefully. Writing to his classmates in time for the fifth reunion, he had this to say:

> The hope of the nation lies in the young China, the students—and there are thousands of them—who shall be trained in modern lines. . . . After seeing all this, one becomes more and more convinced that our Yale in China has a place, and a very important one, in developing all-round leaders, thoroughly disciplined mentally, morally, physically, and imbued with that faith and ideal of service for which mother Yale stands.[47]

Optimistically he continued:

> The opportunity grows on me daily. It is the chance to help lay the foundations of an institution which will influence the educational standards of an entire nation, and which will train men to carry out in China those ideals of Christian service which have so characterized the older Yale. Personally, I can think of no place where I would rather be.[48]

Thus the young Latourette kept ardently at work, following the disciplined daily schedule of the school, situated in temporary quar-

[45] *Ibid.*, p. 135.

[46] William Richey Hogg, *Ecumenical Foundations: A History of the International Missionary Council and Its Nineteenth Century Background* (New York, Harper & Brothers, 1952), pp. 98 ff.

[47] *Yale College. A History of the Class of 1906*, Vol. II, p. 416.

[48] *Ibid.*, p. 417. For a readily accessible comment on further undertakings of Yale-in-China, see Latourette, "Williams, Frederick Wells," *DAB*, Vol. 20, p. 261.

ters outside the city's north gate. Repeatedly he was struck by the glare of contrast between things traditionally Chinese and things imported from the industrialized West. The daily walk around the city gave him not only exercise but also the visible evidence of this East-West encounter. For relaxation and inner peace he played on the little organ in the school's chapel.[49]

Before long, the climate and health hazards began taking their toll. The heat and humidity of summer and the cold dampness of winter in unheated houses, plus the perennial problems of sanitation,[50] eventually brought him low. His chosen life work was not yet two years in progress when, in 1912, he was sent back to the United States. Until 1917 his association as a staff member of Yale-in-China was continued. Much as he longed to return to Ya-li, physicians ordered him to remain in the United States.[51]

Deeply disappointed, he nevertheless could draw comfort from the recognition ever accorded by the Student Volunteer Movement to the "detained volunteers,"[52] as well as to the oneness of the Church throughout the world.[53] Amid the calm of recuperation he now saw a new prospect opening before him. He could become an interpreter of the Orient to the Occident. Specialists on the Far East in academic circles, he noted, were at that time so few that he could "number them on the fingers of two hands with fingers left over." Therefore he felt that he could fulfill one aspect of his missionary purpose by promoting in North America the study of Far Eastern history.[54]

In this unexpected way the school of experience seemed to prepare Latourette for a range of unparalleled service to the broadened study of Christian history. Not far from his birthplace he entered upon his new teaching career. Through the kindness of William Trufant Foster, president of up-and-coming little Reed College in Portland, Oregon, he was given his first opportunity to teach a course on the history of the Far East. His colleagues on the faculty were bright young scholars trained at Harvard, Columbia, Chicago, California, and other leading universities. Beginning as a lecturer, Latourette

[49] *Yale College. A History of the Class of 1906*, Vol. II, p. 416.
[50] *Ibid.*
[51] K. S. Latourette to E. T. Bachmann, April 27, 1960.
[52] *Addresses and Papers*, Vol. I, p. 129.
[53] *Ibid.*, p. 131.
[54] K. S. Latourette to E. T. Bachmann, April 27, 1960.

soon became an assistant professor and seems to have enjoyed thoroughly his two years, 1914–1916, at Reed.[55]

Once again came the pull to the East, this time to Baptist-related Denison University in Granville, Ohio, where he spent the next five years. Beginning as associate in 1916, he became full professor in 1917. In 1918 the position of university chaplain came his way, and to fulfill its requirements he was ordained to the Baptist ministry.[56] Having by-passed the usual formal theological training, he would find his change of status from layman to ordained minister important for his future work. Alongside his chaplaincy he retained his professorship in history. Indeed, the five years at Denison saw the beginning of his literary career and marked the first step toward the realization of his aim to promote, as a missionary, the study of Far Eastern history.

A word about his first four books is in order. In 1917, two appeared. Yale University Press published his doctoral dissertation, *The History of Early Relations between the United States and China, 1784–1844;*[57] and reference has already been made to the favorable reaction of reviewers.[58] It was a product of painstaking scholarship and maturing erudition with ample documentation and a 55-page bibliography—characteristics which have been associated with his major works ever since.

Latourette's other book of 1917 appeared as the product of his initial work at Reed College and constitutes the first expression of his resolve to demolish student ignorance about the Far East. *The Development of China*, published by Boston's Houghton Mifflin Company, was a 275-page introduction designed for the layman. Reviewers called it scholarly and restrained, fair-minded and readable, an excellent textbook "for students and for all who desire to get at the story of China, especially at the more recent history since 1894." The author's disposition to be appreciative of the Chinese, the

[55] Dorothy Johansen and Charles M. Gates, *Empire of the Columbia* (New York, Harper & Brothers, 1957), pp. 538–539. Thirty years later Latourette acknowledged his indebtedness to Reed College and dedicated his book *A Short History of the Far East* (New York, The Macmillan Company, 1946) to W. T. Foster, Reed's first president, p. xi. See above, p. 142.

[56] *Who's Who in America, 1950–1951.*

[57] See this also in *Transactions* of the Connecticut Academy of Arts and Sciences, Vol. 22, pp. 1–209.

[58] See above, p. 236. Also *American Historical Review* (hereafter, *AHR*), Vol. 23 (1918), pp. 408–409.

British, and the missionaries was duly noted, as was his readiness to criticize where an objective criticism was due.[59]

One might venture a preliminary evaluation of Latourette's historiography as a blend of the objective use of the historical method (its German rootage mingled with the American) and of the subjective identification of the author with his subject. Here something of the restrained but deep love of a people reached some of the best minds in the Student Volunteer Movement. Therefore his point of view and his plan of presentation bear exact scrutiny.

"The eyes of the world," he wrote in the Introduction, "are more and more turned toward China. We are coming to be profoundly interested in the fate of that greatest of Asiatic peoples." Then he went on to sketch his reasons in global terms:

> No other existing nation can look back over as long a past of continuous development as can China. When the foundations of Greece and Rome were being laid and when the Hebrew prophets were in the midst of their ministry, a nation was being shaped and a civilization formed which have come down through the centuries with a comparatively unbroken history. There have been changes, but none of them as violent as those which have shaken the West during the same period.[60]

Then he made comparisons, claiming that only two cultural groups, that in India and that in the Mediterranean Basin, "have had as dominant an influence over as large a section of mankind."[61] He reminded the reader of the spread of Chinese culture not only over China proper but also over the outlying cultures of Mongolia, Manchuria, and Tibet, as well as over the culture of old Japan. What the Mediterranean world was to the Germanic people of northern Europe, China was to the outlying lands of Asia.[62]

In presenting the development of China, Latourette departed from the usual European preoccupation with the distant past and gave considerable space to newer developments. His presentation thus brought (1) the development of China to the time when contact with Euro-

[59] *Book Review Digest, 1918.*
[60] *Development of China,* p. ix.
[61] The use of the term "influence" here already suggests its later and typical application to the life of Jesus, e.g., in Latourette's book *Anno Domini.* See below, p. 254.
[62] *Development of China,* pp. x–xi.

peans first began to have a strong effect, or about 1832; (2) a description of the civilization of China as it was before that contact; (3) the history since the contact with the Europeans; and (4) the changes and problems brought on by that contact.[63] We can see here the methodical plan which was to characterize most of Latourette's later writings.

The following year, 1918, Macmillan published his companion volume, *The Development of Japan.* By some it was called the "best brief history of Japan." He drew praise for telling about the achievement of Japan forthrightly, and not falling for the temptation of applying the "yardstick of European advancement." He had "no fad to exploit, no theory either pro or anti-Japanese to put over."[64] Again, this look on Japan, like the one on China, was for students. Its dispassionate tone seemed an application to Far Eastern history of what Leopold von Ranke had raised as a standard for European history: simply tell what happened.[65] Whatever their merit, these books have subsequently passed through many editions, with additions but few revisions.

The fourth book, *Christian Basis of World Democracy,* was published by Association Press in 1919[66] and was intended for the thoughtful student in the postwar era. Its significance would seem to lie not in the field of history but in that of empirical Christian social ethics. Here Latourette set himself the task to ascertain the kind of international order that would result "if the teachings of Jesus were carried out." It was an idealistic work, with a strong reliance upon the social gospel. His six areas of attention included (1) the Gospel of an Ideal World, (2) Worldwide Honesty and Good Will, (3) Christian Individualism and Collectivism, (4) Some Means of Achieving an Ideal World, (5) International Neighborliness, and (6) Patriotic Hypocrisy.[67]

In short, these four books published prior to 1920, and before the author was thirty-five, seem like sure signs pointing to his future as

[63] *Ibid.,* p. xii.
[64] *AHR,* Vol. 24 (1918), p. 128.
[65] James Westfall Thompson and Bernard J. Holm, *A History of Historical Writing* (New York, The Macmillan Company, 2 vols., 1942), Vol. II, pp. 181 ff.
[66] The only copy in the San Francisco Bay area libraries appears to be at St. Margaret's House (Episcopal), in Berkeley, Calif.
[67] *Book Review Digest, 1919,* p. 293.

a historiographer. Stated provisionally, these are: objective repor-
torial narration, on the one hand, and a moral-influence interpretation, on the other. But presently the stage of his activity was again
shifted; this time back to his university alma mater.

3. *The First Fifteen Years at Yale,* 1921–1936

Latourette began his long and productive teaching of missions at
Yale in 1921, just fifteen years after having earned his A.B. there.
In 1906, amid the remarkable advance of Christian commitment
among collegians for service overseas, the chair of missions had been
established at Yale. Eight years later it was endowed with a gift of
$100,000, given in memory of D. Willis James of New York by his
widow and son. James, a Presbyterian, had been generous in sharing
his wealth with various Christian enterprises.[68] The purpose of the
professorship was originally twofold: to develop an interest in missions among the students generally, and to provide missionary training for those aiming to serve overseas.[69] The first incumbent was
Harlan Page Beach, who gave distinction to this professorship during its first fifteen years (1906–1921). One of his courses was required of all students in the Divinity School, but his elective courses
did not draw large numbers. Beach's scholarship was directed toward
his special interest in missionary geography and statistics.[70]

Through his two-volume *Geography and Atlas of Protestant Missions* (1901), as well as through his collaborated work in this field,
Beach laid an invaluable groundwork for the global study of Christianity.[71] In connection with the Edinburgh Conference on World
Missions in 1910 he, along with James S. Dennis, Samuel Zwemer,
and Charles H. Fahs, brought out the *Statistical Atlas of Christian
Missions;* and in 1916, the year of the Panama Conference, which
was the first meeting in Latin America to co-ordinate Protestant mis-

[68] Olaf Guttorm Myklebust, *The Study of Missions in Theological Education.*
An historical inquiry into the place of world evangelization in Western Protestant ministerial training with particular reference to Alexander Duff's chair of
Evangelical Theology (Oslo, Egede Institut, 2 vols., 1955, 1957), Vol. II, p. 80.
[69] *Ibid.,* p. 81.
[70] *Ibid.,* p. 82.
[71] *Ibid.,* Harlan P. Beach, *A Geography and Atlas of Protestant Missions*
(New York, Student Volunteer Movement for Foreign Missions, 2 vols., 1901,
1906).

sionary efforts.[72] Beach and Burton St. John published their *World Statistics on Christian Missions*.[73] With his productive work at Yale tuned to the practical developments in Christian world missions, it may also be noteworthy that he laid down his professorship in 1921, the year of the organization of the International Missionary Council, only to be co-editor with Fahs in 1925 of the *World Missionary Atlas*, which anticipated the Jerusalem Conference of the IMC in 1928. While still at Yale, Beach was doing much to enlarge and catalog the Day Missions Library, and to make it one of the largest and most valuable centers anywhere for study and research in the worldwide history and ongoing work of Christian missions.[74]

In this well-prepared setting, Latourette became the second incumbent of the chair of missions. A historian by training, his major course in the field of missions dealt with the history of the worldwide expansion of Christianity. Moreover, he soon found himself giving practically all the courses on the Far East that Yale had to offer. Therefore in 1927, at the suggestion of the chairman of the history department, his task was entitled the "D. Willis James Professorship of Missions and Oriental History."[75] While the missions remained his central concern, his teaching responsibilities were set as a broad base of Christian and secular history. Indeed, his previous scholarly attainment, plus his personal missionary commitment, now had splendid opportunity for development.

Not only Yale but the Church at large had taken note of Latourette. In 1921 he became a member of the board of the American Baptist Foreign Mission Society.[76] That same year he was named a trustee of Yale-in-China. In 1922 he came on the executive committee of the World Student Christian Federation and the same year attended its international conference in Peking.[77] In 1929 the Foreign Missions Conference named him to its important committee on reference and counsel. He also became a member of a committee of the International Missionary Council, attended its meetings in Wil-

---

[72] Latourette, *A History of the Expansion of Christianity*, Vol. VII, p. 172.

[73] Myklebust, *op. cit.*, Vol. II, p. 82.

[74] Latourette dedicated all seven volumes of his *opus magnum*, *A History of the Expansion of Christianity*, to Beach.

[75] K. S. Latourette to E. T. Bachmann, April 27, 1960.

[76] He held this position 1921–1925, 1935–1947, serving as president 1946–1947. *Who's Who in America, 1950–1951.*

[77] He served on this WSCF committee 1922–1924.

liamstown (1929), Herrnhut (1932), and Northfield (1935).[78] Like-wise in 1929 the IMC asked Latourette to undertake a world-wide survey of the then current scholarly materials being produced on missions. He presented his completed report at Herrnhut, whereupon he was made chairman of a small internal "Research Group," whose task was to gather information on mission studies, wherever under-taken, and to give counsel when requested. This committee worked in close co-operation with the editors of *The International Review of Missions* and soon became responsible for the publication of such scholarly studies as Alfred W. Wasson's *Church Growth in Korea* and James Thayer Addison's *The Medical Missionary.*[79]

Although properly involved in such an extracurricular array, La-tourette's first fifteen years at Yale found him not only devoted as a teacher but also productive as a scholar. If 1929 was significant for his appointment to extra duties in the current task of Christian mis-sions, the reason was not far to seek. For in that year there appeared his comprehensive and imposing work on *The History of Christian Missions in China.*[80] Lauded as a definitive work, by its scholarship and excellent documentation it made a welcome asset to those en-gaged in the missionary task. Not only was it exhaustive, but it was imparital and moderate as well. It was especially noteworthy in that it included the first full account of Roman Catholic missions in China.[81] A Chinese reviewer, however, challenged the author's claim that Chinese Christians have produced no significant Christian litera-ture of their own and noted that few Chinese sources had been used in the study.[82]

Especially amid our currently ominous relations with Red China, Latourette's conclusion to this study is a sobering reminder:

The historian does not cease to be impartial when he declares that the presence and the labor of the missionary were most fortunate for China. Defects the missionary enterprise undoubtedly had. Sometimes it did evil. On the whole, however, it was the one great agency whose primary function was to bring China into contact with the best in the

[78] *Who's Who in America, 1950–1951.*
[79] Hogg, *op. cit.,* pp. 279, 421.
[80] New York, The Macmillan Company, 1930, pp. 930.
[81] *AHR,* Vol. 34 (1929), p. 848.
[82] *IRM,* Vol. 18 (1929), p. 605.

Occident and to make the expansion of the West a means to the greater welfare of the Chinese people.[83]

Five years later, in 1934, Latourette published his two-volume work on *The Chinese: Their History and Culture*.[84] "This work stands alone," exulted one reviewer, himself experienced in China. For nothing like it had appeared in English, bringing the clarity, wealth of detail and competent direction through the rich mazes of Chinese life and culture.[85] Another, who recognized the value of this study, criticized its style, saying, "The author has the obsessive impartiality of the 'scientific historian,' which keeps him from positive statements and makes his paragraphs soggy with qualifications, but which, ten years ago, was held up as the ideal of historical writing; today, in the midst of a society violently in motion, the reader asks for something more."[86] At any rate, this work was a product of Latourette's courses on China at Yale, and a massive follow-up on his continuingly popular work on the *Development of China*, published seventeen years earlier. With the appearance of this erudite study he joined the small but select company of American sociologists.[87] Besides, almost all his writings to date had dealt with Asia. But a change was imminent.

Climaxing his first fifteen years at Yale, Latourette brought out a modest little work entitled *Missions Tomorrow*.[88] Here was evidence that his teaching about missions at Yale and his extracurricular contacts with the actual missionary task were pointing to a practical fusion. Reviewers welcomed this book. One even praised it as a "prospectus of a modern Acts of the Apostles, the work of inspired Christian scholarship, . . . statesman-like in its world view and faithful to the Gospel of Christ."[89] In any case, it was the product of many contributory elements, which he gladly acknowledged. Besides his regular work and unrivaled resources at Yale, his lecture-

---

[83] *A History of Christian Missions in China*, p. 843.

[84] New York, The Macmillan Company, pp. 506 and 389.

[85] M. Searle Bates, in *AHR*, Vol. 39 (1934), p. 709.

[86] Isidor Schneider in *The New Republic*. Quoted in *Book Review Digest, 1934*, p. 541.

[87] Cf. Latourette, *Biographical Memoir of Berthold Laufer, 1874–1934*, pp. 43–68.

[88] New York, Harper & Brothers, 1936, pp. 220.

[89] L. L. Riley in *The Churchman*. Quoted in *Book Review Digest, 1936*, p. 574.

ships at Southern Baptist Theological Seminary (1930 and 1936), his Student Lectureship in Missions at Princeton (1935), and at Union Theological Seminary in New York (1936), all gave him helpful prods, as did also articles prepared for such publications as *Christendom, The International Review of Missions, The Missionary Review of the World, Religion in Life, The Review and Expositor,* and *The Yale Review.*[90] Personal friends, like the dynamic A. L. Warnshuis and Esther Strong, secretaries of the International Missionary Council, and many others, helped to shape and stimulate his thinking. In a fitting way, this book was a synthesis of many experiences and provides us with a suitable pause in Latourette's career at Yale.

Missions Tomorrow, moreover, appeared in the midst of an era which was still troubled over questions and uncertainties raised by the Laymen's Foreign Missions Inquiry. Chaired by the noted professor of philosophy at Harvard, William Ernest Hocking, and undertaken by an earnest team of laymen, the results of the inquiry had come before the public in 1932 under the challenging title *Re-Thinking Missions.*[91] Most of it had been written by Hocking and his friend Rufus Jones, the Quaker philosopher, and the general impression—if not the correct one—was that foreign missions as such were under attack. The onetime SVM leader and lifelong promoter of missions, Robert E. Speer, with his sharp analysis, *Re-Thinking Missions Examined,*[92] was probably the most incisive of the many who entered the heated debate.

Over against this situation, Latourette prefaced his *Missions Tomorrow* by declaring, "Some of us believe . . . that the needs of the new day for what the gospel has to offer are fully as great as are those of the one now ending. We are convinced that Christian missions, if rightly modified and faithfully supported, have an even greater function in the decades immediately ahead than they have had in the decades immediately closing." Speaking as a thoughtful historian and a forward-looking Christian he added:

[90] *Missions Tomorrow,* p. xvi.
[91] William E. Hocking, chairman, the Commission of Appraisal, *Re-Thinking Missions. A Laymen's Inquiry after One Hundred Years,* New York, Harper & Brothers, 1932, pp. xv + 349. Following this angle volume came the seven volumes of supporting material and findings, published as the *Laymen's Foreign Missions Inquiry,* New York, Harper & Brothers, 1933.
[92] Hogg, *op. cit.,* p. 421, n. 120; also p. 446. Speer's book was published in New York by Revell in 1933.

No one with an eye for the facts of the present world can avoid moments of doubt. Some of us, however, while perplexed, are not despairing. We would like to see still more done. We are not always sure what that should be. We are, however, convinced that, partly because of the achievements in the century which is just behind us, but chiefly because of our faith in God, the decades ahead may prove the most fruitful in the history of the world-wide Christian movement. Difficult and perilous the new day seems destined to be, but also marked by hope.[93]

Latourette wrote *Missions Tomorrow,* not primarily for the expert or for the missionary in the field, but mainly "for those who form the mainstay of the churches in the Anglo-Saxon world from which the major part of the support in personnel and money has come and continues to be drawn for the Protestant"[94] wing of the missionary enterprise. It is intended for mature students, for pastors, and for thoughtful laymen and laywomen, "some of whom may be wondering whether the missionary enterprise may not have been a mistake" or whether "amid all the clamorous needs of the world today, there continues to be reason for it." He noted that many earnest Christians were considering a redirection of effort away from foreign missions to evangelization at home, or to economic and social reconstruction, or to the reduction of the danger of war. "It is for those who are raising such questions that these pages are primarily intended." As to his own position or bias, he described himself as "thoroughly committed to the Christian missionary enterprise."[95] Reassuringly he added, "It scarcely needs to be said that the author is the mouthpiece of no organization or group."[96]

In short, this little book was Latourette's way of bringing all his own resources of knowledge, experience, and insight to bear objectively on an anxious situation. He did so as a careful historian. For him, *Missions Tomorrow* gave implicit notice of a new and monumental task he was setting himself.[97]

---

[93] *Missions Tomorrow,* pp. xii and 200.
[94] Protestant here includes Anglican.
[95] *Missions Tomorrow,* pp. xiii–xiv.
[96] *Ibid.,* p. xv.
[97] See pp. 1 ff., regarding the nineteenth century. Cf. pp. 171–172. (A question: Was Latourette one of the three sent by John R. Mott to press "on the younger churches the importance of this consciousness of the long Christian past"? P. 172.) Latourette was research chairman of the International Mission-

4. Opus Magnum, 1937–1945

Kenneth Scott Latourette's seven-volume masterpiece, *A History of the Expansion of Christianity*,[98] has become the standard work in its field. It is monumental and it is moving. With astounding comprehensiveness and almost limitless erudition, its 3,500 pages—complete with thousands of footnotes and scores of bibliographical lists —not only convey an enormous body of knowledge but also lay the basis for a necessary and overdue reorganization of the teaching of Church history.[99] This work is challenging both by what it says and by what it leaves unsaid. For even such an encompassing work as this cannot answer all the questions it raises; indeed, there are vital questions, theological in the main, which can best be asked after rather than before a survey such as this is available. This presentation will, therefore, be descriptive, while a critique will be embodied in the analysis of Latourette's historiography as a whole, which comes at the conclusion of this chapter.

There are, of course, solid and imposing reasons why *The Expansion*, as we may call it, has become the standard work in its field. But behind the objective reasons lie all kinds of subjective ones. Personally I learned of the first volume in 1937 just as I was finishing theological seminary and preparing for a graduate year in Europe and the Near East. By the time the last volume was out, in 1945, I found myself embodying the missionary outreach as a regular part of the teaching of Church history. In my case a combination of circumstances had driven home the conviction that the missionary aspect of Christian history, as well as the ecumenical, belongs in the mainstream, and not simply in the quiet elective pools, of theological study.[100]

---

ary Council and published his first report in 1932. See *IRM*, Vol. 21, pp. 532–546. This put him in an advantageous position to undertake a global project in historiography.

[98] Cited hereafter as *HEC*. Harper & Brothers, in New York, published the seven volumes as follows: 1937, Vol. I, pp. xxiv + 412; 1938, Vol. II, pp. ix + 492; 1939, Vol. III, pp. ix + 503; 1941, Vol. IV, pp. ix + 516; 1943, Vol. V, pp. ix + 526; 1944, Vol. VI, pp. ix + 502; 1945, Vol. VII, pp. xiii + 542.

[99] See below, pp. 268–269 (*The Madras Series*, Vol. IV, n. 195a.)

[100] This was my experience while teaching after 1942 at the Chicago Lutheran Theological Seminary, Maywood, Illinois, and while completing my doctoral work at the University of Chicago.

The seven volumes of *The Expansion* were completed during momentous years that changed the course of world history, and the appearance of each successive volume can hardly be dissociated from events then of global attention. At Harper, these volumes came from the press over a period of nine years that included both the cataclysms of World War II, which tore the nations apart, and the formative process of the World Council of Churches, which appeared as the Spirit of God drawing Christians together.

As always, Latourette's base of operations was Yale. In addition to his teaching he was involved more than ever in practical commitments as well. The familiar setting and the unrivaled resources, especially of the Day Missions Library, enabled him to work with scholarly efficiency. Gratefully he dedicated each successive volume to his predecessor, Harlan Page Beach (1854–1933), whose amassing of materials was making his own work far more possible.[101]

In 1937 came Volume I, *The First Five Centuries*. That was the year of ecumenical landmarks in Life and Work, at Oxford, and in Faith and Order, at Edinburgh; and in that year Latourette was named to the International Board of the YMCA.[102] In that first volume he built upon and carried forward Adolf Harnack's *Mission and Expansion of Christianity in the First Three Centuries*,[103] a book which in 1902 opened up a new perspective in the history of the early Church. In this volume, moreover, the author stated his purpose, described his viewpoint as that of one trained in the objective school of historiography, noted his credentials and the resources at his disposal, and set forth seven questions that would guide his method of procedure.[104]

These questions, long familiar to many, nevertheless bear repeating here: (1) What is the Christianity which spread? (2) Why did it spread? (3) Why has Christianity suffered reverses and at times only partial successes? (4) By what process did Christianity spread? To these basic four were added three corollary questions that sought to examine the problem of relationship between the Gospel and the

[101] See above, n. 74.

[102] *Who's Who in America, 1950–1951.*

[103] English edition, James Moffat. New York, G. P. Putnam's Sons, 2nd ed., 2 vols., 1908, based on Harnack's German original, *Die Mission und Ausbreitung des Christentums in den ersten drei Jahrhunderten* (Leipzig, Hinrichs, 1902, pp. xii +561).

[104] *HEC*, Vol. I, pp. ix–x, xv–xviii.

world: (5) What effect has Christianity had upon its environment? (6) What has been the effect of the environment on Christianity? (7) What bearing do the processes by which Christianity spread have upon the effect of Christianity on its environment, and of the environment upon Christianity?[105] From these questions it was evident that the author's historical treatment would be governed more by sociological than by theological considerations, although the latter were implicit, and could become explicit in the mind of the Christian reader.[106]

Here, too, came the matter of periodization. Leaving room for his now familiar later interpretation of fluctuating recessions within an over-all advance of Christianity,[107] he indicated four broad periods: (1) the first five centuries, (2) the thousand years from 500 to 1500, (3) the three centuries from 1500 to 1800, and (4) the decades from 1800 to the present.[108] It was on these decades that he would center his main attention.

In 1938, Volume II came out under the provocative title *The Thousand Years of Uncertainty*. In that year Latourette had entered upon what became a decade of annual lectures at the Canadian School of Missions, and at Utrecht he had also assisted in the drafting of a constitution for the incipient World Council of Churches.[109] En route to the Madras meeting of the International Missionary Council, he was honored by the Chinese government with the Order of Jade.[110] The delegates heading for Madras had with them Hendrik Kraemer's remarkable study book, *The Christian Message in a Non-Christian World*, published earlier that year by the IMC and inevitably raising provocative questions among mission leaders in many lands with its emphasis on Biblical realism and other incisive issues.[111] In that year, too, Hitler was promising the German people a thousand-year Reich of greatness, and Japan was pressing its claims ever farther over Asia and the South Pacific. Amid such conditions, *The*

[105] *Ibid.*, pp. x–xv.
[106] *Ibid.*, p. xvii.
[107] Cf. *The Unquenchable Light* (New York, Harper & Brothers, 1941), p. 171.
[108] HEC, Vol. I, pp. xviii–xix.
[109] Ruth Rouse and Stephen Neil (eds.), *A History of the Ecumenical Movement, 1517–1948* (Philadelphia, Westminster Press, 1954), p. 704.
[110] *Who's Who in America, 1950–1951*.
[111] Foreword by William Temple, Archbishop of York. London and New York, Harper & Brothers, 1938, pp. xvi + 455.

Thousand Years of Uncertainty challenged the modern Christian to consider his heritage. Even in the year 1500, Latourette claimed, "the hypothetical visitor from Mars might not have been able to determine whether in the ten centuries since the year 500 Christianity had won more than it had lost."[112]

In 1939, the year of the World Conference of Christian Youth, with its hundreds of delegates converging on Amsterdam from seventy-one countries, Latourette's Volume III appeared, heralding *Three Centuries of Advance*. The years 1500 to 1800 had seen the rise of the Reformation and the recovery of the Gospel, yet at the cost of the visible unity of the Church in Europe. The sixteenth and seventeenth centuries, marred by the conflicts of the Counter-Reformation, had also witnessed the unprecedented expansion of Roman Catholic missions around the world, while in the eighteenth century Protestant missions overseas began their belated and initially modest rise. Whoever read *Three Centuries of Advance* in the latter part of 1939 was appalled by the outbreak of the long-threatened war between the totalitarian Axis powers and the Western democracies. Many places usually accessible to scholars were suddenly either out of bounds or in imminent danger. Included were libraries Latourette had been using for research, like the Congregation for the Propagation of the Faith at Rome, the British Museum, the Morrison library on China, relocated at Tokyo; also the North China Branch of the Royal Asiatic Society at Shanghai, and other key places as well.[113]

With the appearance of these first three volumes Latourette's work reached a plateau, requiring a respite of sorts before he undertook the next big push. The years 1940–1941 thus found him publishing two small books that were by-products of his *opus magnum* and at the same time fuller disclosures of his interpretation of the history of Christianity. In *Anno Domini*,[114] the product largely of lectures given in Boston and at the Canadian School of Missions, he set forth "a comprehensive and chronological survey of the influence of Jesus on the stream of human history."[115] To him the very term *anno Domini* suggests a pervasive influence of Jesus, greater and "more widespread in its effect upon individual men and upon human society

[112] *HEC*, Vol. II, p. 3.
[113] *HEC*, Vol. III, p. ix.
[114] *Anno Domini: Jesus, History and God* (New York, Harper & Brothers, 1940).
[115] *Ibid.*, p. xi.

than [that of] any other who has ever appeared on earth."[116] Indeed, this is so "because God is at work through him, both judging and reconciling men to himself."[117]

Within human history this influence of Jesus, according to Latourette, is a pulsating reality that is chronologically measurable in its ebb and flow through the centuries. Indicating this in *Anno Domini*,[118] he developed it at length in *The Unquenchable Light*.[119] This, just to recall, is his tide table with its five advances and four recessions: up to A.D. 500 there is the first advance; then, to 950, the first recession; from 950 to 1350 a second advance, and then a recession to 1500; from 1500 to 1750 a third advance, followed by a recession to 1815; from 1815 to 1914 a fourth advance, followed by a recession to about 1940. Despite the deepening war, was the world entering upon a fifth advance? "In the past," he maintained, ". . . each ebb has been followed by a fresh advance and each advance has set a new high mark for the influence of Jesus in the total life of mankind. The presumption is that that in general will be the course in the future." Then, in anticipation of his own continuing task with *The Expansion*, he concluded, "A century and a quarter ago we could not have been sure from observed experience that this is so."[120] But in 1940 he believed it was so.

Volume IV of *The Expansion* appeared in 1941 under the thrilling caption *The Great Century* and was the first of a trilogy of volumes describing the missionary enterprise from about 1815 to 1914. This year of publication was the one that closed with Pearl Harbor and plunged the United States into mortal combat across the vast Pacific. This volume set the stage for depicting the story of what was hitherto the most extensive geographic spread of Christianity.[121] Where the previous global outreach had been almost entirely Roman Catholic, this new advance found Protestants most often in the forefront;

---

[116] *Ibid.*, pp. 8, 204.

[117] *Ibid.*, p. 9. Cf. review by R. E. E. Harkness, of Crozer Theological Seminary: "A biography of Jesus of 2,000 years" may be confusing the issue by ascribing much to Jesus that probably came from other sources. *Journal of Religion*, Vol. 21 (1941), p. 255.

[118] Pp. 204–205.

[119] The William Belden Noble Lectures, Harvard, 1940–1941. See above, n. 107.

[120] *The Unquenchable Light*, p. 171. See also the review by John Foster in *IRM*, Vol. 31 (1942), p. 472.

[121] *HEC*, Vol. IV, p. 2.

and by far the larger number of them were of the English-speaking peoples.[122] To be sure, the imperial expansion of Britain played a highly important part, but a phenomenal expansion of European-rooted peoples was under way, and a world culture seemed in the making. Because the origins of this culture were in the Occident, this was of advantage to Christianity.[123] Here, more than ever, the interacting influences of Christianity and the environment became exceedingly complex; the complexity was compounded, moreover, by the diversified character of Christianity itself, as well as by the fact that, in Latourette's proper understanding of the term, Christianity is not the Gospel as such but is man's response to the Gospel.[124]

Besides this groundwork, Volume IV handled with fine discernment as well as with unprecedented comprehensiveness the missionary activity carried on during the nineteenth century within the confines of Europe and the United States. For example, his 280 pages on home missions in the United States remain unexcelled in some important respects.[125] This, together with other studies, made the volume prerequisite to an understanding of the process that was currently making Christianity geographically world-wide for the first time in its history.

In 1943, the year of campaigns in North Africa and in the South Pacific, Latourette brought out Volume V, *The Great Century in the Americas, Australasia and Africa.* Wartime had, of course, brought changes in his teaching routine, but he continued to make full use of the resources of the Yale libraries as well as of others, notably the Missionary Research Library in New York. Foreign libraries, where he had done research earlier, received grateful recognition.[126]

This volume, like its predecessors, broke new ground. For the first time the missionary advance from Greenland and Canada to the far reaches of Latin America made composite sense. So also did that in

---

[122] *Ibid.,* p. 14.

[123] *Ibid.,* p. 21.

[124] See, e.g., K. S. Latourette, *Challenge and Conformity. Studies in the Interaction of Christianity and the World of Today* (New York, Harper & Brothers, 1955), pp. 116 ff. Cf. above, n. 117. Has Latourette here rectified the "confusion" that results from a too easy ascription of "influence" to Jesus?

[125] Review by Robert Hastings Nichols, in *Church History,* Vol. 10 (1941), p. 293.

[126] *HEC,* Vol. V, p. ix.

Australasia, the Pacific Islands, and Africa south of the Sahara. The inner logic of this volume flowed from that of Volume IV and its attention to the home bases of this outreach.[127]

In 1944, with Nazi rockets ripping London and the invasion of "Fortress Europe" from Britain as well as from North Africa punctuating the year with souped-up fury, Volume VI went on sale under the timely title *The Great Century in North Africa and Asia*. In contrast to the story in Volume V, Christianity in North Africa and Asia faced mainly ancient and advanced cultures, notably those formed by Islam and by the venerable religions of India, China, and Japan. Yet even against such odds "Christianity made amazing progress."[128] Meanwhile, the author's cultivated sense of responsibility for the quality of the spiritual life in his own community earned him the status of honorary pastor of Calvary Baptist Church in New Haven.[129]

When V-E Day in 1945 marked the unconditional surrender of Germany, and V-J Day did the same of Japan, and when atomic bombs had unleashed the first terrifying portents of massive annihilation, Latourette's final volume came out under the paradoxical but brave banner *Advance Through Storm*. Here, in "what must for the time being be the final volume," the industrious historian was telling as nearly as possible the story of the Christian world mission during the three decades that followed the year 1914. The storms it had been facing during those decades had taken heavy toll, as living memory everywhere testified. Into an amazing composite the author had drawn the diversified epic of the most missionary faith in the youngest generation of mankind.

Having brought the story down to the present, what was left for the author to do but to cast one long backward glance and then to look ahead? Looking back he noted that, despite the diversifications induced by the environment, Christianity through all ages and lands had preserved a remarkable continuity and family likeness. Pointing to the reason for this, and revealing the theological premise on which he had raised his monumental narrative, Latourette said simply:

> It was no accident that the religion which arose from Jesus was called Christianity and his followers Christians. In the designation, the Christ,

[127] *Ibid.*, p. 2.
[128] *Ibid.*, p. 5.
[129] *Who's Who in America, 1950–1951*.

which implied his humanity and divinity, was the symbol of the secret of the persistent life and growing power of the faith. Not always was loyalty to him a warrant of life. Many groups which had it died out. However, only those who cherished that loyalty continued through the centuries.[130]

Although to some readers his judgments might seem to be more swayed by sentiment than governed by doctrine, what he said actually appeared like an afterglow of the lay theology of the Student Volunteer Movement for Foreign Missions. Far from being simply backward looking, that theology—and the commitment it elicited—looked forward as well.[131]

Therefore, as he closed this volume, and with it this *opus magnum*, Latourette turned to the future. Wary of prophecy, especially on the part of the historian, he nevertheless ventured to assert that the record of Christianity "seems to presage a continuing expansion in the area covered and in the effect upon human-kind as a whole."[132] Again, as in *Anno Domini* and in *The Unquenchable Light*, as well as periodically in *The Expansion* itself, he reaffirmed his theory of alternating periods of advance and recession, with the periods of recession growing demonstrably shorter each time. He confidently claimed, "This has been the case by whichever of the criteria the advance and recession have been measured." And his three criteria throughout *The Expansion* had been these: (1) the geographic extent of Christianity, (2) the vitality of the movements issuing from Christianity, and (3) the influence of Christianity upon the human race.[133]

Applying these three criteria to the war-ravaged world of 1944, he came up with three remarkable conclusions. First, as to geographic extent, he said, "Never had any faith been so rooted among so many peoples as was Christianity in A.D. 1944." Second, as to vitality, men were still far from coming into accord with the life, teachings, and

---

[130] *HEC*, Vol. VII, p. 492.

[131] Characteristic of Mott was his irrepressible forward look. See Basil Mathews, *John R. Mott, World Citizen* (New York, Harper & Brothers, 1934, pp. 469), passim. This, of course, is inherent in the watchword "The evangelization of the world in this generation." Mott's influential book by that title, as well as others of his books, engrafted this "futurism" on the members of the Student Volunteer Movement and on many others besides. *Addresses and Papers*, Vol. I, p. 376.

[132] *HEC*, Vol. VII, p. 493.

[133] *Ibid.*, p. 494.

death of Jesus. Yet in A.D. 1944 such an accord was "more nearly approached by larger numbers of people and possibly by a higher proportion of professing Christians than in any other age. Certainly the trend was in that direction."[134] Third, and last, as to the effect of Christianity upon the environment, he has this to say:

> The very fact of the progressively wider extension of Christianity made for an increasing influence. Certainly in A.D. 1944 Christianity was affecting more deeply more different nations and cultures than ever before. If its influence had declined in some, it had begun or increased in others, and the latter outnumbered the former.[135]

This was Latourette, the cautious historian and confident missionary, speaking at the peak of his performance as a scholar. The faith which moved him was not simply an "American optimism," as some may have suspected,[136] but a buoyant and spiritual reality. In this faith, as we shall see later,[137] theological considerations were implicit rather than explicit. This faith, it seems to me, made him alternately a pilgrim through the centuries of the Christian era, a mendicant begging information around the world,[138] and, finally, a general, marshalling armies of facts and interpretively putting them at the disposal of the Church that is militant in earth and triumphant in heaven.

Yet even for one not necessarily sharing such an estimate, like a writer in the *American Historical Review*, reflections on the completed seven-volume work could elicit another form of praise: "No parallel work has ever appeared in any language. . . . [This] is a panoramic narrative of compelling excellence meeting the highest standards of craftsmanship and marking a milestone in New World historiography."[139]

So much for a description of *The Expansion*. We shall return to it in the larger setting of a general critique in the closing portion of

---

[134] *Ibid.*

[135] *Ibid.*

[136] See Ernest A. Payne's very illuminating essay on Latourette's *HEC*, which he read to the Oxford Society of Historical Theology, May 9, 1946. *Journal of Theological Studies*, Vol. 47 (1946), p. 149.

[137] See also below, pp. 267–269.

[138] *HEC*, Vol. VII, p. vii.

[139] See review by Lowell Ragatz, of George Washington University, in *AHR*, Vol. 51 (1945), p. 96.

this presentation. Meanwhile, there is more to be said about the author's further career as historian and friend.

5. *"The Expansion of Latourette,"* 1946–1960

Through a curious slip I have found myself occasionally telescoping the title and author of that huge missionary monograph into "The Expansion of Latourette." The slip may be felicitous as a title for a description of Professor Latourette's amazing productivity since the completion in 1945 of *The History of the Expansion of Christianity*. Indeed, our attention may be so fascinated by a work of great magnitude that we tend to overlook what happened next; and in many a historian's life *opus magnum* has also spelled *finis*. But in Latourette's case this is not so. He has flourished as never before. Thus, the decade and a half since 1946 presents us with a full pattern in two parts: first his life, and then his books.

1. Latourette's life in recent years has covered a broad range of activity. In terms of writing—not to forget his numerous articles, reviews, and other writings—the fifteen volumes he has published between 1946 and 1960 are about equal to all that he produced up to 1945, and this omits revised editions of earlier works. In terms of people, his other activities have gone on apace. At Yale he became director of graduate studies in the Department of Religion in 1946 and was honored in 1949 by his appointment as Sterling professor—a rank of high distinction in the University. Although retiring from teaching in 1953, his emeritus status seemed to stimulate new enterprise on his part. His continued residence in his Divinity School apartment, plus the ready access to resources long familiar, proved an ideal combination.

Since 1946 he has cultivated not only his chosen fields of history but also a world-wide company of friends. A string of lectureships in the United States, Canada, Latin America, Britain, Scandinavia, Germany, as well as in Asia and Africa, have given him incentive and multiplied his contacts with generations of scholars and students, pastors and missionaries, and many others. He has continued to be active in connection with the International Missionary Council, the American Committee for the World Council of Churches, and the International Committee of the YMCA. In 1948 he became a member of the Japan Christian University Foundation, being made president of it in 1951; he has served long on the United Board of Christian Colleges in China; and in 1955 he was president of the Far Eastern Association. He has continued his services, consultative or otherwise, in many other agencies of the Church, the government, the academic community, or the local congregation.[140]

Honors have come his way, including over a dozen doctorates *honoris causa*. Among the learned societies which elected him to membership is the American Catholic Historical Association. President of the American Society of Church History in 1945,[141] he is one of the few Church historians to hold the presidency of the American Historical Association, a position which he filled in 1948 and climaxed with his address on "The Christian Interpretation of History." His own denomination, the American Baptist Convention, elected him its president for 1951–1952. Although his travels since the end of World War II have taken him to many parts of the world, he has always returned to his writing with a high sense of duty. A lifelong bachelor, his children are his books, and to those brought forth since 1946 we turn next.

2. Latourette's books, during this postwar period, can be grouped in the main under four headings: (a) Far Eastern history, (b) missionary and ecumenical history, (c) general history of Christianity, and (d) period history of Christianity. Only some of these works shall we be able at this time to give more than the briefest notation, but even that much may reveal a meaningful pattern and help to set the stage for the final section of this study.

a. Far Eastern history, as we have seen, had claimed Latourette's attention from his student days.[142] World events had, meanwhile, turned attention to Asia with extraordinary urgency. Relatively few Americans were prepared to understand properly their relationship to the great Asian peoples, for many of whom the end of World War II meant the emancipation from dependency and the beginning of independent nationhood.

To help meet the demands of this sort of situation, Latourette was on hand with two kinds of books. First of all there were his books on China and Japan, which had originally appeared during and following World War I and had been reissued or revised ever since.

[140] *Who's Who in America, 1960–1961.*
[141] *Ibid.*
[142] See above, pp. 234 ff.

In 1946 Houghton Mifflin brought out a sixth revised edition of his *Development of China*.[143] Also in 1946, Macmillan published two-volumes-in-one as a third revised edition, his standard work of *The Chinese, Their History and Culture*.[144] In 1947 came his *History of Japan*, which was practically a fifth revised edition of his early book *Development of Japan*.[145]

This, however, was only the beginning of Latourette's productivity. His professorship at Yale involved teaching courses on the Far East. Of his three books in this field between 1946 and 1952, the major one was his *Short History of the Far East*. Published by Macmillan in 1946,[146] it was the fruit of lectures on this subject extending back to his Reed College days. Appropriately the book was dedicated to Reed's first president, William Trufant Foster, who had also launched Latourette on his teaching career. By 1957 a third revised edition had come out and, like his other works of the Far East, was meeting the need for a forthright popular textbook that paid proper attention especially to the modern period and would introduce college and university students to a subject of growing magnitude. The two other books were short monographs, also of practical interest: *The United States Moves Across the Pacific: the A.B.C.'s of the American Problem in the Western Pacific and the Far East*, came from Harper in 1946,[147] and *The American Record in the Far East, 1945–1951* from Macmillan in 1952.[148]

A reading of these books, and also of their reviews, reveals not only substantial content but dedicated scholarship. Here was the prolongation of Latourette's missionary commitment, redirected as it had been by illness in 1912.[149] This leads us to an assortment of his specifically Christian books.

b. Missionary and ecumenical history required repeated interpretation and ever fresh restatements for denominationally and cultur-

[143] Boston, Houghton Mifflin Company, 1946, pp. 343.

[144] New York, The Macmillan Company, 1946, pp. 847.

[145] New York, The Macmillan Company, 1947, pp. 290. *Development of Japan* had appeared in a fourth revised edition in 1938, pp. 272. *History of Japan* came out in a revised edition in 1957, pp. 299. There was little, if any, real revision; rather a continuation of the historical narrative into the present.

[146] Pp. 665. Revised editions have continued to come out, being supplemented by an account of latest developments: 1952, pp. 730; 1957, pp. 754.

[147] Pp. 174.

[148] Pp. 208.

[149] See above, p. 241.

ally diversified audiences. This activity might be called Latourette's teaching-at-large. The books which were its product appeared between the years 1946 and 1957. At the outset, however, two exceptions to this rule should be noted. The one was his booklet on Buddhism,[150] part of a series designed to promote a popular understanding of living world religions. The other was his concise and informative monograph on the history of foreign work and world service of the YMCA's of the United States and Canada. Entitled *World Service*,[151] its appearance in 1957 gave a striking interpretation of a world-wide Christian and cultural operation.

Now to the other books. As précis or, more aptly in some cases, as by-products of *The Expansion* we may here briefly take up five of them. We must bear in mind that their purpose was pedagogical and that, as a result, the historian was here not simply informing about the past but also describing the present and prognosticating the future. Indeed, to me these works suggest a practical combination of the erudite historian and the perennial Student Volunteer—an angle, as I see it, implicit in his presidential address to the American Society of Church History in 1945.[152]

Taking these books in order, the first to appear was an edited volume entitled *The Gospel, the Church and the World*.[153] As Book III of the noteworthy Interseminary Series of 1946, it was designed to help widen the horizons of theological students and to give them historical perspectives commensurate with the tasks of the new day.[154] Latourette's own chapter was a thumbnail sketch of *The Expansion*, plus a provocative set of generalizations pointing toward the future.[155]

In 1948, the year of the formation of the World Council of Churches, came *The Christian Outlook*.[156] Here again was an epitome of *The Expansion* with a forward view added. The content had been tried out on audiences at nine different universities and theological schools in the United States, Canada, and England. Latou-

---

[150] *Introducing Buddhism* (New York, Friendship Press, 1956, pp. 64).

[151] New York, Association Press, 1957, pp. xiv + 489.

[152] *Church History*, Vol. 15 (1946), pp. 3–16.

[153] The Interseminary Series (New York, Harper & Brothers, 1946), Vol. II, Book III, pp. 225.

[154] *Ibid.*, pp. x–xi.

[155] *Ibid.*, pp. 83–110.

[156] New York and London, Harper & Brothers, 1948, pp. 229. The English edition bore the title *The Prospect for Christianity*.

rette's presidential address to the American Historical Association, in 1948, still further condensed the substance of *The Christian Outlook* but was weighted to set forth "the Christian interpretation of history."[157] In commenting on both the address and *The Christian Outlook*, a British reviewer feared that too much condensation resulted in dilution rather than concentration; he expressed a judgment that might apply not only to these two items but to some of the others here before us as well when he wrote:

> The material of which Dr. Latourette is master affords much food for thought. . . . His genius, however, is pragmatic rather than speculative, comprehensive rather than critical, buoyant rather than profound. It shines out finely in the assertions that evangelization is the test of Christian vitality, and that it is the duty of every Christian to realize the unity of the Church in his own life.[158]

For a Protestant, to be sure, this would not be easy. As Latourette had pointed out in his 1945 address, while Christianity is becoming more and more world-wide, "Protestantism is becoming more Anglo-Saxon and American." This, in turn, meant growing strength for the radical wing of Protestantism[159] and greater problems in reconciling such positions with those of Anglicans and Eastern Orthodox in the ecumenical movement.

Against the background of *The Expansion*, also in 1948, came the stimulating little book *Tomorrow Is Here*.[160] Done in collaboration with his able young graduate assistant William Richey Hogg, this was a report and interpretation of the first postwar meeting of the International Missionary Council. Held at Whitby, Ontario, in July, 1947, "the conference was marked by resolute pleas for giving the Gospel to the entire world." Even the old watchword of the Student Volunteer Movement seemed to rise to new relevance for the tomorrow that had come.[161]

With the Amsterdam assembly of the World Council of Churches leaving its imprint in many quarters, Latourette's next work, *The*

[157] *AHR*, Vol. 54 (1949), pp. 268–276.
[158] Martin Wight, in *IRM*, Vol. 38 (1949), p. 490.
[159] *Church History*, Vol. 15 (1946), p. 13.
[160] New York, Friendship Press, pp. 145.
[161] Cf. *Missions Tomorrow*, 1937, singled out as the work to which this book is the sequel.

Emergence of a World Christian Community,[162] was timely. Published in 1949, when the first chilling blasts of the cold war were boding ill and the Berlin blockade was on, this little volume reminded its readers that the nations are "slowly and painfully learning to work together, but it is an open question whether they will do so in time. . . . A spiritual and moral tie is desperately needed which will hasten wholesome cooperation and assure its success. The most hopeful prospect of such a tie is the growing world Christian fellowship." Therein lay his purpose of describing historically the emerging world-wide Christian community. The Christian faith, as religions go, was still young. He ventured to say, "Compared with the millenniums which have thus far been marked by the presence of civilization, Christianity is a very recent feature of the human scene."[163] The author's propensity to think chronologically and evolutionally, to the apparent exclusion of eschatology, left some serious questions unanswered. Nevertheless he saw in Christianity "the hope of our bewildered and distraught race."[164]

Likewise, in 1949, his booklet on *Missions and the American Mind* presented a provocative summation of the role of the Christian missionary enterprise in shaping significant elements of thought and action among Americans throughout their history.[165] Although little appreciated by most people, these elements have "contributed to the view that every man, whether in the United States or in any other country of the world, is of infinite worth. . . . On the world scene it has been one of the chief sources—historically, indeed, the original impulse—of movements for world peace and world organization."[166]

In 1950, the Tipple Lectures at Drew University caught the biographical dimension of the missionary enterprise and subsequently appeared as the book *These Sought a Country*.[167] Skillfully he portrayed William Carey as "the inspired scholar who sought India and the world"; Samuel Mills, who ventured courageously to Burma; Hudson Taylor, who "sought China's millions"; Timothy Richard,

[162] New Haven, Yale University Press, 1949, pp. 92. These were the Rockwell Lectures at Rice Institute, Houston, Texas.
[163] *Ibid.*, p. 59.
[164] *Ibid.*, p. 86.
[165] Indianapolis, National Foundation Press, 1949, pp. 40.
[166] *Ibid.*, p. 3.
[167] New York, Harper & Brothers, 1950, pp. 156.

who "sought all China"; and Joseph Hardy Neesima, who "sought a country in order that he might transform his own" Japan. Of these five men, as of all true Christian witnesses, a word from the Epistle to the Hebrews seems applicable; for in the light of the obedience of their faith "God is not ashamed to be called their God."[168]

Taking up the challenge being flung at the Gospel by opposing forces, Latourette published *The Christian Mission in Our Day* in 1954.[169] The product of lectures delivered at four schools in the United States and at the Universities of Lund, Copenhagen, and Helsinki,[170] this book also revealed its lineage from *The Expansion*. So far as I can gather, however, it also sounded a theological note which had been noticeably absent in Latourette's earlier works, namely, eschatology.[171]

Since eschatology is a matter of basic importance to any historian who goes at his work as a Christian, a few quotations may be helpful. While eschatology does not permeate his book, it comes in near the end, as a paradox. Recapitulating first the old way, typical also of his own characteristic thought, Latourette asks, "Is God gradually, even though by uneven stages and with occasional temporary reverses, to transform human society within a continuation of the historical process as we have thus far known it? Many have believed and even now believe that this is to be. . . ." He then adds the already familiar observation that, despite the magnitude of evil in the world, "Christianity is more deeply rooted among more peoples, and exerting a wider influence upon mankind than ever before."[172]

However—and this is the noteworthy departure—"against this expectation, what may be called this utopianism, are the testimony of history and the Scriptures. The paradoxes which we have noted seem to preclude such a culmination in history." Then he goes on, "The New Testament is emphatic that there is to be an end of history. . . . For us the precise manner and hour of the culmination must remain a mystery. Yet while living in instant expectation of that event we are not disappointed if it is greatly delayed."[173] Pre-

---

[168] Hebrews 11:16, which also suggests the title of the book.
[169] New York, Harper & Brothers, 1954, pp. 192.
[170] *Ibid.*, p. 10.
[171] *Ibid.*, p. 178.
[172] *Ibid.*, p. 178.
[173] *Ibid.*, p. 179.

cisely in this state of expectancy, as Latourette points out, the Christian takes up his task in full earnest. "In the meantime," he says,

> . . . we are not to be idle. We are to be witnesses. . . . We must labor to permeate all the features of human society with the teaching of Christ.[174] We must aim at nothing less than winning all the nations to discipleship, incorporating them into Christ's Church, and teaching them to bring all aspects of this life into conformity with Christ's commands. Even though we know that, by a paradox, the goal is not to be attained within history, we must press forward toward it. . . . We can do so, knowing, not merely wistfully hoping, that neither things present nor things to come can separate us from the love of God which is in Christ Jesus our Lord.[175]

Perhaps the meeting with Scandinavian and other European theologians helped Latourette to a clearer theological position.[176] In any case, upon his return from a year of research in Europe, he brought out *Challenge and Conformity*, being studies in the interaction of Christianity and the world of today.[177] Growing largely out of lectures delivered originally at the Universities of Copenhagen, Aarhus, Uppsala, and Oslo, and in the theological school of Bethel-Bielefeld, Germany, this small book reflected another aspect of Latourette's latter-day encounter with European Christians and scholars. In taking up his subject he makes case studies of three geographic areas: Europe, the United States, and portions of the non-Occidental world. His purpose is to delineate how Christianity has responded to the varying environments in which it is found, and how it has transformed them.[178] Here again we notice the pedigree of Latourette's basic work, *The Expansion*. But there is also something more that grows inevitably out of mission history, and that is the general history of Christianity with all its inner conflicts and external involvements. Actually, the compass of this book is too small to do more than point to a much larger historiographical task. Yet it stands

---

[174] It may be asked whether this use of Christ represents any meaningful change over against Latourette's usual reference to the teachings of Jesus. Christ, eschatology, and final judgment under divine authority belong together theologically.

[175] *The Christian Mission in Our Day*, pp. 178–181.

[176] See below for the criticism of Martin Wight, p. 278, and of J. S. Whale, p. 277, in regard to Latourette's neglect of eschatology.

[177] New York, Harper & Brothers, 1955, pp. 126.

[178] *Ibid.*, pp. 9–11.

chronologically in between two works of related intent but of much vaster format to which we shall presently turn.

Not another book but a chapter deserves mention before we leave this section, and that is Latourette's contribution to *A History of the Ecumenical Movement, 1517–1948*.[179] His monograph culminated in the rise of the International Missionary Council and showed impressively how important for the ecumenical movement as a whole was the missionary enterprise of the nineteenth and twentieth centuries.[180] From missions and ecumenics, however, it is but natural to consider the whole purview of the history of Christianity and to recast what has been long traditional into what ought to be excitingly contemporary.

c. The general history of Christianity proved to be an irresistible temptation for Latourette, and he entered the field with such resolve that he produced the first major American compendium in a generation. *A History of Christianity* was published by Harper in 1953. Its 1,516 pages and weighty bulk might intimidate the fastidious, but the reputation of its author made the work immediately attractive to many. Here, at last, was a textbook whose scope matched developments of the modern day; for the first time in a general history of the Church was embodied the story of its missionary enterprise. Nor was this textbook thereby simply a condensation of the seven-volume *History of the Expansion of Christianity*. Rather, because of this substantial parentage, this book could stand solidly on its own feet.

What Williston Walker's standard text had been to the fathers in the twentieth century, Latourette's should be to the sons. True to past form, it was Yale for Yale. Indeed, it may even be charged that a Yale tradition has infiltrated the field of American Church history textbooks. Latourette, as we have seen, was indebted to Williston Walker, under whom he took his one course in Church history. Walker's book, *A History of the Christian Church*, published in 1917, was in turn a replacement for the work of another Yale man, George Park Fisher, whose *History of the Christian Church* (1888) had ushered in this American line. Fisher was influenced by the

[179] Ruth Rouse and Stephen Neill (eds.) (Philadelphia, Westminster Press, 1954). Chapter 8, "Ecumenical Bearings of the Missionary Movement and the International Missionary Council," by Kenneth Scott Latourette, pp. 353–402.

[180] Cf. Hogg, *op. cit.* (see above, n. 46), done under Latourette's guidance.

German fashion of writing Church history with stern objectivity, to the severe exclusion of the author's preferences, and Walker followed lowed suit. In Latourette, this cultivated objectivity continued, but the book itself, whose title accentuated Chrisianity rather than Church, was in scope and treatment an implicit declaration of independence from European-bound historical perspectives. While we shall return to this matter of scope in the final section, there are other things to claim our attention first.

Among these is the question of the author's presupposition. In contrast to 1937,[181] he seems to deal more openly with the limitations of "objective" historiography and about the real difficulties of telling "what actually happened." Now, as then, he is aware of his personal bias; but now it seems to be more clearly stated. "One is either for or against Christianity," he asserts; "there is no neutral or strictly objective ground." Reason has its legitimate role, yet "truth is not attained by reason alone." For the insight "born of faith can bring illumination." Underlying all the chapters "is the conviction that the faith which is stimulated by contact with the Christian Gospel, the faith which is the commitment to God of the whole man, body, mind, and spirit, the commitment which is the response in love to God Who is love and Who in His love revealed Himself in Jesus Christ, opens the mind towards the true understanding of history." Latourette recognizes, of course, that the believer's commitment to God, though ever so earnest, is nevertheless incomplete. "We should, therefore," he adds, "never claim infallibility for our interpretation of history. Yet so far as the faith which follows commitment has been given to us, we must seek in its light to perceive the road which man has thus far traversed."[182]

Resolutely, Latourette endeavors to present the history of Christianity—of man's response to the Gospel—"in its relation to the total story of mankind." His aim, though manifestly impossible to full attainment, he believes to be at least partly attainable as a summary story. Thus he hopes to bring the highlights in the record of Christianity in a useful manner "to the thoughtful student, whether he be clergyman or layman, Christian or non-Christian." He trusts that this

[181] *HEC*, Vol. I, pp. xvii–xviii. Cf. *A History of Christianity*, pp. xx–xxi (cited hereafter as *HC*).
[182] *HC*, p. xxi.

work will be welcome as a textbook in colleges, universities, and theological schools.[183]

Basing the work on the best available books, monographs, and articles of specialists, he has endeavored also to examine a fair proportion of the original sources and thus to make his own account as factually accurate as possible.[184]

The pattern into which Latourette shapes his narrative arrests attention. Following a sketching of the pre-Christian course of mankind, he devotes over thirty pages to the life and ministry of Jesus. This is basic to his subsequent, and characteristic, notation of the influence of Jesus throughout the Christian era.[185] Then comes a periodization already familiar from his seven-volume *Expansion,* and other writings.[186] In the process he breaks with the traditional *horizontal* approach, which the German historians had made standard by their neat periodization, especially in the first five centuries. His description of Christianity's external sweep across the Graeco-Roman world, and then his portrayal of its internal structuring through polity, doctrine, worship, and discipline make for a certain amount of repetition and chronological surprise.

As in *The Expansion,* so here in this handbook, Latourette is intent upon telling the epic of the faith. It matters little to him, it seems, what the nature of this faith is; for he is telling the history of Christianity, and Christianity is not the same thing as the Gospel—as he made clear at the outset. The Gospel is indeed coming to all the world; but while its message is the same for all, what is spreading is the response to the Gospel; the response to the influences of Jesus, who himself is the Good News for all men, and this response is not the same among all.

Noteworthy also is his world-wide perspective. Traditional German Church historiography had been—and still is for the most part—severely European and globally provincial.[187] Latourette here makes

---

[183] *Ibid.,* p. xxii.
[184] *Ibid.,* p. xxvi.
[185] Cf. *Anno Domini*—see nn. 114 and 117 above.
[186] See above, p. 253. Cf. *The Unquenchable Light*—see n. 119 above.
[187] This condition, as well as a generally "Western" orientation of Church history, has led the World Council of Churches, through its Division of Studies, to promote conferences of Church historians from all parts of the world. The latest was conducted at the Ecumenical Institute, Bossey, near Geneva, in August, 1960. Reports on earlier sessions are available from the World Coun-

amends. Indeed, he is the first American to produce a major compend of Christian history that gives both Continental Europe and also the Anglo-Saxon peoples their due. Yet he does not overdevelop the American portion of his narrative; for his outlook is persistently comprehensive and ecumenical. As George H. Williams has pointed out: "The vantage point is ecumenical, surely not primarily American." The founders of the Bay Colony in Massachusetts get little more preferential treatment than those who brought the faith to the Belgian Congo.[188]

Still other matters might be mentioned, such as Latourette's apparent position toward the doctrine of the Church, and of man,[189] but these must wait for the general appraisal at the end.

In view of its excellences and handicaps—not least of which is its ponderous bulk—it would be interesting to know how extensively Latourette's *History of Christianity* has become a text in our colleges, universities, and theological schools; or how much the recently revised "Walker" has re-established itself as the standby, albeit without treatment of Christianity outside the Occident and with only a short concluding section on the ecumenical movement.[190] Thus the struggle for a reorganized global presentation of the history of Christianity continues to be waged chiefly, though not exclusively, by Latourette.

d. Period history, long a favorite among historians, has summoned forth what promises to become Latourette's crowning achievement. His currently appearing *Christianity in a Revolutionary Age*, four volumes of which are already out, addresses itself with methodical determination to the nineteenth and twentieth centuries.[191] Admit-

---

cil's Geneva headquarters. Typical of the German orientation is the perennially popular handbook of Karl Heussi, *Kompendium der Kirchengeschichte* (Tuebingen, Mohr, 11th ed., 1957).

[188] *AHR*, Vol. 59 (1954), p. 589.

[189] E.g., E. A. Payne, *Journal of Theological Studies*, Vol. 47 (1946), pp. 146, 152; or Robert H. Fischer, review in *Journal of Religion*, Vol. 34 (1954), p. 142. Cf. below, pp. 277–278.

[190] Williston Walker, *A History of the Christian Church*, revised by Cyril C. Richardson, Wilhelm Pauck, Robert T. Handy (all of Union Theological Seminary, New York) (New York, Charles Scribner's Sons, 1959, pp. 585).

[191] *Christianity in a Revolutionary Age. A History of Christianity in the Nineteenth and Twentieth Centuries*. Vol. I, *The Nineteenth Century in Europe. Background and the Roman Catholic Phase* (New York, Harper & Brothers, 1958, pp. xiv + 498); Vol. II, *The Nineteenth Century in Europe. The Protestant and Eastern Churches* (1959, pp. ix + 532); Vol. III, *The Nineteenth Century Outside Europe. The Americas, the Pacific, Asia, and Africa* (1961,

tedly, the closer we come to the present the more difficult becomes the problem of historical perspective and the higher rises the mountain of available materials.

Surely, the time for a proper appraisal of this latent and again monumental effort of Latourette must await the completion of these projected five volumes. Nor is it necessary to rehearse the author's sources, credentials, qualifications, viewpoint, and a number of other matters which he discusses in the Preface; for with these we are already somewhat familiar.

The purpose, however, of choosing this subject and period and of undertaking this all-out effort concerns us very much indeed. As the author points out, Christianity is seen by many as a moving force and as occupying a position in the modern and especially Western world that has become so changed as to invite the application of "post-Christian era" not only to the twentieth but also to the nineteenth and even to the eighteenth century. But such a characterization, while understandable, the author brands as "hasty and naïve."[192]

In rebuttal, he tells why he has entered upon the venture at this time and in this chosen way. With the year 1815 as his starting point for the nineteenth century, he asserts, "The period is one in which Christianity first became world-wide. To be sure, it was seriously threatened and that threat mounted as decade followed decade in the breath-taking speed and bewildering multiplicity of the era." He notes that by forces "which issued from what was once called Christendom and in which to no small degree Christianity had entered as a causative factor, all mankind was being made a neighborhood." Quarrelsome though it was, this neighborhood took on the semblance of "one world." In it, by the mid-twentieth century, "Christianity was represented by organized churches in all but two of the countries which claimed political independence." Although in most countries outside the traditional Christendom these churches were small minorities, "they were growing minorities," becoming rooted in indigenous leadership and self-support.[193]

---

pp. viii, 527). Vol. IV, *The Twentieth Century in Europe. The Roman Catholic, Protestant, and Eastern Churches* (1961, pp. viii, 568). Vol. V, *The Twentieth Century Outside Europe. The Americas, the Pacific, Asia, and Africa: the Emerging World Christian Community* (to be published 1962). (Cited hereafter as *CRA*.)

[192] *CRA*, Vol. I, pp. vii, ix.

[193] *Ibid.*, pp. vii–viii.

Latourette sees clearly that his subject is beset with paradox. On the one hand, Christianity is in danger of decline; on the other, it shows amazing vigor and a world-wide spread. The very contrariness of this situation "would in itself make some such work as is here attempted imperative for an understanding of history and the current human scene."[194]

Other paradoxes complicate the situation still further, as, for example, the expansion of Europe in the nineteenth century versus its decline in the twentieth; the modern rejection by colonial peoples of Europe's political rule, and the acceptance by those same people of its science and industry and homogenized life.[195] In the light of such development, claims the author, this is not a post-Christian era but an era when the paradoxical character of the human situation is more dramatically than ever before us. Hence the title of this work, *Christianity in a Revolutionary Age*, and its subtitle, *A History of Christianity in the Nineteenth and Twentieth Centuries*.

The main outline of the work is this: the first three volumes present the historic background and the nineteenth century. Volume I, *The Nineteenth Century in Europe*, published in 1958, brings the background and the Roman Catholic phase. Very quickly the author sketches the origin of Christianity and a summary of its history through the eighteenth century, closing this introductory part with the French Revolution and the era of Napoleon. Then follows an account of Roman Catholicism in Europe, compressed into some 230 pages.

Volume II, appearing in 1959, continues the European account with over 400 pages devoted to the Protestant phase. While Roman Catholicism has had its full-scale histories of the period, this is, I believe, the fullest and most complete coverage thus far accorded nineteenth-century European Protestantism. This gathering of chunk-like state churches and dispersed fragment-like minorities into an orderly, if not exactly attractive, whole has rendered English-speaking Protestants a great service. The less than one hundred pages on Greek and Russian Orthodoxy are helpful but show up the limitations of compression.

Volume III, published in 1961, covers the course of Christianity during the nineteenth century outside the traditional Christendom

[194] *Ibid.*, p. viii.
[195] *Ibid.*

and includes the Americas, Asia, Africa, and Australasia. Volume IV published in 1961, and V, scheduled to come out in 1962,[196] cover the twentieth century since 1914 and repeat the method of presentation devised for the first three volumes.

Although Latourette's *Christianity in a Revolutionary Age* draws on his previous major works, these five volumes are essentially a new work.[197] Portions of the four pertinent volumes of *The Expansion* are here recast with perspectives and emphases occasionally altered. His one-volume *History of Christianity*, which devoted about one-fourth of its space to the nineteenth and twentieth centuries, he likewise regards as a resource for the present work.

Christianity in a Revolutionary Age, as things now appear, will be the climactic achievement, crowning an unusually long and productive career. But to close our study of Latourette as historian and friend at this point would be to content ourselves largely with compilation and recital. His career is open-ended and invites discussion, especially since behind all this lifetime of scholarship there appears also a profounder involvement.

6. *The Mission of a Historian—and a Critique*

Kenneth Scott Latourette is manifestly a man of conviction and of Christian commitment. As one who has known him almost exclusively through his books, I cherish the thought of being nonetheless counted among his friends as well as among those whom his lifework has influenced positively. From my present vantage point on the Pacific coast, and with memories of historical studies that extend eastward not to Yale, but alas! to Harvard, I see Dr. Latourette in what, I trust, is a properly large perspective. To me he appears as one in whom a redirected missionary career and scholar's disciplined training have been blended into a life of memorable achievement. To say this is not a subtle form of self-justification for the time and effort expended on the preparation of this study, but rather an honest way of expressing that kind of appreciation which many undoubtedly share.

Somewhat impersonally I have headed this concluding part "The Mission of a Historian," for no scholar ought to be without his high purpose; but I should especially like this heading understood as de-

[196] K. S. Latourette to E. T. Bachmann, April 27, 1960.
[197] See *CRA*, the author's Introduction.

noting Latourette as a historian with a mission. The justification for this kind of caption may seem to lie in his life as a whole. As generalizations go, to call him a historian with a mission would therefore hardly demand documentation. But headings and footnotes always refer beyond themselves, and here we must turn to a specific place for the clue and its context.

In his comments on "The Place of Church History in the Training of Missionaries"[198]—which is the shortest piece of his that I have read—Latourette, at Christmas time in 1938, presented the conferees at the Madras meeting of the International Missionary Council with a far-reaching fourfold challenge. In effect, his four points still bear repeating today as overdue imperatives: reorganize, rename, oversee, and amplify the teaching of Church history.

Latourette's spelling out of these four points makes them read like the platform to which he pledged his career. They bear quotation, especially as we keep in mind the previous parts of this chapter. This is what he said:

> First of all I have a profound conviction that the teaching of Church history is in need of reorganization not only in the preparation of missionaries, but also in the training of the ministry of both the older and younger churches. The following suggestions are, therefore, intended for the general courses in Church history in both East and West.
>
> In the second place, I much prefer the caption *The History of Christianity* to *Church History*. This is not from any desire to belittle the Church. It is, rather, in part from a desire to exalt the Church. Much of Church history as now taught is too narrow. It is chiefly concerned with the Church's internal history. . . . All this is, of course, important and in any comprehensive survey of the Church must be continued. However, most courses in Church history have far too little of the effect of the Church upon its environment, of the effect of the environment upon the Church, and of the geographic spread of the Church. . . . A change . . . can probably best be achieved by a frank alteration in the name. In the history of Christianity we must attempt to trace the entire course of the stream which issues from our Lord and of its contributions to mankind.

[198] *The Madras Series*, Vol. IV, *The Life of the Church* (New York, International missionary Council, 1939), pp. 254–258. It is useful to note the subhead of this important series: "Presenting papers based upon the meeting of the International Missionary Council, at Tambaram, Madras, India, December 12th to 29th, 1938."

In the third place, and as a corollary to what has been said, the study of the history of Christianity must be ecumenical in its outlook and scope. . . . I should be . . . insistent that the history of Christianity be so taught that leaders of the Church, both missionary and national, possess a comprehension of the world-wide Christian movement and something of an understanding of all the main communions and of the progress and achievements of Christianity in all the lands which it has entered.

In the fourth place, I cherish a profound conviction that in the study and teaching of the history of Christianity much more attention should be devoted to the post-Reformation period and especially to the nineteenth and twentieth centuries. . . . One ought not, of course, to belittle the importance of the first four centuries, of the Middle Ages or of the struggles connected with the Reformation. However, to pass over lightly the period since the Reformation (as is so often the case) gives the student the impression that nothing especially significant has occurred since that time and that Christianity is a waning force. . . . [Yet] never before has it molded the human race so profoundly, so widely, or in so wide a variety of environments. . . . We need to re-apportion the space and to see that the last three centuries, and particularly the past century and a half, have their due.

This plea for comprehensiveness and a reorientation of preparation has found its most impressive response in Latourette himself. Although the first two volumes of *The Expansion* had already appeared by the time he was making this plea in 1938, the decades that followed have seen him stick resolutely to these four points, aiming with unrelaxed motivation to reorganize, rename, oversee, and amplify the study of the historic faith to which all mankind is potential heir. It is with this broad vision that Latourette's writings in Far Eastern history were also to be included; for they deal in almost prophetic anticipation with the coming center of gravity of world history.

Latourette's efforts, of course, have not been single handed, and he has won co-workers in his cause. But he himself has been the one plodding on, going ahead at his pedestrian pace while others were more swiftly and traditionally going around. As a pioneer, operating within the limits set for his work, the product of his scholarship has drawn recurring choruses of astonished commendation. That one man—not unassisted, as he was ever first to admit—could accomplish so much and over so long a period has raised repeated admiration from fellow scholars and mission men the world over.

Among scholars, however, it is not always a favor to have a pioneer work accepted uncritically. So, too, in Latourette's case his work could be appreciated most when it was criticized constructively. Here let me simply cite some examples of such criticism, and after that go on to conclusions of my own.

The series of reviews by J. S. Whale, which appeared in the *International Review of Missions* in the wake of the successive volumes of *A History of the Expansion of Christianity*, culminated in a brief but telling climax with Volume VII.[199] This English Congregationalist challenged some of Latourette's optimistic generalizations and registered uneasiness over the ethicizing interpretation of Christianity that characterized his work as a whole. Besides, he charged, "The philosophy of history with which Dr. Latourette is working is not that of the Hebraic-Christian eschatology of the New Testament but rather the evolutionary perfectionism which dreams of a Utopia achieved by human efforts within the time process."[200] Whale goes on to say that this "familiar distortion of what the Bible means by the Kingdom of God is not substantially different from those blatant doctrines of man's self-sufficiency which abound to-day (amid a world catastrophe which gives them all the lie)." With benevolent candor he concludes that such Christian idealism permeates *The Expansion*, especially its seventh volume, and "is not essentially different from the Nazisms or Marxisms of our time, in spite of the mere façade of Scriptural phrases behind which it innocently hides itself."[201]

Eight years later, with the appearance of *A History of Christianity*, at least one reviewer again took exception to the ethical idealism and to the seemingly shallow understanding of the nature

[199] *IRM*, Vol. 34 (1945), pp. 427–429. Cf. Whale's earlier reviews of *HEC*, as the successive volumes appeared: Vol. II, *IRM*, Vol. 28 (1939), pp. 579 ff.; Vol. III, *IRM*, Vol. 29 (1940), pp. 274 ff.; Vol. IV, *IRM*, Vol. 30 (1941), pp. 406 ff.; Vol. V, *IRM*, Vol. 32 (1943), pp. 436–439. Vol. VI was reviewed by the Swedish Lutheran missiologist Professor Knut B. Westman, at Uppsala, *IRM*, Vol. 34 (1945), pp. 199–202, who raised no theological issues but praised the erudition of the author and the comprehensiveness of the work. Note how Latourette himself could be critical, e.g., of Edward R. Hardy's *Militant in Earth* (New York, Oxford University Press, 1940), pointing out its weaknesses where it dealt poorly with the modern period after having made an excellent presentation of the ancient and medieval eras. *IRM*, Vol. 30 (1941), pp. 265.
[200] *IRM*, Vol. 34 (1945), p. 429.
[201] *Ibid.*

of man with which Latourette still clothed his narrative.[202] For another reviewer, in 1938, the fact that Latourette apparently contented himself with the role of the recorder "who endeavors to avoid an estimate of the ethical and social worth of what he observes" gave him an uneasy feeling. It was as though "Hamlet has been left out of the play."[203]

With fine penetration the English Baptist historian Ernest A. Payne wished that throughout his survey, and at least in his account of the nineteenth- and twentieth-century Christian expansion, "Dr. Latourette had given more attention to the Christian message itself, to doctrinal and theological issues and controversies." Payne questioned "whether there is enough in these volumes about the Church, its faith and order as well as its life and work." The question of eschatology seemed to Payne to cast serious doubts on Latourette's metaphor of the tide-like pulsation of Christianity's advance through history.[204] Criticism along similar lines came from Harvard's George H. Williams in reviewing *A History of Christianity* in 1954.[205]

Repeatedly Latourette pauses at the semicolon of the present[206] and then, on the basis of the past record of Christianity, cautiously estimates its future. In *The Christian Outlook* (1948) he sees Christianity as still young; although "eventually the human race will disappear. That may come by a sudden catastrophe, and perhaps fairly soon."[207] However, as Martin Wight, of London's Royal Institute of International Affairs, commented, "It may be questioned whether Dr. Latourette touches the real problem of the prospect for Christianity." Wight objects to the claim that "the Church has survived many cultures," because this confuses a culture with an epoch; and of epochs in the Western world there have been the Roman Empire, the Middle Ages, and so on. He adds, "In the more precise historical perspective of Spengler or Toynbee there has so far been only a single generation of Christian cultures or civilizations, comprising the sister Christendoms, Byzantine and Western, both now probably *in extremis*." Here, warns Wight, "lies the ambiguity of the Christian

[202] Fischer, *op. cit.*, pp. 142–143.
[203] David Muzzey, *AHR*, Vol. 44 (1938), p. 866.
[204] *Op. cit.*, p. 152.
[205] *AHR*, Vol. 59 (1954), pp. 589–590.
[206] *HEC*, Vol. VII, p. 1.
[207] Pp. 24, 183, 194.

era—its suggestion of a colossal failure."[208] Moreover, when citing the Great Commission that the Gospel must first be preached among all nations, Wight asks why Latourette does not include the Scriptural word "and then shall the end come" (Mark 13:10; Matthew 24:14). For, he observes, "the unification of the world by Western civilization has perhaps for the first time in a loose sense fulfilled this requirement." There is foreboding in such an observation, with a serious inquiry as to the kind of faith being spread by today's Christians. Here is the real threat of possible apostasy in the New Israel, drawing upon itself the wrath of God and surviving only as the saving remnant. Our Lord asked the question: "When the Son of man cometh, shall he find faith on the earth?" (Luke 18:8) And a question it remains.[209]

Over against such criticism, valid as it may be, there remains the fact that Latourette's historiography emanates from a different premise from that of *Church* history as such. Here we must return to his Madras "platform" of 1938, where he clearly states his case. He is not promoting *Church* history, but the history of *Christianity*. Likewise, he is not writing about the Christian faith, but about the Christian *religion*. He is not writing as a specialist in historical theology but as a sociologically informed historian who places "the story of Christianity in the setting of universal history."[210]

Consistently throughout his career Latourette has adhered to this position, and from it have proceeded his books. Far from being beyond criticism, his books are attempts to blaze trails where relatively few historians have as yet ventured. His career is a bold adventure, clearing ground on which others should build. It must be remembered that he never set out to write *Church* history; for that would have involved him in many problems with which others must wrestle.[211] What he has been seeking all these years is something broader than Church history, and yet something intended *for* Church history. What he has done, as I see it, is to emancipate Church history from its traditional provincialism and geographic limitations.

Because of Latourette Church historians are not likely to be the

---

[208] *IRM*, Vol. 38 (1949), p. 490.
[209] *Ibid.*
[210] *HC*, p. xvii.
[211] Payne, *op. cit.*, p. 152.

same again. They will henceforth have to operate with much broader horizons and more inclusive perspectives.

As a historian Latourette is also a deeply committed Christian. His contribution to the history of Christianity is noteworthy in three directions, one outward, another inward, and a third upward. Outward, his work is done in such a way as to be useful in conversation with the modern secular man or with the adherents of non-Christian religions. Inward, it is a prod to ecumenical conversation among the Christian communions and sects. Upward, it contains the elements of a truncated theology whose leading edges point beyond his own work to that of others who should folow. To go into this subject further would indeed be tempting but, in a favorite phrase, "that would prolong these pages unduly."

To conclude, it was at Madras that Latourette gave this ever timely admonition:

> A knowledge of the history of Christianity is of quite first-class importance to leaders in the Church the world around. It is to be hoped that it will be of such a nature as to promote that catholicity of outlook and understanding and that comprehension of the continuing vitality of the Gospel which are of the genius of the faith.[212]

---

[212] *The Madras Series*, Vol. IV, p. 258.

CHAPTER IX

My Guided Life

KENNETH SCOTT LATOURETTE

My first word must be one of very great appreciation for this privilege and the honor that you have done me. I have been deeply touched. I might give way to emotion, but I do want to express my very great gratitude for the honor, and for this goodly fellowship of which I am very proud to be a member.

I often think as one hears these tributes to folk like myself, who are about to pass off the stage, of the story they used to tell of Oliver Wendell Holmes. You remember he lived to a great age well along in his eighties. It is said that in his later years some woman called on him and said, "Oh, Dr. Holmes, just think of the obituaries!" Dr. Holmes said that reminded him of what happened in Paris during the siege of 1870 (the Franco-Prussian War). It seems they ran short of food, so in one home they killed their dog and ate him. As they were finishing, the mistress said, "Oh, wouldn't Fido have loved these bones!"

It is rather presumptuous even to think of doing what your committee has asked me to do tonight. It is almost like undressing in public—to try to tell one's autobiography. And obviously, even in

Note: The following address was given by Kenneth Scott Latourette at the dinner in his honor, June 15, 1960. The place was Union Theological Seminary, Richmond, Virginia. The recording library of that institution taped the address. This set of pages has been transcribed from the tape. The address was not prepared as a paper, nor had Dr. Latourette anticipated its publication. The reader may note certain references not fully covered. For instance the paper "Latourette, Historian and Friend" had been read that very afternoon. Dr. Latourette refers again and again to Eugene Exman of Harper & Brothers, who was present. Dr. Exman was a former student of Dr. Latourette and more recently has been of immeasurable help as written materials have poured from Dr. Latourette's pen. (W. C. Harr) an intimate group like this, one can't tell all of it. I remember Robert Speer said in his later years when a young friend proposed to write his biography, "Rex, if you do, I'll get up from my grave, take my shin bone, and whack you over the head." Nevertheless Rex Wheeler wrote—and very well—and I believe he is still living. Dr. Speer said that if the Lord would forgive him his sins he would try not to have anyone remember his virtues.

And now for my story. I think I can tell it rather rapidly. I've thought about writing an autobiography. Eugene Exman here has asked me to do it. I haven't promised him I would. I think if I did I would have as title words from Kipling's Explorer, you remember, "Behind the Ranges." Although tonight, if I were choosing a title, it would be the one which was chosen by a great English Methodist who lived into his nineties and died in the present century. His autobiography was called "My Guided Life." I think I would also take a quotation from Shakespeare: "There's a divinity that shapes our ends, rough hew them how we will." And then I'd take a passage of Scripture, "I being in the way, the Lord led me" (Genesis 24:27).

Well, the story is roughly this. I was born in Oregon, in Oregon City, the oldest town in the state. My people were all pioneers, coming out in covered wagons. My father and mother were both born out there. They were college classmates at Pacific University, which when they attended it eighty years back was the best of the colleges on the west coast. I think there is no doubt about that, as I look at the curriculum and know what was meant by it. Ours was a very deeply religious home. My father was a lawyer and a banker, and modestly successful in that small town. Father and Mother were both very active in the Baptist Church—the oldest existing Baptist Church west of the Rockies. That is where I was reared, baptized, and later ordained. Family life centered around my father's business and, of course, the home and the church. In the good old custom of those days, not too widespread even then, we had family worship. It came as often as sunrise. Nothing interfered with it. We children were frequently very pressed with many things we wanted to do, but my father with a twinkle in his eye would announce a hymn like "No Time to Pray." We would keep on with our devotions. I can never be too grateful for that. One of the things we did in family worship which we children finally became old enough to appreciate was to memorize Scripture. Passage after passage, chapter after chapter, I remember now from that family custom. I think I learned more Scripture there than by any other way. The church was largely in the Moody tradition. As the older people here know, in those days the Moody gospel songs were much sung. We had in the formal morning service a more stately hymnal, but for the informal services the Moody-Sankey hymns were used.

We were taught as children that the Gospel is summed up in John 3:16. The older I grow the more I see in that—the more I am convinced that here is the heart of the Gospel. I like to remember that John 3:17 goes on to say that God sent His Son into the world not to condemn the world but that the world (the world that crucified Him) through Him might be saved.

And perhaps back of that goes what was said this afternoon, that I am accused of being an optimist! As I said to our friend who read the paper, "By nature, I am a pessimist." Faith has never been easy for me. I have almost envied people for whom faith is easy.

Well, I was reared in that home and educated in the public schools in town.

I went off to college, to our Baptist college, not to where Father and Mother had graduated. Father was a trustee, and had taught there soon after he had graduated from college. It was at McMinnville, Oregon, and was then called McMinnville College. Latterly, because of some generous donors, it has come to be Linfield College. I was there three years. It was a kind of junior college but was a very good college. I have often said that the best teaching I had there was better than the best I had at Yale and the worst teaching I had was not as bad as the worst I had at Yale. I am very grateful to Linfield. In my day life there was very simple. I think the student body never had an enrollment of more than 175. Most of them were in the preparatory department, in the commercial department, and in the department of music. There were, I think, six in our class.

The college had an endowment of about $50,000 and a debt of about $45,000. My father carried most of the debt. He was the source from which they very often paid the faculty. Life was simple. Some students for the lark of it, and others from necessity, kept bachelors' hall, the nearest approach to a fraternity, and for over half of my three years I was a member. Six of us rented a four-room house for two dollars a month. The total cost of room, food, light, and heat was a dollar a week apiece. So you can see what salaries

must have been like in Linfield in those days. While I was there, I
became president of the Young Men's Christian Association in the
college, being elected at the end of my sophomore year. I had entered college as a sophomore.

The first student Christian summer conferences in that area were
held in 1903 and 1904 under the auspices of the student Young Men's
Christian Association. I went to the first two. Dan Poling, by the
way, was there. His father was president of a college still more on
the poverty side, which expired later. I learned to know Dan very
well, and we have been friends across the years.

Things were said at those conferences, particularly the first one,
which challenged me.

The first I had heard from childhood, but it hadn't sunk in—that
in asking what one is to do in life one should say, "Not what I want
to do, but what would God have me do."

The second has meant a great deal to me through the years. The
name now used is "The Quiet Time," isn't it? We used to call it
"The Morning Watch." Did you ever see a little pamphlet called
The Morning Watch? I think Mott wrote it. At home we had had
family morning worship. I had knelt at my bed at night, but the
idea of getting off alone by oneself in the morning was new to me.
I remember how the first few mornings I did it, I went into the
woods where it was very quiet, but there didn't seem to be any God
there! Nobody was listening! But I have kept that up all the years
since through thick and thin. I keep it up still. I may say along with
that (this is a kind of confession, you see) that I believe profoundly
in intercessory prayer. One of the great privileges of a teacher is to
remember his students one by one all over the world. I don't know
how God uses our prayers. It seems almost presumptuous for us to
tell Him what He should do. He is a God of love. I do believe that
in some way He uses our prayers. And from time to time I have
seen what seem to me to be amazing answers to prayer. I need not
detail them here. All of you have known them. At other times the
answer has been "No." And one has not always known why.

Well, the third thing held up at that conference was the missionary cause. I suppose that not many of you have read Speer's pamphlet, *What Constitutes a Missionary Call.* Did you ever read that
or Sherwood Eddy's *The Supreme Decision of a Christian Student?*
If you remember Speer's little pamphlet you'll recall that it said in

substance that everybody in the United States, or practically everybody, has had a chance to hear the Gospel. There are millions of people on the other side of the ocean who have never had that opportunity. Unless one can show some valid reason why he should not be a missionary, if he is a Christian he must be a missionary.

I had never thought of being a missionary or a minister. I had intended to follow my father in banking and law. By the time my college course was finished I was an only son. The other sons had died. About the last honorable thing I wanted to be was a missionary. But there was that seeming obligation. To me the great struggle was as to where my duty lay. As an only son, was it my duty to stay with my father and see him through his later years? But there were those challenging words of our Lord, "He who loves father and mother more than me is not worthy of me" (Matthew 10:37a, Revised Standard Version), or "If any one comes to me and does not hate his own father and mother and wife and children and brothers and sisters, yes, and even his own life, he cannot be my disciple" (Luke 14:26, Revised Standard Version).

I thought that through during the next year. If anyone asked me what I was going to do I told him that I was going to law school and then join my father. At the second conference to which I went, just at the end of senior year, I did decide. I remember pacing the beach night after night struggling with the problem. I finally signed the Student Volunteer Movement declaration card, which some of you will remember as reading, "It is my purpose if God permits to become a foreign missionary."

I felt as if I had signed my death warrant. I hadn't the slightest desire to be a missionary. I hated the thought, but it seemed to be a clear duty. I remember the next year. (I was out of college for a year. My father thought it wise, inasmuch as I was young, for me to have a little more business experience. I had been out of school for a year between high school and college, and had done a little work on the side, so entered college as a sophomore.) I remember talking with one of the Jewish customers in my father's bank one day on the trolley. He asked me what I was planning to do with my life—quite the thing to ask of a lad of twenty! I said I was planning to be a missionary. I have never forgotten the look of horror on his face, nor his voice. "What you do that for? Your father's got lots of money. If you want to be a minister, he can send you to a good seminary. Our rabbi, he gets five thousand dollars a year." No money in being a missionary! Well, I did decide to be a missionary. Really it was from a pure sense of duty. Those of you who have read Leighton Stuart's story will remember this was his experience.

I wanted to go east to college. Our colleges in the west were good but not as advanced as some of the eastern ones. I knew nothing whatever about them except their names. I wrote to Harvard, to Princeton, to Brown, to Williams, and to Yale. My first letter to Yale was addressed to Yale University, Hartford, Connecticut. It shows how little I knew about it. The other colleges would not accept students beyond the junior year. They had a general rule forbidding it. Yale had the custom, thanks to its dean, of admitting about twenty men to each senior class from other colleges. These men, already holding degrees, came for just a year. The dean said it was good for Yale to have these sober-minded youth and that it was good for their classmates. There was a condition. Yale required both Greek and Latin for admission. I had had Latin but no Greek. My first degree had been a bachelor of science, and I dodged Greek. So I had to get Greek. I have always been proud of the fact that the year when I was working eight hours a day, in the businesses which my father was conducting, I got Greek on the side without a tutor. My father and mother had had it in college but they had forgotten it. They still had their first Greek books and I had the use of them. I didn't even know the pronunciation. Finally, near the end of the year a teacher of Greek helped with it. I am glad to say that I passed the Yale entrance examinations in Greek. I went to Yale entering senior year . . . what they then called a "scrub senior." It was a nickname given to those of us who came to do our senior year.

I often remember as I pass the New Haven Green of my first arrival. I had saved money by not going Pullman. I had some rough nights on the train, and after riding day coaches I was desperately tired. I came to the Green, stretched out on the grass, and a policeman ordered me to get up.

Since I had been connected with the Christian Association in the west, I made a beeline for the Christian Association, which we call Dwight Hall. That was much of my life during the years at Yale.

The question came up as to what I should do in getting ready for missions. Should I take a divinity school course? I had no prejudice against the ministry but I had never thought of it as a possible vocation. I considered going to Rochester Theological Seminary, where my uncle had been a generation or more before. That school had the reputation of being the best of the Baptist seminaries in the North. Then, just as the paper was saying this afternoon, Yale-in-China was being organized. The Yale Missionary Society had been founded by a group of young Yale graduates of the classes of 1898, 1899, and 1900. In 1900 Horace Pitkin, a Yale graduate, had been killed by the Boxers. China was just being opened up. Yale men said, "Why shouldn't we go to China collectively and start a Christian mission?" After exploring the situation they decided that the best service they could give would be in an educational mission. It was to be frankly Christian and frankly missionary. Later it developed into a medical school, a secondary school, a nursing school, a hospital, and a share in a college.

I had been at Yale only a few months when it was suggested to those in charge that I go out to China. That seemed to me to be the solution to my problem. I had found much of appeal in college life. I am not sure whether it was the appeal of scholarship. But I enjoyed college life. I had been very active in every extracurricular activity except athletics. I have been glad I didn't take part in them because athletics were pretty crude in that day in the college where I had been.

I had had Sunday School classes of boys in their early teens. Many of us when in late teens or early twenties were interested in boys a little younger than we. I was much interested in students and, like many of my friends, thought some of going into student work. A chance to combine that interest in students with teaching seemed to be the answer to my problem. So I was under appointment. That meant graduate work, to get ready to teach in China.

I had taken no history at Linfield. At Yale I was allowed to elect anything that I wanted. They had no requirements . . . except a certain number of class hours. I majored in history because I had read a lot of it as a boy and enjoyed it. I had some work in geology, and some economics. So I canvassed the possibilities of a doctorate . . . including one in economics or geology. The reason I finally settled on a doctorate in history was that I could get it more quickly than I could in either of the other subjects. This may have been a slight indication as to where my abilities lay.

Inasmuch as I was going to the Far East I took all the work on that region which was being offered at Yale. This was three courses. I'm afraid my interest wasn't too great in much of my graduate work. I was much more involved in Dwight Hall. In those days we were at the peak of a certain Bible study development. In my first year of graduate work I was asked to have charge of the normal class for the class of 1909, where the boys were having groups to teach their own classmates. So I had that class and when they moved on to junior year I took the next sophomore class . . . and so on. I had three successive sophomore classes. The result was that by the time I took my doctor's degree we had a thousand men in voluntary Bible classes! I am afraid they didn't learn very much Bible. I have often wondered whether it did any good. I have a Bible, one of my most cherished gifts, signed in the handwriting of Robert Taft, the late ex-Senator. He was the secretary for the groups in his class. He wouldn't teach one, but he said he'd go around and get the record of each group each week. I have that Bible inscribed by him and signed by the other boys in his class (1910), who led the groups.

I think a lot of this bears on what happened later. With my profound conviction about missions, whenever I saw a likely boy, I had him read *What Constitutes a Missionary Call*, or I talked to him about it. So far as I can know, this was responsible for several boys going abroad. Some of you know a few of them: John Reisner, Rex Wheeler, and a few of the people in Yale-in-China. Many of the names you wouldn't know. The old China hands will know Billy Roberts (Bishop Roberts). After taking my doctor's degree I traveled for the Student Voluneeer Movement for a year and made some lifelong friends . . . several still among my dearest friends.

Then I went to Yale-in-China. I think if anybody had told me even on the day I sailed that it was all off, that I needn't go out, I would have thrown up my hat and given three cheers, and taught in some college, or perhaps gone into student work. I went to China. I must say that when I did arrive and came to know my colleagues and began to be familiar with China, I was profoundly grateful that I was there. I was profoundly grateful also to have a share in the missionary enterprise. At the end of the first year I was taken with amoebic dysentery. Until that happened I had never been ill a day in my life. Some of you know that back in those days the treatment for dysentery was pretty rough, ipecac taken in great quantities, and then you kept still so that you could keep it down. When I had dysentery later the treatment was kerosene enemas! They have better treatment for it now. By the way, that latter treatment was prescribed by a Harvard medical school graduate! After sticking it out for another eight months I came home in March, 1912. I expected to go back in the autumn, even buying a round-trip ticket on the Yangtze River steamer. When I reached home and had a chance to let down the bottom dropped out. It was two years before I could do part-time work. If anybody is in that particular kind of hell I know what corner of hell they are in.

When I was beginning to do a little work I went to a man whom I had never met, the president of Reed College in Portland. It happened to be the nearest college to my home, an hour or so away by trolley. I thought if I could teach part-time there, getting back on my feet, it might be useful.

He and I looked one another over. I told him my story. He smiled. It was late in July, 1914. He told me the budget for the next year was made up and that course offerings had been decided upon. "Come back in a few weeks and I'll see what I can do," he said. In the meantime war broke out in Europe. When I came back he said, "Well, you can come and teach one course. You can stay here as much as you like. You can advise the Christian Association. You can give a course one semester on the Far East, and in the other semester one on Europe since 1870. You can give some extension lectures in the public library on the 'Background of the European War.' I think we can find you six hundred dollars." The second year I taught half-time. At the end of that year there was obviously neither the money nor the need for another full-time man in history at Reed. So I began casting about and I couldn't find a thing. I finally accepted an appointment in the high schools in Portland, on the condition that if something opened up in a college I would take it.

While I was at Reed I debated whether I should go ahead with student work (the Young Men's Christian Association as they called it in the colleges) or teaching. I felt that in the former there was not a lifework. But I was interested in teaching. My primary concern, you see, was students, not a subject. Just at the last moment a chance opened up to go to Denison, for a year's appointment. I was told by the grapevine route that if they liked me it would be permanent. I had been there only a few weeks when the president called me in and said he'd be glad to have me stay. I became the chairman of the Department of History and Political Science; I was the only full-time man in history.

I liked Denison very much. Gene Exman and I were there together. He was a student and I was a faculty man. I was not very much older. The difference in our ages is more obvious now than then, I think. He looks much younger, and I have acquired gray hair and a bald head.

While I was at Denison I was ordained to the Baptist ministry. I was helping the Christian Associations and became chaplain for the University . . . an experiment they didn't repeat for many years after I left! It was a great lot of boys there and several have become distinguished, especially in church work.

I ought also to say that in my first year at Denison I was visiting in New Haven and Dr. Harlan Beach talked with me. He held the first university chair of missions in this country. He had only four or five years to serve before becoming emeritus, and he spoke to me about succeeding him. So they gave me what they called at Yale a "hold-off." This meant that I would not accept anything elsewhere without letting them know. They didn't promise me the chair. They said they would consider it. I promised to let them know if I was tempted to leave Denison.

I had not had a divinity school course. The only work I had had in the Yale Divinity School was in Church history under Williston Walker, and that had been applied on my general graduate work for a Ph.D. I went back and asked the Denison president, "May I give a course in missions?" I told him the story. It's very presumptuous to tell a president that you want to give a course which might help you to leave his institution. But I did give the course, on "The Expansion of Christianity," and Gene Exman took it.

In 1920 after World War I, I had a good many invitations to leave, among them one from the University of Chicago to become the professor of missions, and that was the one I looked at the hardest. One came from Northwestern to help Ned Soper. I knew there was an invitation on the way from the University of Wisconsin to teach Far Eastern history. The minister to China had developed that interest while there and they were looking for a successor.

Duty-bound, I told Yale. Then they asked me to come. I had a terrible time making that decision. Should I, or should I not, stay in a small college? I liked Denison. I lived with the students. They were the sort of boys I had been reared with, and I would have preferred to stay. But again came that conviction which had sent me out as a missionary. In general, I believe it to be sound. I remember as they were presenting missions in those early days, they said, "If you saw a fire and on one side everyone was working to keep it from spreading then someone had better get busy on another side where it is spreading. Shouldn't you level your hose where no one else is working?" So to my mind the principle has been this: what is it that God wants done? Who is there to do it? Is there some ability which the Lord has given me to help do it? In other words how can I best work with God? Is there something that ought to be done which no one else is doing?

I had already seen this in Far Eastern history. When I began teaching it I could count such teachers in American universities on the fingers of my two hands and have some fingers left over. Somebody ought to be doing it. Here was a Christian obligation. There needed to be a sympathetic interpretation of the peoples I had come to know. I pressed the American Historical Association to do more about it on their annual programs.

When the invitation came from Yale I said to myself, "Now here's an opportunity to do several things." One, I could help through the chair of missions to prepare missionaries. Two, prospective ministers could be made acquainted with missions. Three, undergraduates could be helped and their Christian faith stimulated. Fourth, various mission boards in New York City could be served. The upshot was that there came a clear conviction that the thing to do was to go to Yale. I went. It was a very strange experience. My colleagues were often talking about things of which I knew nothing . . . eschatology, apocalypticism, and so on. The great scholars on the faculty were experts on the Bible, and while I knew the text of my Bible, the critical studies I knew only vaguely. I had read a little theology, but not much. My first ten years on that faculty were frankly very rugged. This was true for a number of reasons. I don't have time to go into them here, and it isn't necessary, anyway. I did a lot of things which seemed to me to be worth doing. I helped in Dwight Hall. I taught the history of the Far East and they eventually added Oriental History to the title of my chair. For many years I was giving practically all the work offered at Yale on the Far East.

I tried to help further Far Eastern studies in the country at large. A committee was being organized by the American Council of Learned Societies and I became involved in it. I knew perfectly well that if I was going to continue with missions I couldn't hope to become a first-class sinologist. I subsequently became president, for a while, of what is now called the Association for Asian Studies.

Then to my amazement a few years ago, I was made the president of the American Historical Association! I have never known why. My presidential address was on the subject "The Christian Understanding of History," which some of the hearers didn't enjoy. I may say that when I finished the address Catholic priests at the dinner came up and told me the theology was perfect. I may add that the printed supply of the address was soon exhausted. A few years ago the Methodists reprinted it.

Service on many boards and committees claimed me. I put in on the average at least a day a week in New York, on committees of one kind or another. At the height of my folly I was serving on thirty-three boards and committees in New York and New Haven, including four mission boards. I am deeply interested in international relations, and I served with John Foster Dulles on the Federal Council's Committee to Study the Bases of a Just and Durable Peace.

I have tried to serve in a variety of ways that I haven't ventured to mention or outline. I have written a good many books, which they were talking about in this afternoon's meeting, but I don't need to go into all that. I have been interested in the World's Student Christian Federation, the World Council of Churches, the International Missionary Council, and in my own denomination. I may say that I am a Baptist by heredity, inertia, and conviction.

As I look back across the years the titles with which I began this talk I think still hold: "My Guided Life"; "There's a divinity that shapes our ends rough-hew them how we will"; "I being in the way, the Lord led me. . . ."

And so as this stage of life begins to draw to a close I am profoundly thankful. And I may say here, knowing I am talking to a number of former students of mine, that the most rewarding part of life has been the friendship of these men. I went into teaching, as I said, because I was primarily interested in students. They have been my great joy through the years. I have boasted repeatedly that I have fourteen honorary degrees from universities and colleges in five different countries, but the greatest honor is that I have had seventeen namesakes in six different countries. Whenever a student is willing to name a son for you I think it the greatest compliment that can be given to anybody.

When the time came to be "emeritus" I said, "What shall I do?" Many invitations would be coming to go to this campus or that, for it really doesn't cost much to secure a man who has a retirement allowance! And the invitations did come and they continue to come. I said to myself, "I've been a reasonably good teacher but certainly not one of the great ones. My life has been with students. I'll stay on right here at Yale where I am 'Uncle Ken,' particularly in the Divinity School." Undergraduates who know me best call me by the same name.

I have three groups which meet at the fireside in my little apartment in the Divinity School. I say to the groups, "I'm your host, you elect your leaders, have your programs. I'll always be here." And they meet. I've had something of this sort ever since I've been teaching. One comes to know informal groups of students very well. I have a similar group in the undergraduate college where I am a fellow, and an undergraduate group in the church where I am a member.

I have tried to write and some of you have had to endure the products of the writing. Gene Exman here has had to look after much of it. At Denison, Eugene Exman was interested in a religious vocation. He went on to the University of Chicago and then went into religious publishing. When he got to Harper's he knew I was working on the series *The Expansion of Christianity*, and he came to me. I often think of it, Gene. When we were talking about a contract I said, "Gene, you'll lose money on it." He explained to me that Harper was interested in producing books which were worth while and that maybe they didn't need to make money on all their books. But I think they did make a little on mine.

In conclusion I want to say my life has been a guided life. Many things I wouldn't reveal to you. God has had to forgive a lot. The older I grow the more I am aware of His mercy. As I look back the more I am convinced, in spite of all the sins . . . not just blunders . . . that the good Lord has been forgiving and is using me.

SELECT BIBLIOGRAPHY OF
KENNETH SCOTT LATOURETTE

Compiled by
Helen B. Uhrich, Ralph Norman, and Raymond P. Morris

BOOKS AND BROCHURES

The American Record in the Far East, 1945–1951. New York: Macmillan, 1952. Pp. 208.
   Issued under the auspices of the American Institute of Pacific Relations.
Anno Domini: Jesus, History and God. New York: Harper, 1940. Pp. xv, 248. Translated into German by H. Doebeli. St. Gallen: Vadian-Verlag, 1949. Pp. 310.
   Part of the material employed in the Powell Lectures at the Canadian School of Missions, Toronto, in 1938; and in lectures under the Lowell Institute in King's Chapel, Boston, 1939. Chapter VI, "The Meaning of the Story," reprinted as Behold Thy King. New York: Published by Harper for the Student Volunteer Movement, 1940, 1942. Pp. ii, 203–240.
Biographical Memoir of Berthold Laufer, 1874–1934. Presented to the Academy at the autumn meeting, 1936. Pp. 43 68. In National Academy of Sciences, Washington, D.C. Biographical Memoirs. 1938. Vol. XVIII, 3d Memoir.
   Issued separately, 1937. Contains: "Bibliography of Berthold Laufer," pp. 57–68.
Challenge and Conformity: Studies in the Interaction of Christianity and the World of Today. New York: Harper, 1955. Pp. 126.
The China That Is to Be. Eugene, Oregon: Oregon State System of Higher Education, 1949. Pp. ix, 56.
   Condon Lectures.
China under the Republic. New York: The Institute of International Education, 1921. Pp. 23.
   International Relations Club, Syllabus No. IX.
The Chinese: Their History and Culture. New York: Macmillan, 1934. 2 v. Second edition, revised (2 v. in 1), 1934. Third edition, revised (2 v. in 1), 1946. Fourth edition, revised, expected to appear 1964. Translation of third edition into Spanish: *Los Chinos, su Historia y su*

Cultura. Traducción de Miguel de Hernani. Buenos Aires: Editorial Sudamericana, 1949. Pp. 975. Also translated into French and Japanese.
Christian Adventure at Yale: Seventy-five Years of the Yale Young Men's Christian Association. Prefatory note by Sidney Lovett. New Haven: Yale University, 1956. Pp. 24.

Published in celebration of the seventy-fifth anniversary of the founding of the Association.
The Christian Basis of World Democracy. New York: Association Press, 1919. Pp. xii, 193.

"Daily readings" largely from the Gospel of Matthew, with comments which consider the bearing of the principles contained in the selection on the international or national problems of our age.
The Christian Outlook. New York: Harper, 1948. Pp. xii, 229. (English edition: *The Prospect for Christianity.* London: Eyre & Spottiswoode, 1949. Pp. 222.) Translated into Swedish: *Det Kristna Perspektivet,* by Knut B. Westman. Stockholm: Westerberg, 1949. Pp. 245.
The Christian World Mission in Our Day. New York: Harper, 1954. Pp. 192. (English edition: London: Eyre & Spottiswoode, 1954. Pp. 191.) Translated into Norwegian: *Den Kristne Verdensmisjonen i Vår Tid,* oversatt av Sigmun S. Kostøl. Oslo: Ansgar Forlag, 1956. Pp. 157.
Christianity in a Revolutionary Age: A History of Christianity in the Nineteenth and Twentieth Centuries. New York: Harper, 1958–1962. 5 v. (English edition: London: Eyre & Spottiswoode, 1959–1962.)

Contents: I. The Nineteenth Century in Europe: Background and the Roman Catholic Phase. II. The Nineteenth Century in Europe: the Protestant and Eastern Churches. III. The Nineteenth Century Outside Europe: the Americas, the Pacific, Asia, and Africa. IV. The Twentieth Century in Europe: the Roman Catholic, Protestant, and Eastern Churches. V. The Twentieth Century Outside Europe: the Americas, the Pacific, Asia, and Africa; the Emerging World Christian Community.
Correspondence of the Reverend Ezra Fisher, Pioneer Missionary of the American Baptist Home Mission Society in Indiana, Illinois, Iowa, and Oregon. Edited by Sarah Fisher Henderson, Nellie Edith Latourette, and Kenneth Scott Latourette. Portland, Oregon: Privately printed, 1916. Pp. 487.
Desafío a los Protestantes. Buenos Aires: Editorial "La Aurora," 1957. Pp. 158.

Cátedra Carnahan, 1956.
The Development of China. Boston: Houghton, Mifflin, 1917. Pp. xi, 273. Second edition, revised, 1920, pp. xiii, 287. Third edition, revised, 1924, pp. xiii, 309. Fourth edition, revised, 1929, pp. xiii, 322. Fifth edition, revised, 1937, pp. xi, 333. Sixth edition, revised, 1946, pp. xi, 343.

The Development of Japan. Published under the Auspices of the Japan Society. New York: Macmillan, 1918. Pp. xi, 237. Second edition, revised, 1926, pp. xiii, 245. Third edition, revised, 1931, pp. xiii, 258. Fourth edition, revised, 1938, pp. xi, 272. Fifth edition, revised as: *The History of Japan*, 1947, pp. vi, 290. Sixth edition, revised, 1957, pp. vi, 299.

The Emergence of a World Christian Community. New Haven: Published for the Rice Institute by Yale University Press, 1949. Pp. iv, 91.
 The Rockwell Lectures on Religion at the Rice Institute, Houston, Texas, 1948.

The Gospel, the Church and the World. Edited by Kenneth Scott Latourette. New York: Harper, 1946. Pp. xvi, 229. Interseminary Series, v. 3. Translated into Japanese, 1946. Pp. 331.

A History of Christian Missions in China. New York: Macmillan, 1929. Pp. xii, 930.

A History of Christianity. New York: Harper, 1953. Pp. xxvii, 1516. (English edition: London: Eyre & Spottiswoode, 1954.) Translated into Spanish: *Historia del Cristianismo.* Traducción por Jaime C. Quarles & Lemuel C. Quarles. El Paso, Texas: Casa Bautista de Publicaciones, 1958–1959. 2 v.

The History of Early Relations between the United States and China, 1784–1844. New Haven: Yale University Press, 1917. Pp. 200. (Transactions of the Connecticut Academy of Arts and Sciences, v. 22.)
 The author's doctoral dissertation at Yale, 1909, but not published as a thesis. Reprinted, without permission, in Peking, *ca.* 1936.

A History of Modern China. London and Baltimore: Penguin Books, 1954. Pp. 234. (Pelican Books: The Pelican History of the World, v. 1.) Translated into Italian: *Storia Della Cina Moderna.* Introd. di Luciano Petech, traduzione e appendice di Annibale Vasile. Rocca San Casciano: Cappelli, 1959. Pp. xiv, 275.
 Universale Cappelli, 25/26.

A History of the Expansion of Christianity. New York: Harper, 1937–1945. 7 v.
 Contents: I. The First Five Centuries. II. The Thousand Years of Uncertainty, A.D. 500–A.D. 1500. III. Three Centuries of Advance, A.D. 1500–A.D. 1800. IV. The Great Century, A.D. 1800–A.D. 1914. Europe and the United States of America. V. The Great Century in the Americas, Australasia, and Africa, A.D. 1800–A.D. 1914. VI. The Great Century in Northern Africa and Asia, A.D. 1800–A.D. 1914. VII. Advance through Storm, A.D. 1914 and After, with Concluding Generalizations.
 Spanish translation of Vol. 7: A Traves de la Tormenta; Historia de la Expansión y las Luchas del Cristianismo desde el año 1914 en adelante. Traducción por D. E. Hall. Buenos Aires: Editorial "La

Aurora," 1952. Pp. 498; Translated into German: *Geschichte der Ausbreitung des Christentums:* Gekürzte deutsche Ausgabe, von Richard M. Honig. Göttingen: Vandenhoeck & Ruprecht, 1956. Pp. 482. Theologie der Oekumene, Bd. 4.

Introducing Buddhism. New York: Friendship Press, 1956. Pp. 64.

Japan: Suggested Outlines for a Discussion of Japan, Her History, Her Culture, Problems, and Relations with the United States. New York: Japan Society, 1921. Pp. 39. Second edition, revised, 1923, pp. 44. Fifth edition, revised, 1928, pp. 47. Sixth edition, revised, 1929, pp. 48. Seventh edition, revised, 1934, pp. 53. Eighth edition, revised, 1936, pp. 68.

Latourette's contribution in the eighth edition is limited to historical and political evolution of Japan and Japan's foreign relations. The section on art and literature is revised and expanded by Harold Gould Henderson; the sections on population, family and social life, and manners and customs are revised and expanded by Douglas G. Haring.

Master of the Waking World: An Approach to the Christian Understanding of History. Nashville: Tidings, 1958. Pp. 27.

Adapted and slightly altered from "The Christian Understanding of History," published in the January, 1949, issue of *The American Historical Review.*

Missions and the American Mind. Indianapolis: National Foundation Press, 1949. Pp. vii, 40.

Fundamental American Principles Series. Published for the National Foundation for Education in American Citizenship.

Missions Tomorrow. New York: Harper, 1936. Pp. xvii, 220.

Perspective on the World Mission. New York: American Baptist Foreign Mission Society. Pp. 12.

Problems of Peace in East Asia: A Statement of the Committee on the Far Eastern Settlement, Kenneth S. Latourette, Chairman. New York: Federal Council of Churches of Christ in America, 1947. Pp. 14.

A Short History of the Far East. New York: Macmillan, 1946. Pp. xiv, 665. Revised edition, 1951, pp. xiv, 730. Third edition, 1957, pp. xiv, 754. German edition: *Geschichte des Fernen Ostens in den Letzten Hundert Jahren.* Ubersetzt von Ursula Michaelsen. Frankfurt am Main: Metzner, 1959. Pp. 350.

These Sought a Country. New York: Harper, 1950. Pp. 156. The Tipple Lectures at Drew University, 1950.

Tomorrow Is Here: The Mission and Work of the Church as seen from the Meeting of the International Missionary Council at Whitby, Ontario, July 5–24, 1947. By Kenneth Scott Latourette and William Richey Hogg. New York: Published for the International Missionary Council by the Friendship Press, 1948. Pp. xiv, 145.

Reprinted, with subtitle: A Survey of the World-wide Mission and

Work of the Christian Church. London: Edinburgh House Press, 1948. Pp. xii, 129.

Toward a World Christian Fellowship. New York: Association Press, 1938. Pp. vii, 64. Translated into Chinese. Shanghai, Assoc. Press of China, August, 1939.
   Hazen Books on Religion.

The United States Moves Across the Pacific: the A.B.C.'s of the American Problem in the Western Pacific and the Far East. New York: Harper, 1946. Pp. ix, 174.

The Unquenchable Light. New York: Harper, 1941. Pp. xi, 191. (English edition: London: Eyre & Spottiswoode, 1948. Pp. xvii, 160.)
   The William Belden Noble Lectures at Harvard for 1940.

Voyages of American Ships to China, 1784–1844. New Haven: Connecticut Academy of Arts and Sciences, 1927.
   Transactions of the Connecticut Academy of Arts and Sciences, v. 28.

What Can I Believe about Christian Missions? New York: Student Volunteer Movement, 1931. Pp. 32.

What Is Christianity? Philadelphia: Judson Press, 1940. Pp. 7.

World Christian Community in Action: The Story of World War II and Orphaned Missions. By Kenneth Scott Latourette and William Richey Hogg. New York: International Missionary Council, 1949. Pp. 42.

World Service: A History of the Foreign Work and World Service of the Young Men's Christian Associations of the United States and Canada. New York: Association Press, 1957. Pp. 189.

ARTICLES AND CONTRIBUTIONS IN BOOKS

American Protestant Denominations and Missions, in *The Church and the World*, ed. Francis P. Miller. New York: Association Press, 1926, pp. 61–69.

China and Japan, in *The Study of Nations:* An Experiment of Social Education, by Harriet E. Tuell. Boston: Houghton, Mifflin, 1919, pp. 125–149.

China as Interpreted to the Occident by the Recent Books, in *China Mission Year Book*, 1924. Shanghai, Christian Literature Society, pp. 450–456.

China, the United States and the War in *League of Nations*, vol. II, Special Number, July 1919. Boston, World Peace Foundation, pp. 167–191.

The Christian Church in the Last Seventy Years, in *The Annual Report* of the *American Historical Association* for 1942, vol. III. Washington, 1944, pp. 67–72.

Also issued as a reprint, Washington, 1944.

The Christian Future, in *The Coming-of-Age of Christianity*, ed. Sir James Marchant. Chicago: H. Regnery, 1951, pp. 119–142.

The Christian Mission in Asia, in *East and West:* Conflict or Co-operation? ed. Basil Mathews. New York: Association Press, 1936, pp. 85–111.

Christianity, in *China,* ed. Harley P. MacNair. The United Nations Series, gen. ed. Robert J. Kerner. Berkeley and Los Angeles: University of California Press, 1946, pp. 301–311.

Christianity and the Peace Movement, in *The Church, the Gospel, and War,* ed. Rufus M. Jones. New York: Harper, 1948, pp. 93–110.

The Church and the World in the Nineteenth Century, in *Leo XIII and the Modern World,* ed. Edward T. Gargan. New York: Sheed & Ward, 1961, pp. 51–62.

The Church on the Field, in *Interpretative Statistical Survey of the World Mission of the Christian Church:* Summary and Detailed Statistics of Churches and Missionary Societies, Interpretative Articles, and Indices, ed. Joseph I. Parker. New York and London: International Missionary Council, 1938, pp. 239–242.

Community and Church: An Historical Survey and Interpretation, in *Church and Community,* by Kenneth Scott Latourette, Ernest Barker, Marc Boegner, and others. London: Allen & Unwin, 1938, pp. 1–17.

Prepared in connection with the World Conference on Church, Community, and State, Oxford, 1937.

The Early Evangelical Missionary Movement in Latin America, in *From Missions to Mission in Latin America.* New York: The Committee on Coöperation in Latin America, Division of Foreign Missions of the National Council of Churches of Christ in the U.S.A., 1958, Part I, pp. 3–14.

An address at the Study Conference of the Committee at Buck Hill Falls, Pa., November 6–8, 1958.

Ecumenical Bearings of the Missionary Movement and the International Missionary Council in *A History of the Ecumenical Movement, 1517–1948,* ed. Ruth Rouse and Stephen Charles Neill. Philadelphia, Westminster Press; London, S.P.C.K., 1954, pp. 353–402.

Epilogue, in *Forward through the Ages,* by Basil Joseph Mathews. New edition. New York: Friendship Press, 1960, pp. 253–259.

History and the World Mission of Christianity, in *Students and the World Mission of Christianity:* Report of the North American Student Consultation on the World Mission of Christianity, December 27, 1939 to January 1, 1940 at the University of Toronto. New York, 1940, pp. 88–91.

Medieval Thought: Christian Conceptions of Life, in *Chapters in Western Civilization*, ed. Contemporary Civilization Staff of Columbia College, Columbia University, vol. I, third edition. New York and London, Columbia University Press, 1961, pp. 33–64.

The Missionary Outlook Today, in *Official Report* of the Baptist World Alliance, Eighth Congress, Cleveland, 1950, ed. Arnold T. Ohrn. Philadelphia: Judson Press, 1950, pp. 217–222.

Opportunities: In the Far East, in *Protestantism:* A Symposium, ed. William K. Anderson. Nashville: Commission on Courses of Study, The Methodist Church, 1944, pp. 217–225.

The Place of Church History in the Training of Missionaries, in *The Life of the Church*. The Madras Series, IV. New York and London: International Missionary Council, 1939, pp. 254–258.
Papers based upon the meeting of the International Missionary Council, Madras, India, December 12 to 29, 1938.

Pre-Nineteenth Century Evangelism; Its Outstanding Characteristics, in *Studies in Evangelism*, ed. William Paton. London and New York: International Missionary Council, 1938, pp. 9–21.

The Propagation of the Gospel by the Roman Catholics, in *Christian World Mission*, ed. William K. Anderson. Nashville: Commission on Ministerial Training, The Methodist Church, 1946, pp. 29–37.

Religious Coöperation, in *The United States in the Postwar World:* Addresses Given at the 1945 Summer Conference of the University of Michigan, ed. W. B. Willcox and R. B. Hall. Ann Arbor: University of Michigan Press, 1947; London: Oxford University Press, 1948, pp. 65–77.

The Religious Situation in the United States Since 1939, in *World Christian Handbook*, ed. Kenneth G. Grubb. London: World Dominion Press, 1949, pp. 77–87.

Roman Catholic Missions, in *Interpretative Statistical Survey of the World Mission of the Christian Church:* Summary and Detailed Statistics of Churches and Missionary Societies, Interpretative Articles, and Indices, ed. Joseph I. Parker. New York and London: International Missionary Council, 1938, pp. 262–264.

Serving Overseas, in *They Seek a Country*, ed. Gaius Jackson Slosser. New York: Macmillan, 1955, pp. 191–209.

Trends of Thought in Recent Books on China, in *China Mission Year Book*, 1923. Shanghai, Christian Literature Society, pp. 307–314.

In *What I Believe*, selected and arranged by Sir James Marchant. London: Odhams Press, 1953, pp. 49–56.

ARTICLES IN PERIODICALS

American Historical Review. Articles: "Chinese Historical Studies during the Past Seven Years," XXVI, July, 1921, pp. 703–716; "Chinese Historical Studies during the Past Nine Years," XXXV, July, 1930, pp. 778–797; "The Christian Understanding of History," LIV, January, 1949, pp. 259–276.

The Americas. Article: "The Contribution of the Religion of the Colonial Period to the Ideals and Life of the United States," XIV, April, 1958, pp. 340–355.

Annals of the American Academy of Political and Social Science. Articles: "Peace with Japan," V. 257, May, 1948, pp. 142–150; "The Present Status of Foreign Missions," V. 256, March, 1948, pp. 63–71.

Church History. Articles: "The Christian Church in the Last Seventy Years," XII, March, 1943, pp. 28–34; "A Historian Looks Ahead: The Future of Christianity in the Light of Its Past," XV, March, 1946, pp. 3–16.

International Review of Missions. Articles: "Charles Harvey Fahs," XXXVIII, January, 1949, pp. 75–76; "The Church in the Anglo-American World: the Post-war Situation," XXXVI, April, 1947, pp. 232–252; "Distinctive Features of the Protestant Missionary Methods of the Nineteenth and Twentieth Centuries," XXVI, October, 1937, pp. 441–452; "History and the Indigenous Church," XVII, January, 1928, pp. 101–118; "Indigenous Christianity in the Light of History," XXIX, October, 1940, pp. 429–440; "The Light of History on Current Missionary Methods," XLII, April, 1953, pp. 137–143; The Missionary Awakening among Roman Catholics in the United States," XXI, July, 1922, pp. 439–444; "Missions and Wars," XXXI, October, 1942, pp. 394–399; "Pre-Nineteenth Century Evangelism: Its Outstanding Characteristics," XXVI, July, 1937, pp. 309–321; "Pre-War Christian Groups in Asia in Post-War Planning," XXXIII, April, 1944, pp. 138–146; "The Problems of Realizing the Church Universal," XXV, July, 1936, pp. 297–305; "Research and Christian Missions," XXII, October, 1932, pp. 532–546; "Retaining the Christian Character of Educational Foundations," XVII, October, 1928, pp. 663–674; "Rethinking Missions after Twenty-Five Years," XLVI, April, 1957, pp. 164–170; "Roman Catholic and Protestant Missions in China: Some Comparisons," XVI, April, 1927, pp. 161–181; "The Study of the History of Missions," XIV, January, 1925, pp. 108–115; "A Suggestion toward a Reorientation of Mission Policy," XXIII, July, 1934, pp. 405–413; "Toward a Comparative Study of the Spread of Religions," XX, July,

1931, pp. 367–380; "The Training of the American Missionary to China," VII, October, 1918, pp. 445–455; "The Vitality of the Younger Churches: A Question and a Possible Answer," XXVIII, December, 1939, pp. 480–490; "What Can We Expect in the World Mission?" XL, April, 1951, pp. 141–148; "The World Fellowship of Christians and World Peace," XXVIII, July, 1939, pp. 347–358.

Journal of Religion. Articles: "Have We Passed the Age of Religion?" XVI, October, 1936, pp. 419–431; "New Perspectives in Church History," XXI, October, 1941, pp. 432–443.

Pacific Affairs. Articles: "The Future of Japan: An American View," with M. Searles Bates, XVII, June, 1944, pp. 190–194; "Problems Confronting Christian Missions in the Far East," XXI, June, 1948, pp. 176–185.

Religion in Life. Articles: "Achieving a World-Wide Fellowship of Christians," V, Spring, 1936, pp. 243–253; "Blind Leaders of the Blind: Some Reflections on a Current Tendency in American Higher Education," IV, Winter, 1935, pp. 45–51; "Christ the Hope of the World: What Has History to Say?" XXIII, Summer, 1954, pp. 323–333 (with response by Reinhold Niebuhr, pp. 334–340; F. Ernest Stoeffler, pp. 341–351); "The Condition of Religion in the United States," VII, Summer, 1938, pp. 335–345; "Developments in the 'Younger Churches' Since Edinburgh, 1910," XXIV, Summer, 1960, pp. 352–362; "The Effect of the Missionary Enterprise upon the American Mind," XII, Winter, 1943, pp. 53–70; "The Humanist and the Christian: A Study in Similarities and Contrasts," XIV, Autumn, 1945, pp. 478–487.

Yale Review. Articles: "Present Conditions in China," XII, April, 1923, pp. 562–578; "The Question of China," VII, October, 1917, pp. 101–117; "What Is Happening to Missions," XVIII, Autumn, 1928, pp. 65–81.

Articles of importance are also to be found in the following periodicals: *America, American Scholar, Atlantic Monthly, Christendom, Christian Century, Christian Education, East and West Review, Educational Review, Far East Quarterly, Foreign Affairs, Journal of the American Oriental Society, Journal of International Education, Journal of International Relations, Journal of the North China Branch of positor, School and Society, Yale Journal of Biology and Medicine.*

Further information on periodicals, articles, and reviews by Latourette (over 710 reviews in 48 periodicals) and of the Latourette's books may be obtained in the following indices: *The Catholic Periodical Index; The Education Index; Index to Religious Periodical Literature; International Index; Readers' Guide to Periodical Literature* and the *Book Review Digest.*

ARTICLES IN ENCYCLOPEDIAS

Dictionary of American Biography, ed. Dumas Malone. New York: Scribner, 1928–1936. Articles on: Rosewell Hobart Graves, Andrew Patton Happer, Virgil Chittenden Hart, Chester Holcombe, John Glasgow Kerr, Hiram Harrison Lowry, William Alexander Parsons Martin, Calvin Wilson Mateer, David Washington Cincinnatus Olyphant, Alvin Pierson Parker, Peter Parker, Watts Orson Pye, Samuel Isaac Joseph Schereschewsky, Devello Zelotes Sheffield, Albert Leroy Shelton, Jehu Lewis Shuck, Arthur Henderson Smith, David Tappan Stoddard, Ellen Maria Stone, John Van Nest Talmadge, Rudolf Bolling Teusler, Fennell Parrish Turner, Guido Herman Fridolin Verbeck, Andrew Watson, Channing Moore Williams, Frederick Wells Williams, Samuel Wells Williams, Matthew Tyson Yates, Wing Yung.
Supplementary volume, 1941. Articles on: Harlan P. Beach, James Hoover Matthews, and Berthold Laufer.

Encyclopaedia Britannica. 13th edition (1926). Articles: "China," I, pp. 614–627; "Chinese Eastern Railway," I, pp. 627–628; "Chinese Literature," I, p. 628; "Manchuria," II, p. 785; "Mongolia," II, p. 940. 14th edition (1929). Articles: "China," V, pp. 530–546; "Chinese Eastern Railway," V, pp. 565–566; "Chinese Literature," V, pp. 570–574; "Formosa," IX, pp. 514–516; "Manchuria," XIV, pp. 785–786. (1955 edition) Articles: "China," V, pp. 508–549 (with L. H. Dudley Buxton, "Country and People," with Carl W. Bishop, "Aesthetic Development;" With Edward Altham, "Defense;" with Percy Maude Roxby, "Production and Industry"); "Chinese Literature," V, pp. 570–574; "Chinese Eastern Railway," V, pp. 565–566; "Formosa," IX, pp. 520–522 (with Joseph W. Marlow); "Manchuria," XIV, pp. 781–786 (with Percy Maude Roxby); "Mongolia," XV, pp. 710–714 (with Percy Maude Roxby and Nicholas N. Poppe; "Missions," XV, pp. 596–601 (with W. Paton).

Encyclopaedia Britannica Book of the Year. Articles: "Foreign Missions," 1938, pp. 273–274; (in part by K. S. Latourette); 1939, p. 273; 1940, p. 298; 1941, pp. 301–302; 1942, p. 288; 1943, pp. 294–295; "Missions, Foreign," 1944, p. 448; 1945, p. 454; 1946, p. 486; 1947, pp. 506–507; 1948, pp. 486–487; "Missions, Foreign (Religious)," 1949, pp. 470; 1950, pp. 451–452; 1951, p. 463; 1952, p. 467; 1953, p. 464; 1954, pp. 467–468; 1955, pp. 510–511; 1956, p. 447; 1957, p. 510; 1958, p. 448; 1959, pp. 447–448; "Religion," 1955, pp. 655–656; 1956, pp. 592–593; 1957, pp. 654–655; 1958, pp. 588–590; 1959, pp. 587–588.

Encyclopaedia of the Social Sciences, ed. E. R. A. Seligman. New York: Macmillan, 1930–1935. Articles: "Hung Hsiu-ch'üan, VII, p. 552; "Missions," X, pp. 536–546; "Ricci, Matteo," XIII, p. 380; "Xavier, Francis," VI, pp. 409–410.

Die Religion in Geschichte und Gegenwart. 3, völlig neu bearbeitete Auflage. Tübingen: J. C. B. Mohr (Paul Siebeck), 1959. Article: "Japan: I. Politisch-ethnologisch," III, pp. 535–538.

Weltkirchen Lexicon: Handbuch der Ökumene, ed. Franklin H. Littell und Hans Hermann Walz. Stuttgart: Kreuz-Verlag, 1960. Articles: "Ausbreitung des Christentums," Cols. 114–116; "China," Cols. 214–215.

Also articles in: *American People's Encyclopedia, Collier's Encyclopedia, Encyclopedia Americana,* and *World-Scope Encyclopedia.*

Editor, Chinese terms, in: *Webster's New International Dictionary of the English Language.* Second edition. Springfield, Massachusetts, 1934.

BOOKS AND ARTICLES ON LATOURETTE

Gli Studi di Storia Religiosa negli Stati Uniti e l'Opera di K. S. Latourette, di Domenico Sella. Firenze: Sansoni, 1958. Pp. xvii, 153.

Pubblicazioni della Facoltà di Lettere e Filosofia dell' Università di Milano, 27.

"Kirchengeschichte als Universalgeschichte: Das Lebenswerk von K. S. Latourette," von Ernst Benz, in *Saeculum: Jahrbuch für Universalgeschichte,* I, 1950, pp. 487–507.

Also issued as a reprint München, 1950.

"Latourette, Kenneth Scott," in *Twentieth Century Encyclopedia of Religious Knowledge:* An Extension of the New Schaff-Herzog Encyclopedia of Religious Knowledge, ed. Lefferts A. Loetscher. Grand Rapids, Michigan: Baker Book House, 1955, p. 643.

"Latourette, Kenneth Scott," by W. Richey Hogg, in *Weltkirchen Lexicon: Handbuch der Ökumene,* hrsg. Franklin H. Littell und Hans Hermann Walz. Stuttgart: Kreuz-Verlag, 1960, Col. 836.

"Weltgeschichte—Kirchengeschichte—Missionsgeschichte; die Kirchengeschichtsschreibung Kenneth Scott Latourettes," in *Kirchengeschichte in Ökumenischer Sicht,* von Ernst Benz. Leiden, E. J. Brill, 1961, pp. 13–38.

Also listed in: *International Who's Who; Who's Who; Who's Who in America; Dictionary of American Scholars.*

Manuscripts, including personal and professional correspondence, together with a definitive bibliography by and about Kenneth Scott Latourette, may be found in the Day Missions Collection of the Yale University Divinity School Library.

INDEX

National Association of Evangelicals, 208, 225
National Christian Council, 1–2, 3, 9, 10, 12, 13
National Council of Churches, 178, 207, 224, 226
Nationalism, 202
  and Christian churches, 43–44, 60–61
  in Madagascar, 145–146
Native churches, *see* Aglipayan, Batak, Buganda, Burma, Chinese Christian, Malagasy, Philippines, Sudan, Thailand, Timor
Natives as clergy, 72, 109–110
New Guinea, 68, 69, 80–81
New Tribes Mission, 219
New Villages, 31, 35, 39
New Zealand, 28, 38
New Zealand Missionary Council, 73
Nigeria, 85, 87, 91, 103, 107, 108, 112
Northern Rhodesia, 99
Norwegian Lutheran Church in Madagascar, 136, 150, 160, 161
Nyasaland, 98–99

"Orphan missions," 96–97
Orthodoxy and faith boards, 194–197

Pacific Islands, United Church of, 75
Palace Church, 119–120, 121, 122, 123, 125, 127, 134
Paris, Evangelical Mission Society of, 62, 74, 145
Partnership of missions, 101, 115, 174–177
Philippines, 28, 34, 36–37, 39, 46, 48, 49, 52–53
Politics and Christian missions, 89
Portugal in Africa, 98
Presbyterian Church, 7, 8
  United, in the U.S.A., 206
Presbyterian Church of Australia, 29
Presbyterians
  in Korea, 34
  in Malaya, 34
  in Thailand, 36, 40
Prime Minister Rainilaiarivony, 118, 119, 120, 121, 126–127, 134
Publications for Christian education, 13, 57–58, 80, 216–217

Queen Ranavalona II, 118, 119, 120, 121, 123, 126–127

Racism, 90, 92–93, 192
Radio and films, 58–59, 184–185, 214–215
Rainisoalambo, 151–154
Reed College, 241, 289
Refugees, relief of, 14, 41–42
  in China, 15–16
Revival in Soatanona, 150–166
Research by Protestants, 186–187
Roman Catholics, 6, 34, 68, 222, 273
  in Africa, 87, 113
  in China, 247
  see also Jesuits

Schools in Africa, 85, 87–88
  in Madagascar, 144
Self-propagation of church, 116–167
Seventh Day Adventists, 9, 18, 57, 79, 207, 208
Sierra Leone, 85, 89–90, 103
Silberman, Prof. Leo, 91
Soatanana, revival in, 150–166
South Africa, 99
Southern Baptist Convention, 9, 192
Southern Baptists, 34, 40, 57, 202, 207, 208
Southern Rhodesia, 99
Student Volunteer Movement, 227, 234, 237, 238–239, 241, 243, 285
Studies, missionary, 187
Sudan, Association of Churches of Christ in the, 107–111
Sudan United Mission, 108, 110, 111
Sumatra, 27, 29
Sundkler, Prof. B., 92–93
Swiss Brethren, 37

Tambaram conference, 109; *see also* Madras conference
Tananarive Churches, evangelism of, 127–131
Tanosy tribe, 124–125, 133–134
Thailand, 25, 26, 27, 31, 33, 34, 36, 37, 39–40, 46, 47, 48, 51, 52, 54
Timor, 25, 27, 29, 44
Tongues, speaking in, 193, 195
Training of missionaries, 121, 137, 187–188
Translation work, 213–214

True Jesus Church, 7

United Christian Youth Movement, 41
United Church of Canada, 8
United Church of Christ in the Philippines, 34, 39, 49, 57
United Church of the Pacific Islands, 75
United Lutheran Church, 207
United Missions, 100–101

Walker, Williston, 235
West, impact of on Pacific Islands, 62–66

Whitby conference, 21, 29, 174
Williams, Frederick Wells, 235–236
Witnessing, urgency of, 174–175
Women in the church, 45–47
World Council of Churches, 41, 42
opposition to, 192
World Ecumenism, developments of, 41–43
Wycliffe Bible Translators, 205, 210–211, 214, 221–223

Yale, 234, 235, 236, 245–246, 247–248, 262, 286–288, 290, 291–292
Yale-in-China, 234, 237, 240–241, 287
YMCA and YWCA, 56